DATE			

When the Phone Rings, My Bed Shakes

Memoirs of a Deaf Doctor

Philip Zazove, M.D.

Gallaudet University Press
Washington, D.C.

Gallaudet University Press
Washington, DC 20002

Published 1993
Printed in the United States of America

Library of Congress Cataloging-in-Publication Data

Zazove, Philip, 1951–
When the phone rings, my bed shakes : memoirs of a deaf doctor / Philip Zazove.
p. cm.
ISBN 1-56368-024-6 (acid-free paper) : $22.95
1. Zazove, Philip, 1951– 2. Deaf physicians—United States—Biography. I. Title.
R154.Z39A3 1993
610′.92—dc20
[B] 93-6384
CIP

The paper used in this publication meets the minimum requirements of American National Standard for Information Sciences—Permanence of Paper for Printed Library Materials, ANSI Z39.48-1984. ∞

To Katherine and Rebecca

And those who follow. . . .

With love

FOREWORD

A. J. Cronin, Walker Percy, Richard Selzer, Oliver Sacks, Melvin Konner, Perri Klass: these are all physicians who became renowned as writers. And now Philip Zazove, M.D., has joined their ranks.

His absorbing memoir *When the Phone Rings, My Bed Shakes* makes me pleased and honored to call Phil a colleague as well as a friend. To be sure, I am not a doctor, but a fellow writer—a fellow *deaf* writer.

Deaf? There might be some argument about that, but it won't come from me. Technically, Phil has a "profound" hearing loss, one great enough so that he depends on speechreading for nearly all his communication. At the same time, he has some hearing, enough so that in certain circumstances he can carry on a telephone conversation. But I am not going to quibble over the fine points of an audiogram.

Phil's experiences as a person whose hearing is impaired mirror those of all of us who consider ourselves deaf. He speaks with an odd "accent." As a child he suffered jeers from hearing youngsters. Even today he has a hard time making sense of group conversations. Most of all, he has had to overcome the greatest handicap we face: the low expectations of people with "normal" hearing. Doing so is always a struggle, and only a sentimental ignoramus who has never had to endure such a battle would claim it is character-building.

As a youngster who was born with a severe hearing loss in 1951, Phil was fortunate. His extremely supportive parents are both physicians, and they relied on hearing aids and speech therapy to prepare their bright, personable, and capable child for an education in the public schools with his hearing peers. This was mainstreaming before the term was invented, and Phil took to it easily. So much so that he entered Northwestern University with a robust self-image.

Despite his sterling academic credentials at Northwestern, however, Phil had a difficult time persuading a medical school to accept him. School after school turned him down until Rutgers, and later Washington University, decided to take a chance. And they were not disappointed; deafness, like the famous prospect of being hanged, wonderfully concentrates the faculties. Phil did himself proud.

Philip Zazove is an experienced physician—a member of one of the noblest and most exclusive of all the professions—yet he must deal, every day, with a world that lacks sound. He does it with a singular lack of bitterness and self-pity, with a great deal of patience and resourcefulness, with wry humor, and with an astonishing compassion for his fellow human beings.

He does this in the company of an extraordinary wife—Barbara, herself a physician. She is hearing, and like many hearing spouses of deaf people, she is possessed of a flexibility and depth of understanding rare in any human being. So much, in fact, that Phil gave up his successful Utah practice in order to accommodate the needs of her career.

But I am getting ahead of a story Phil tells better than anyone else could.

In this book he tells us about many things: how a deaf doctor listens to a patient's heart; how a deaf doctor keeps in touch with his answering service; how a deaf doctor wakes up to a phone call from a pregnant patient about to deliver in the middle of the night (thus the title of his book); and, most interestingly, why a deaf doctor would choose family practice, a specialty that requires subtleties of human communication beyond the capabilities of most people who can hear.

Readers will also revel in stories that have nothing to do with deafness and everything to do with compassion and delight in the illimitable variety of human beings. Phil Zazove, you must remember, is a doctor who writes. His tales of his early days practicing in a small town in Utah are rich in both humor and tragedy. His patients include a ninety-year-old man who fancies himself tough as nails, so stubborn that it takes all Dr. Zazove's wiles to get him to hold still long enough to be treated; an adorable little girl who likes to stuff things up her nose, with smelly consequences; a pregnant lesbian fearful that her father, who has links to the underworld, might harm her—and, Phil fears, possibly him too; and an elderly woman addicted to both meprobamate and monologues, who seems to turn up every time Phil faces a professional crisis.

There are also deeply touching stories of cancer and death and personal involvement in the sufferings of others. Philip Zazove is an empathetic and caring human being, and that, more than anything else, is why he became a family practitioner.

Though he grew up in the hearing culture, he learned sign language as a medical student in order to minister to signing deaf patients. They flock to him, not merely because he speaks their language and can preserve the confidential doctor–patient relationship without need for an interpreter, but also because he shares their problems and, just as important, knows their potentialities.

And this, in the end, defines Philip Zazove, physician. "Some day in the future," he writes, "I hope my descendants will look back at my life . . . and say, 'He helped destroy the stereotype that once prevailed about people who are deaf. He showed them they can do anything hearing people can.' "

Who could hope for a better legacy?

HENRY KISOR

PREFACE

It doesn't seem that long since I received the envelope from Rutgers Medical School. But it is. It was before anyone knew what a video cassette or compact disc player was, before the space shuttle, the personal computer, or the minivan became household words. It was even before President Nixon resigned from office. I remember hesitating before opening the envelope. It was, after all, just like the others, a thin one. Then I took a deep breath and read the letter. "It is with great pleasure that we inform you that the faculty of Rutgers Medical School has voted to accept you." I did not finish the paragraph—I was too busy jumping for joy.

That same year, 1974, thousands of others across the country received similar letters from medical schools. However, mine was a special case. A major difference separated me from everyone else, one that made it particularly hard to get accepted: I am almost totally deaf.

The word *deaf* is not a precisely used term. There is a whole spectrum of "deafness," ranging from mild hearing loss to total inability to perceive sound. Still, as Oliver Sacks explains so well in his book *Seeing Voices,* the word *deaf* is often used to denote anyone with a hearing impairment. This is unfortunate. The extent of the loss plays a crucial role in dictating how a person functions in society, as well as determining whether he or she can speak like most people or must use sign language.

Sacks himself describes three broad categories of people with hearing loss: those who are hard of hearing, those who are severely deaf, and those who are profoundly deaf. The hard of hearing group is by far the most common. It consists of people who hear well enough to converse relatively easily with others in society. People who are severely deaf traditionally have had much more difficulty doing this. Today, however, because of technological improvements in modern hearing aids as well as other equipment, even this group can hear speech and converse orally. People who are profoundly deaf, on the other hand, have no hope of ever hearing speech and must lipread, use sign language, or both. These are the people who were once called "deaf-mutes."

I have been classified as having a "profound" loss. It is so great in most frequencies—ninety decibels or greater—that I depend on reading lips. This would put me in the third category. However, I can hear a few sounds in the lower frequencies (below one thousand cycles per second). And with enough amplification, I can often use the phone. I even understand a rare word without reading someone's lips. So I probably belong in the ill-defined area where the second group meets the third. Regardless, many (if not most) people consider me deaf, and I occasionally refer to myself in this book as being so.

I was a senior in high school when I first conceived of writing this book. As part of my application for a college scholarship available for persons who are deaf, I was required to have an interview. That is how I met Catherine Munro, a hearing person who was, at the time, a deaf educator for the state of Illinois. Our encounter turned out to be more than the usual perfunctory meeting. She was excited about my plan to become a physician—there are very few physicians who are deaf or profoundly hard of hearing. Since I was going to be a pioneer of sorts, she persuaded me to undertake two projects.

The first was to learn sign language. I had been one of the first persons with my degree of hearing loss to be mainstreamed in Chicago area public schools and thus had not learned this language. Most people who are deaf have difficulty communicating with physicians and often bring an interpreter when seeking medical care. As a result, some of the details are lost during translation, and the deaf person loses the confidential doctor–patient relationship. By learning American Sign Language, I could help alleviate this problem.

I began to learn American Sign Language the summer after my first year of medical school. A classmate and I went to the weekly meetings of a northern New Jersey deaf club where we studied the basics of the language. I'll never forget the enthusiasm and enjoyment shown by the members teaching us. Since then, I have improved my signing and can now converse in it, though I am not as fluent as I would like to be.

Mrs. Munro's second request was for me to write about my experiences as a doctor. There are few role models for people who are deaf, and she believed a book about a physician with a profound hearing loss would help fill this void. So after several years of private practice, I sat down to write my story. I have tried to highlight, where appropriate, how my life is different from those who hear normally. In some fundamental ways, and some not so fundamental, it is vastly different. Many of these differences will interest hearing people, as will the solutions I have devised to compensate for them. I am sure other deaf people will find all of them familiar.

Another reason I wrote this book is that people often ask me, "What's it like to be a family doctor, especially one who's deaf?" This story is my answer.

Long hours, patients' expectations, difficulty in making some diagnoses, and the emotional commitment required—these factors combine to make medicine a demanding profession. But it is not all worries and heartbreaks; there are funny incidents, glowing accomplishments, and happy times as well. The diversity of experiences that family doctors encounter is fascinating, and these make being a family physician, hearing or deaf, satisfying despite the drawbacks.

But being deaf adds a whole new dimension to being a doctor. In addition to the usual practice of medicine, one also confronts everyday issues such as communicating through masks in surgery and using a stethoscope. How I have tackled these and other problems are all explained in the book.

Everything in this book is true. Thus, in order to protect everyone's confidentiality, I have changed the names of most of the people and places. The only real ones are mine and those of my medical assistant and family. Otherwise, any similarity of names in this book to real persons and places is purely coincidental. Also, where necessary, details have been altered to maintain privacy.

Writing a book is an immense undertaking that requires seemingly endless hours. Despite having read this comment in other prefaces, I had no idea how time-consuming this process really is. Fortunately, my wife understood. I am indebted to her for her patience and understanding on the many evenings I disappeared after the kids went to bed. She encouraged me when I did not think I would ever finish. And she critiqued my manuscript when she had other, more important things to do.

My parents also reviewed the manuscript innumerable times. They made many invaluable suggestions, all of which improved the book markedly. Even more so, I am thankful to them for their unwavering confidence in my ability to make it in this hearing world. Without their encouragement and support, I would not be where I am today.

Others also devoted hours of their time to reviewing the book and offering suggestions. They are, in alphabetical order: LeAnne Davis, Sue Grangroth, Melvin Gray, Arla and Werner Huck, Florence Lerner, Jude Reed, Larry Russell, and David Spendlove. I would like to thank Pam Check for her wonderful editorial assistance, my writer's group for their constructive comments, and Karen and Cami Christiansen for their secretarial help. Ivey Pittle Wallace, the editor at Gallaudet University Press, made many insightful suggestions as well, all of which greatly improved the manuscript. Likewise, I am also indebted to my agent, Susan P. Urstadt, not only for her constructive suggestions but also for her confidence that the manuscript I submitted to her three years ago was publishable.

Finally, I would like to thank my office staff—both past and present—as well as my associates. My prejudice aside, I am convinced that they make up one of the best medical offices that has ever existed. They care about each other as well as the patients, and it shows in the way they treat people.

So Catherine Munro, here it is. It took a long time to write but it's finally done, and I hope you have an opportunity to read it. I also hope the Deaf community will be as encouraged as you predicted many years ago. And for those of you in that community who are wondering if you have a chance to succeed in a hearing world, the answer is a resounding yes. I did it. You can too.

When the Phone Rings, My Bed Shakes

ONE

RRRRRIIIING! RRRRRIIIING! The sharp shrill of the telephone shattered the quietness of the night. I didn't hear it, but my bed began to vibrate. Only half-awakened, I turned over, wishing the shaking would stop. It did, but only for a second.

Rrrrriiiing! Rrrrriiiing! The jarring sound recurred. Each time it did, my bed vibrated. Soon, I realized the phone had to be answered. I groped for it in the dark, knocking the receiver off the hook. Finding it, I mumbled, "Hello?"

No one answered.

"Hello?" I waited again. Still no answer. Then I discovered the phone was upside down. Turning it over clumsily, I repeated once more, "Hello?"

"Can I speak to Dr. Philip Zazove?"

I barely heard a sound and could not understand the voice. "Pardon me?" I murmured sleepily, turning the amplifier on the handset all the way up so I could hear better.

"Dr. Zazove?"

"Yes?"

"This is Mary Dawson at Plymouth Hospital Labor and Delivery," I barely heard her say.

"Please speak louder," I reminded her, trying to wake up.

"Is that better?"

"Yes."

"I have a patient of yours here, Rosie Green, who seems to be in active labor. Her baby is due in four days. She started having contractions last night around 10:00, and they're now occurring every three minutes. The baby's head is still high, but its heart rate seems fine at 140 beats per minute."

"How far is she dilated?"

"Four centimeters."

"Go ahead and admit her," I said. "I'll be there in about thirty minutes."

I replaced the phone in its cradle, lay back on the warm sheets, and snuggled against my wife. The clock read 2:00 a.m. Barbara stretched, having also been awakened by the phone, then curled up and went back to sleep.

Fortunately, Rosie was just in early labor. I had a little time to remain in the comfort of the bed before going to the hospital. I closed my eyes and wondered why I had chosen a profession with such bad hours. There had been so many other possibilities with much more free time. Still, years ago, I picked medicine as my career. That decision initiated a prolonged battle to get into medical school, despite my excellent qualifications, solely because I am practically deaf. Yet, did I spend all that time studying and training just for the privilege of enduring middle-of-the-night interruptions such as this? Why is it that babies always seem to be born at night?

Suddenly, I realized I was drifting back to sleep and opened my eyes with a start. Whew! That had been close. If there was any delivery I didn't want to miss, it was this one. I looked at the clock: 2:05. I still had a few more minutes.

I started musing about what life might be like as a different kind of doctor, one who had few night calls. I'd work normal days like everyone else. And when I went home, I would stay there all night. I'd have more time, both for my family and my other interests. As attractive as the better hours of other medical specialties are, though, I knew I wouldn't be as happy in any of them. Being a family doctor lets me interact with all types of people and deal with many kinds of problems. This variety makes life interesting. As a subspecialist who always did the same things, I would be bored.

I recalled the times in medical school when several of my professors urged me to choose a different specialty. They had mistakenly believed family practice was a fad and wouldn't exist in the future.

Select a field you'll be proud to be a member of, they had argued, one that will still be around in a few years.

I decided to become a family doctor anyway. It was what I wanted to do. But that wasn't the first time I bucked the establishment. I have done so since I was three years old, when my deafness was first discovered. Although my hearing loss isn't total, it is classified as about as severe as one can get; only persons with a total loss hear less. It is severe enough that, for all practical purposes, many people consider me deaf. People I grew up with, went to school with, took classes from—even persons with medical training—often referred to me as being deaf despite the fact that I do hear some sounds. The experts viewed me that way too. At the time they diagnosed me, they wondered about my capacity to become a self-sufficient adult. They even asked questions about how educable I was and advised my parents to consider special classes. It was, the experts proclaimed, the only way I could hope to learn some basic skills. My parents' idea of giving me a chance in public schools was considered ridiculous. There was just no way I could compete successfully with hearing children. Or so the experts said.

I glanced at the clock. It was time to get up. I crawled out of bed and began to feel the excitement build. For in addition to being just the second delivery of my young medical practice (though I had delivered many babies during my residency), this was also not going to be a normal delivery.

Goosebumps erupted on my skin from the coolness of the room, the result of the cold March weather outside. I took a quick hot shower, dressed, and left the house. "Well, Rosie," I thought to myself as I drove off, "I guess we'll find out the answer now."

I first met Rosie Green when she came to my office for a pregnancy test after missing two menstrual periods. The test result was positive. She was amazed, as many young girls are, that she had gotten pregnant so easily. That was supposed to happen to other people, not her. The father, who was eighteen, promptly disappeared when she told him she was expecting.

Rosie was short, squat, and sixteen. The ruddy complexion and pale blue eyes of her cherubic face were framed by straight, limp blond hair that hung two-thirds of the way to her shoulders. Her clothes were simple: faded jeans, old sneakers, and short-sleeved blouses. The most striking thing about Rosie was her apathy. As soon as she spoke, her bland responses, listless mannerisms, and meager choice of words, all contributed to this impression.

Either her mother or her stepfather usually came to her prenatal visits. They were attentive; her stepfather in particular often asked questions or offered suggestions. Rosie, however, spoke only when necessary. At first I attributed this to her feeling shy, embarrassed, or even overwhelmed by the pregnancy. After all, she was only a sophomore in high school. So I strove to stimulate her interest in the pregnancy: what was happening inside her, the child to be, the delivery to come. We discussed things she could do to improve the chances for a healthy baby. I also stressed the responsibilities of being a mother and encouraged her to learn all she could about babies. But she remained apathetic.

Soon I became worried about Rosie's mental capacity to be a mother, let alone a single teenage parent with all the inherent problems of that role. So I reminded her that adoption was a possibility. I tried to impress on her the immense lifestyle changes that occur with having children and encouraged her to prepare for these if she decided to keep the child.

Unfortunately, these efforts all seemed to be in vain. Rosie never seemed interested in her baby. At times, I found myself getting frustrated. I wanted some evidence that she understood what I told her. If only it were possible to look inside her head and see what she really thought.

Seven months into the pregnancy, another problem developed. Rosie's baby wasn't growing as it should. So I decided to do an ultrasound, a safe method of using sound waves to produce an accurate picture of the fetus. Ultrasounds are wonderful additions to modern medical care. Not only have they enabled doctors to better treat their patients, they also make our lives much easier. I don't envy the physicians of yesteryear who had to care for the same problems without this technology. Ultrasounds offer another benefit too: they are exciting for the parents who can see their unborn child's image, including its beating heart.

Usually the test is normal. Sometimes, however, it isn't, most commonly because the baby is due later than expected or is small for its age. There may even be twins. Every once in a while, though, the results are more grave—something is wrong. And this was the case with Rosie. There was very little fluid around the fetus, in the "bag of waters." This situation is sometimes a result of medical problems with the baby. Although Rosie's baby looked okay, we couldn't be sure. So six weeks later, we repeated the ultrasound. There was even less fluid this time. But the baby still looked normal.

It is hard enough when I must tell parents their baby may not be normal. I was even more concerned in Rosie's case. Up to this point, I had worried how she would cope with a normal child. Now she very well might have an abnormal baby. So I called a family conference, hoping her parents' presence would provide Rosie some emotional as well as intellectual support.

As soon as I entered the room, it was obvious her stepfather was very upset. "I've already missed work to take her to those goddamn ultrasounds. Now you want me to come to meetings like this. Look, this is getting out of hand. You better do anything else you want to now because I ain't taking off no more work."

"Mr. Zimmerman," I began after he finished complaining (Rosie had kept her real father's name), "I realize you can't afford to miss much work. Very few people can. But there's an important reason I asked you to come here today. All three of you need to be aware of some possible problems with Rosie's baby. As you know, the first ultrasound suggested there's not much fluid around the baby. This one confirmed that. That means the baby might have lung or kidney problems." After pausing a second to let that sink in, I went on. "Now, I want to emphasize that ultrasounds aren't always right. In fact, I've seen them be totally wrong. And even if it is correct, as best we can tell the baby looks okay. So it could very well still be normal. Either way, though, there's not much we can do at this point. We'll just have to wait and see."

The subsequent silence was disquieting, even for me. I watched them closely, especially Rosie, wishing someone would say something. But no one did. They just sat quietly in their chairs. I began to feel uncomfortable myself, wondering what to say next. Then her parents finally asked a couple of questions about the ultrasound. After answering them, I turned to Rosie and asked if she had anything to say. She remained mute. I emphasized that it wasn't her fault and she hadn't done anything wrong—it was just one of those things that happen. I also stressed the need for hope. For until the baby was born, we wouldn't know whether it even had any problems. Despite this, she didn't say a word. The expression on her face remained unchanged.

The shriek of a siren from a passing ambulance interrupted my reverie. I hadn't heard it until it was right next to me, and even then I had barely heard it for a second. I realized I had seen the flashing light in my rearview mirror a moment earlier but, for some reason, had not responded to it consciously. Whew! I needed to be sure that didn't happen again. I've never been in an accident and don't ever want to be. I depend on my vision more than hearing people do. And there are other adjustments I've made too. For example, after a stoplight turns green, I either wait for another car to go first or check both sides of the intersection to be sure no vehicle is coming. Otherwise I might not hear a siren until it is too late.

I looked down the road in front of me and saw the hospital, a block away. A minute later, I pulled into the empty parking lot and paused to look at the building. It was small but stately. The soft light from several strategically placed spotlights gave the off-white walls a subdued appearance. Only the name on its walls—Plymouth General Hospital—was well lit. A manicured lawn and trees around the one-story building gave the place a friendly feeling.

"I hope the baby's okay," I thought out loud, feeling a little apprehensive. For if it wasn't, there was no telling how Rosie would respond.

My hands a little clammy, I went in the side entrance and walked to the labor and delivery wing. There were two beds in the labor room. In one lay Rosie Green in a hospital gown, watching television, while her mother sat passively in a chair at the foot of the bed. In the other lay a woman in her twenties whose husband sat next to her, intimately involved with helping her breathe through each contraction. I couldn't help but notice the contrast the two couples made.

"Hi, Rosie. How are you feeling?" I greeted her as I drew a curtain between the beds.

There was a nod of recognition. She seemed uneasy, but because of her stoic appearance it was difficult to tell. Even after I began talking, she continued watching TV. I watched her lips closely so I could read them when she spoke, for she could be difficult to understand. Even though I am an expert lipreader, I had a hard time with hers. She barely opened her mouth when she talked.

"Are you having much pain?"

"I dunno," she answered. Then a contraction started. She winced and started to whine. "I don't want the baby. Stop the pains and lemme go home."

"We may be able to give you something for them. Let me examine you first and see how you're doing."

Mary, the nurse, brought me a sterile glove. I donned it and checked Rosie. She was now five centimeters dilated, having made progress since Mary's 2:00 a.m. phone call. Because the baby's heart rate remained normal, I decided to give Rosie something for the pain.

"I'm going to give you some medication through the IV, Rosie. It won't take your pain away completely but should make things more tolerable." Although Rosie continued to avoid everyone's gaze, at least her mother acknowledged my statement.

"Rosie, you're five centimeters dilated. Do you remember what that means?" I asked.

She shook her head.

"That's how dilated your cervix is. It's normally as thick as your nose. During labor, it gradually shortens until it becomes as thin as a piece of paper. At the same time, the tiny channel through the center of it widens to ten centimeters, which is about four inches.

That allows the baby's head to come out." At this point another contraction came, and Rosie lost interest in my explanation.

The next hour went smoothly. Every ten minutes or so, I looked in on Rosie. She continued to make good progress, and the baby's heart tones remained normal. Rosie also remained silent. Between contractions, she just gazed at the TV. At times, I wasn't sure if she was really watching it or just staring at it. It was only when a contraction came that she would move or make a sound. But as soon as that ceased, her passivity returned.

Then, when she reached eight centimeters, Rosie abruptly started to scream. It was as if someone had turned a key in her. She even uttered a few words between her cries. "Yiiiii. I don't want this baby now. Yiiiii! Stop the pain and lemme go home. Yiiiii!"

"Rosie," I said after the contraction was over. "At this point you have no choice but to go ahead with it. It won't be much longer. Look. Try breathing through the contractions like this." I demonstrated again what the nurses had been showing her since she had arrived at the hospital.

"When you feel one coming on, take a deep breath and let it out. Then take another deep breath and let that one out too. Then start breathing short but fast breaths, like a dog does when he pants." I panted rapidly to demonstrate what I meant.

She just stared at me. When the next contraction began, Rosie started screaming again.

"Come on, Rosie, breathe like we talked about," I grasped her arm firmly. "Come on, now. Breathe."

She wouldn't cooperate and continued to cry. I felt myself getting angry and wanted to yell back at her. I had tried so hard to forewarn her about labor, but she had ignored me. And she had refused to attend prenatal classes too. Even now, she wouldn't cooperate with anyone.

But being angry wouldn't accomplish anything. What Rosie needed more than anything else was help. Labor was turning out to be more than she could handle. So I forced myself to calm down and decided to give her an epidural. I hadn't ordered it earlier because her family had requested keeping the cost down, but Rosie was out of control. Epidurals are another wonderful modern advantage that doctors in the past didn't have. They are a popular and safe means of eliminating the pain of labor.

During the next two hours, Rosie dilated steadily. Free of pain, she refocused her attention on the TV. She maintained such a poker face that it was almost as if a mask were glued onto her head. Nothing seemed to get through. Her mother also appeared indifferent about the forthcoming baby.

Then I fell asleep in the doctor's lounge. Next thing I knew, someone was shaking my shoulders. I opened my eyes in time to see Mary's lips by my face saying, "Doctor, did you hear me?"

I jumped up, fearful something was wrong. "No, I didn't."

She said something, but the light in the room was turned way down and I could not see her lips. I walked over to the wall switch and turned the overhead light on. "I'm sorry, I didn't hear you. What did you say?"

"I just checked her and she's ten centimeters, completely dilated. Shall we have her push?"

"How far down is the baby?"

"About zero station, I think."

This meant the widest part of the baby's head had passed through the narrowest point of Rosie's pelvis, a good sign that she should be able to have a vaginal delivery. "Okay, start having her push."

To no one's surprise, Rosie didn't cooperate. In fact, when contractions came, she closed her eyes instead, as if she were trying to escape the situation.

I walked into the room as Mary was trying to coax her. "If you want to get this over with, then push with your contractions. When you feel one coming on, take a deep breath and let it out. Then grab your legs by the knees and pull them back. Then take another deep breath and push as hard as you can. Try to push the baby out, okay? Do you understand?"

There was no response.

"Rosie," I intervened assertively, "did you hear what she said?"

Rosie nodded, her eyes on the TV.

"Good, because you're now going to help get the baby out by pushing when we tell you to. Otherwise, we'll have to let the epidural wear off so you can feel the urge to push."

The next contraction came. Mrs. Zimmerman, Mary, and I all exhorted Rosie. She pushed, but only halfheartedly. After twenty-five minutes of this, Rosie was as nonchalant as ever. I grabbed another sterile glove and rechecked her. Despite her lack of cooperation, the baby was coming down slowly. I told Mary to move Rosie to the delivery room in five minutes. This was before the days of birthing beds; nowadays she would have delivered in the same room.

"If you want to come into the delivery room, we'd be glad to have you," I told Rosie's mother. "In fact, I think it would help her to have you there."

"All right," she answered without much enthusiasm. A short, fat, dark-haired woman with a triangular, heavily wrinkled face, she looked many years older than her forty-five. There was an aura of fatigue about her too. Perhaps she was depressed. Or it may have been just her usual phlegmatic character. Regardless of the cause, I was surprised at how few words of support she expressed for her daughter. Only if something was specifically requested of her would she help, but always without a sense of eagerness. She acted as though if she ignored the situation enough, it would go away—like a bad dream.

It was now 6:30. Because the baby might be seriously sick, and I couldn't care for it and Rosie simultaneously, I called a pediatrician friend who was just starting a private practice after having worked three years with a prepaid health plan.

"John? Philip Zazove calling."

"Yes, Philip."

"I'm sorry to call you so early in the morning but I need your help. I'll be delivering a baby in about fifteen minutes who may have problems. Could you come in to help out?"

"I'd be glad to. Tell me a little about it."

After relating the facts to him, I went to the men's locker room and changed into one of the blue scrubsuits of the hospital obstetrical ward. Five minutes had elapsed by the time I returned to the labor floor. We wheeled Rosie to the delivery room while she lay passively, as if nothing were about to happen.

I walked over to the infant incubator, readied all the instruments we might need for the baby, and checked the oxygen to be sure it was working. Meanwhile, two nurses got both the room and Rosie ready for the delivery.

Then I put my hearing aid on. In those days nurses did not scrub to make themselves sterile, but they still wore masks in the delivery room. Without the aid, I rarely heard anything; with the aid, I could sometimes tell when someone was talking to me, especially if he or she stood right next to me. And when the nurses had my attention, they could then pull down their masks so I could read their lips. Recently it's become even easier. People no longer wear masks when delivering babies, so I have no problem communicating at all. In fact, I often do not even wear my hearing aid; it's much easier for me reading lips than trying to make sense of a few sounds.

I began to scrub. While washing, I looked into the delivery room where I could see what one nurse was saying to Rosie, for the nurse had not yet put on her mask. "Put your legs over here so the doctor can better see what he's doing," she explained as the two nurses helped Rosie do so. "We're also going to clean the area where the baby comes out to reduce the chance of an infection."

Just as the nurses finished, I walked into the room, holding my dripping-clean hands up in the air. While drying them, I talked to Rosie.

"Having any pain?"

"Uh-uh."

She looked at me with her usual expression, but for once, there seemed to be something else in her eyes. Was it interest? Bewilderment? Concern? Fear? At last she was showing some emotion!

"Keep pushing with your contractions. There should be only a few more before the baby comes out," I encouraged her.

At this point John walked into the room, also dressed in blues. After I introduced him to Rosie and her mother, he proceeded to double-check all the instruments.

The baby came steadily down the birth canal. First, a dime-size area of the head appeared. Over the next two to three contractions, it became the size of a quarter and then a half-dollar.

"That's it, Rosie. If you give a good push with the next one, I think you'll have the baby."

She was still impassive, although that flicker of emotion remained in her eyes. Her mother sat stoically on a stool next to Rosie, offering no comfort other than a hand under her daughter's head.

The next contraction began. It was a very tight fit, and I worried the birth canal might tear as the baby delivered. Taking advantage of the numbness from the epidural, I made a small incision, called an episiotomy, to give the baby more room to come out. The head emerged slowly, face down.

"Now stop pushing for a second, Rosie," I requested as I sucked mucus out of the baby's mouth with a bulb syringe. The mucus is removed to prevent it from going into the baby's lungs when the baby takes a breath. Suddenly, Rosie started pushing.

"Stop pushing," I beseeched her as I quickly aspirated the mucus.

"I can't," she shouted and continued to push.

I threw the syringe down and managed to deliver the rest of the baby.

"It's a girl!"

TWO

I LAID THE BABY on Rosie's abdomen. She looked at the child silently, her face a blank stare. There was no apparent reaction. Even Rosie's mother didn't say anything. It seemed strange not to see the usual cooing and expressions of delight. I leaned over and took a closer look at the infant. She was a little smaller than most newborn babies. Her face looked different too, although it was hard to say exactly why. There was something about it that just didn't seem right. Otherwise, she appeared normal.

I glanced at the clock. The baby was now ten seconds old but had not yet taken a breath. I rubbed her chest and slapped both feet, trying to get her to gasp. She wouldn't. I quickly cut the umbilical cord and passed her to John, who was waiting by the incubator. He placed a bag and mask over her mouth and forced oxygen into her lungs. He too looked the baby over carefully, searching for evidence of other problems. Meanwhile, a nurse monitored the baby's heartbeat. Fortunately, that remained okay. Despite their efforts, however, the child wouldn't breathe on her own.

After two minutes, the infant's heart rate began to slow down. John put a tube through her mouth and into the windpipe so he could breathe more effectively for her.

As he turned to Rosie, I saw him say, "I'm going to take your baby to the nursery. She's having trouble breathing, and we can care for her better there. I'll be back as soon as I can to tell you how she's doing."

Rosie just grunted, looking at the baby in his arms with her usual expressionless face.

"Did you understand what he said, Rosie?" I queried as they left.

She nodded slightly as I delivered the afterbirth—the placenta. It seemed intact and normal. "Put twenty units of pitocin in her IV," I told Mary.

Usually the uterus clamps down spontaneously after the placenta comes out. This is nature's way of slowing the bleeding and minimizing the mother's blood loss from the raw surface left in the uterus. To further reduce this loss, most doctors give the mother pitocin, a natural hormone that helps the uterus contract.

I checked the episiotomy. It had not enlarged with the delivery. As I started sewing it, thoughts about the baby started to go through my mind. How was she doing now? Would she live? Was Rosie wondering the same thing?

"How are you feeling, Rosie?" I stood up from the stool so I could see her face.

"Okay," I saw her lips mouth, although I didn't hear a sound. Not hearing her voice would be upsetting for most people since they depend on sounds for face-to-face communication. But I don't. I have never heard most sounds of speech and use lipreading and facial expressions to understand others. Besides, in this case, it was not necessary to hear. Rosie had little to say.

I noticed the bleeding had become heavier and felt Rosie's uterus. It was boggy—not firm as it should be. Still, I wasn't too concerned; this condition is not uncommon immediately after a delivery. I massaged the uterus vigorously with a hand on her abdomen, a maneuver that usually causes it to contract. But this time it didn't. The hemorrhage was still brisk. I inserted my other hand inside and squeezed the uterus with both hands, trying to get it to clamp down.

"Is the IV running in okay?" I asked.

Mary nodded as she checked again.

"It's lactated Ringer's solution, isn't it?"

"Yes, Doctor," she said as she nodded again.

"Let it run in as fast as possible. She needs fluids."

The bleeding remained heavy. I grabbed a sterile gauze square, wrapped it around my first and second fingers, and carefully inserted it into the uterine cavity. Using this as a scraper, I rubbed the inside of the uterus to remove any residual pieces of afterbirth that could be causing the bleeding. None were present. Despite the massaging and scraping, the flow steadily increased. Soon it ran like a faucet turned on full blast. The blood just poured out; it was one of the worst cases of hemorrhage after a delivery that I had ever seen.

I began to feel warm and sweaty. Beads of perspiration ran down my forehead and under my arms. My pounding heart seemed to crawl up into my throat. It was hard to breathe too. When would the bleeding stop? Then I noticed blood was spilling out of the basin at the foot of the bed onto the floor. Rosie had probably already lost at least a liter of blood. Since she had only about six liters of blood in her body, this was a significant amount.

"Have the lab arrange for four units of blood. We may need to transfuse her," I ordered while examining the uterus again. It remained boggy.

"How's her blood presure?"

Mary pulled down her mask and turned around to face me. She had worked with me when I had been a resident physician and knew I could not understand her with the mask on. This was no time to have to repeat herself. "86 over 54," she said clearly.

"Oh, no," I thought to myself. "She's lost so much blood that her blood pressure is starting to drop." After resuming a vigorous massage of the uterus, I told Mary, "Give her .2 milligrams of ergotrate."

Ergotrate is another medicine that makes the uterus contract. Unlike pitocin, it's not natural in humans. However, it too is effective, especially in situations like Rosie's.

"Is the IV open all the way?"

"Yes, Doctor, it is," I saw her slightly frantic but controlled reply, thankful that her lips were so easy to read.

"And you put twenty units of pitocin in the bottle, right?"

"I did."

"Start another IV of lactated Ringer's in her other arm and open it all the way too."

The heat in the room now seemed oppressive. I hadn't remembered it ever being so warm in the room before. It reminded me of a humid day in Miami. Rivulets of sweat ran down my face and coalesced into rivers. My surgical blues were drenched and clung to my body. I wished I could remove my sterile gown and cool off. If only the hemorrhage would slow down. I struggled to remain calm. The ergotrate should work soon. Or would it? There are few things scarier than a full-blown postpartum bleed.

My arms were becoming fatigued but I continued to knead Rosie's uterus, waiting impatiently for the drugs to take effect. Why wouldn't the uterus clamp down? By now Rosie had lost another half-liter of blood. I looked at the clock. It would be at least twenty more minutes before the lab finished readying the blood. Until then, none would be available to give her. A glance back at Rosie revealed things had not changed—the bleeding remained massive. Only one option was left: emergency surgery. I decided to call an obstetrician in to consult. In the meantime, I would begin the preparations for the operation.

Miraculously, before I could inform Mary of my decision, Rosie's uterus became firm. Almost immediately after, the bleeding decreased. The combination of ergotrate, pitocin, and massage was finally working. As Mary's face showed her relief, I felt myself become noticeably more relaxed too. My legs felt wobbly, and I sat on a stool, soaking wet.

I looked at Rosie and her mother. I had been so involved with the hemorrhage that I hadn't even glanced at them, let alone thought about the baby. "How are you feeling, Rosie?"

"Okay."

"Are you dizzy?"

"Naw."

She was still nonchalant. I wondered if she had noticed the excitement or even sensed that something was wrong. Her mother seemed more attentive but did not show any indication she had realized the gravity of the situation.

"I'm going to finish sewing up your episiotomy now. Then I'll go find out how your baby is doing." As usual, there was no reply.

I finished the repair in ten minutes. Since the bleeding remained minimal and her blood pressure was now stable, I pulled off my gown and gloves.

"Keep the IV running at 200 cc per hour," I instructed the nurses. "If the bleeding increases or her blood pressure falls, call me immediately." Turning to Rosie, I continued, "I'm going out to check your baby. I'll be back shortly."

I walked down the cool hallway, shivering a little as the sweat evaporated. It felt so good to finally be out of that hot room and have the wet gown off. Letting out a deep sigh, I felt an immense sense of relief. My muscles ached all over; they must have been more taut than I had realized. I had had visions of Rosie bleeding to death. It was the most wonderful feeling in the world to have everything end up okay.

Around the corner from the labor suite was the nursery. I arrived there shortly, still a little shaken, and found John with the baby. Tubes and lines of all sorts were going into the infant.

"Well, John, how's she doing?"

"Very poorly, Philip. Even though it's been almost an hour, she still hasn't taken a breath. We're giving her one hundred percent oxygen but there seems to be a lot of resistance to the air going in."

That was bad news. It meant the baby's lungs were probably poorly developed.

"Sounds like the baby has Potter's syndrome," I offered.

"It certainly looks like that, doesn't it? Just in case, though, I think she needs to be in a newborn intensive care unit. Since you were in delivery, I took the liberty of calling their transport team to come and take her there."

I looked at the tiny girl. If she did indeed have Potter's syndrome, there was nothing we could do. It would be only a matter of time before she died.

"Thanks for coming in," I told John as I started to leave.

"I was happy to help. You know," he mused, "today is my first day of private practice. Since I haven't even been to the office yet, I'll probably be able to truly say that my first patient in private practice died."

"That's quite a way to start, isn't it?"

"Yeah, it sure is."

I returned slowly to the delivery floor, where Rosie was now in the recovery room. The nurses were closely monitoring her blood pressure and rate of bleeding.

"Any problems?" I asked.

"No, everything seems stable now," Mary responded. "Her blood pressure is up to 102 over 70 and her pulse is 98. The bleeding is normal, maybe even less than usual."

I looked at Rosie. She was pale but otherwise seemed none the worse for her experience. Propped up on several pillows, she lay in bed drinking Seven-Up through a straw. Her mother sat in a chair next to her, watching people walk by in the hall. Neither asked me about the baby.

I sat down and let out another big sigh. "Rosie, let's talk about your baby," I began, trying to get her attention. Watching her closely, I continued, "She isn't doing well. She hasn't taken any breaths of her own and we've been breathing for her through a tube in her windpipe. We think she has a condition called Potter's syndrome. If that's true, neither her lungs nor her kidneys will ever develop, and she'll eventually die. However, we're not one hundred percent sure of this. So we've arranged to transfer her to Primary Children's Hospital. They can do a much better job there of caring for her."

I paused to let this sink in. Neither woman showed much reaction. Unlike Rosie, however, her mother at least looked at me. When nothing was said, I continued. "They'll be bringing your baby by for you to see before taking her to the other hospital. She'll have a lot of tubes coming out of her. Don't let that upset you. That's how we're breathing for her, feeding her, and getting blood for tests."

Another pause. Still no response. "Do you have any questions?" I quietly asked.

Although I was looking at Rosie, out of the corner of my eye I saw her mother start to speak and managed to glance at her lips in time to catch enough words that I understood her question. "How long will she be up there?"

"I don't know. It all depends on several things: how the baby responds to treatment, if she has Potter's syndrome, and if not, what the problem is."

Rosie looked at me briefly. I scrutinized her face for signs of emotion but found none. Then she stared at the open doorway again.

The transport team came twenty minutes later. Before leaving, they brought the baby by Rosie's bed. She was encouraged to touch her daughter but refrained from doing so, instead she stared at it mutely. Even after they left, she remained silent.

"I'm leaving now to go to my office," I informed them at that point. "I'll be back later to see how you're doing. Okay?"

Mrs. Zimmerman nodded while Rosie just watched me. I left the hospital and drove home, suddenly realizing how exhausted I felt. Trudging into my house, I showered again, revelling in the clean feeling. I stood there a long time, feeling my muscles relax under the hot water, pondering the events of the morning. Delivering a baby is usually a happy occasion. This morning, however, was anything but happy. I couldn't take too many deliveries like that. I was amazed at Rosie's apparent lack of emotion and wondered how anyone could be so wooden. After all, it was her very own child, and her first one at that.

I'm sure, I mused, there are times when my deafness makes people think I am aloof or without feelings too. One such time is when I am with a large group of people who are having a conversation. Since I depend on reading people's lips, I must know who's speaking in order to do so. But when the person I am watching stops talking, I don't know who will speak next. So I must quickly scan all the faces to locate the new speaker. By then, I have missed part of the conversation. Furthermore, it is not uncommon for me to find that person only to discover that he has just finished and someone else is talking. In fact, in a larger group it is almost impossible to keep track of dialogue as it jumps around the room.

Try it sometime and see for yourself. Next time you get together with several people, block out their voices with some well-fitted earplugs. See how long you last using only your eyes. I'll bet it won't be long. You'll find it quite demanding—and frustrating too.

So rather than annoy people by constantly asking them to repeat themselves, I remain quiet and unaware of what is being said. If I see people laughing, I sometimes laugh too so I don't stand out. Often I find myself daydreaming. When I do this though, inevitably someone talks directly to me. I usually don't realize this until a nearby person nudges me. Then I feel embarrassed. Everyone knows I wasn't "listening." It gets worse too. After the statement is repeated, I often give a reply that's totally inappropriate in the context of the discussion. Then I feel really foolish. Fortunately, my wife understands. In fact, Barbara has rescued me many times by answering for me as soon as she realizes what's happening.

Likewise, if I am in a darkened place, such as a car at night, I can't understand others. I don't say much then, either. Even in the daytime I have problems maintaining a conversation while driving because I have to take my eyes off the road constantly to look at the other person's lips. That's why my wife usually drives when we're together; we can talk more easily. But such wasn't the case during my high school dating days. Then, being the male, I was expected to drive. To make it worse, most dates were at night. Although it was very difficult to carry on conversations, I would try desperately to do so, leading to some awkward and amusing situations. How I avoided having an accident, I'll never know. In college, it was much easier. There, people usually walked or took public transportation. I did not have to worry about looking two places at once.

Perhaps—my thoughts shifted back to the present—Rosie had similar reasons for not talking. If so, though, why didn't she respond when I talked directly to her? I recalled the flicker of interest she showed just before her daughter was born. She must have feelings of some sort, I decided, but just not know how to express them. I wondered how she would react if the baby died.

Later that day, Rosie's mother visited the baby at Primary Children's Hospital and brought back a picture of her, which Rosie kept at her bedside. The next morning Rosie was discharged from the hospital so she could be with her baby. Despite losing a lot of blood, she was not dizzy and had not required a blood transfusion. I resolved to spend extra time with her over the next few weeks to help her express the emotions I was convinced she must feel. And I wondered how the baby would do.

THREE

As far as anyone knows, I was born deaf. Surprisingly, though, no one suspected it for a few years, least of all me! But more about that later.

My birth itself, in 1951, was not normal. Of course, no birth is routine to the people involved, but mine was definitely out-of-the-ordinary. Perhaps it could best be described as the case of the inexperienced intern. At the end of my mother's labor, when she felt delivery was imminent, she asked the intern to get her doctor. Before doing so, however, he checked her himself and informed her she still had several hours to go. But my mother knew better. She was a physician herself and realized he had mistaken her cervix for the soft spot all babies have when they are born. So she demanded he call her doctor. No sooner had the intern left the room to do so, when out I popped. Fortunately, my father is also a physician and he guided me safely into this world. Upon seeing me, the first words out of his mouth were, "Who in your family has big ears?"

"No one that I know of. Why?" my mother responded.

"Because this kid has wings!"

Although I am happy to say I no longer look like Dumbo, it seems ironic that my ears were my most noticeable feature then. A small baby, I was also quite sickly and intermittently stopped breathing. Nowadays I would be put in a neonatal intensive care unit, but there was no such thing in those days. So instead I was placed in an incubator and sent home. My parents took turns staying up nights, watching me closely to be sure I kept breathing.

Whenever I stopped, they stimulated me as needed until my respiration returned.

It took two weeks before I started breathing normally and no longer had to be observed constantly. From then on, I developed like any other child. I gained weight, grew longer, attained the developmental milestones, and became the typical toddler. I did enunciate poorly, sometimes so much so that only my family could understand me, but no one worried much about that. Many young children have that problem. Even when the possibility was raised that I might have dyslalia, a condition in which a person has difficulty articulating various speech sounds, there was not much concern. I understood others, had a sizable vocabulary, and could communicate my wants easily. In fact, my vocabulary was so large for my age, no one even considered the possibility of a hearing loss, particularly since the condition did not exist in either side of the family.

In retrospect, however, there was plentiful other evidence suggesting I could not hear. In addition to my poor articulation, I never responded when people called me. At the time, that trait was attributed to my being stubborn. Furthermore, when my mother read to me at night, she often noticed I did not seem to pay attention. Several times she tried placing one of her novels inside the book she was supposedly reading to me and read hers out loud instead. I never complained. She believed I was not interested in the story but just wanted someone in the room with me as I fell asleep.

Moreover, I never reacted to sounds normal hearing people react to. Nevertheless, my parents and caretakers always found a plausible explanation for this lack of response. The prolonged time that elapsed before my profound hearing loss was diagnosed is not unusual. Even today, when people are much more aware of how deaf children manifest themselves, the average age at diagnosis remains over two years. In the early 1950s, the delays were even longer. In my case, the fact that both my parents were physicians did not help either—I was almost four years old before they realized how little I heard.

The first person to suggest the possibility that I had a hearing loss was the director of the nursery school I attended. She had noticed that whenever she read a story to the class, I did not understand unless I sat right next to her and watched her face closely. Shortly thereafter, an incident at home confirmed her suspicion. I was talking to my father while he was replacing books on some shelves. His back was toward me and I became upset.

"Daddy, look at me when I talk!"

"Philip, I don't have to look at you to hear you."

"What did you say, Daddy?"

He turned around and repeated himself.

"Yes you do," I insisted.

"Why?"

"How else could you hear me?"

That question led to extensive testing, which confirmed my deafness. I was found to have hearing in only the very lowest end of the normal hearing range for human beings. And even in those frequencies I had a 50-decibel loss, a significant one. In terms of conversational sounds, I could hear vowels and an occasional consonant, provided they were of sufficient intensity. Thus, technically, I am not deaf. However, in many ways I am functionally so. My loss is similar to that of many who consider themselves members of the Deaf community, and many persons—ranging from teachers to patients—consider me deaf. Perhaps most importantly, I suffer from most, although not all, communication difficulties faced by people who are truly deaf. I miss most words in individual conversations and find group conversations extraordinarily difficult to follow. The main advantage I have over the totally deaf is that somehow I manage to understand most telephone conversations, provided they are fully amplified. How this is possible is unclear; the degree and type of my loss are inconsistent with this capability.

At the time my hearing loss was diagnosed, the cause was thought most likely due to anoxia, the medical term for lack of oxygen at birth. Although possible, this conclusion is not fully satisfactory. I had been immediately resuscitated, and lacked any other physical or mental abnormalities. No other apparent reason at the time, however, explained my deafness. My mother's pregnancy had been normal except for bleeding during the first three months, and neither side of the family had any deafness. The cause of my breathing difficulties was also unclear. Knowing what we do now, forty years later, I wonder if the culprit was cytomegalovirus. This virus infects pregnant women, unknown to them and their physicians, and commonly causes hearing losses similar to mine. It can also result in sickly babies, and could have caused the breathing trouble with which I was born. In the 1950s no one knew about cytomegalovirus. Even if doctors had been aware of its existence, however, the outcome would have been the same since no treatment is available.

With the diagnosis of my hearing loss, my parents were informed that the best place in Chicago for me to be evaluated was at Dr. Myklebust's clinic at Northwestern University. Helmer Myklebust, an internationally renowned specialist in deafness, was considered by many to be the premier expert in deaf education for his time. Under his supervision, I received an intensive outpatient evaluation over several weeks. During this time, tests were done to determine the type of hearing loss I had as well as my capabilities for schooling and communication.

Initially, the tests suggested I had "aphasic deafness," a type of deafness due to damage in the hearing area of the brain. With time, however, the clinicians changed their minds and concluded my hearing loss was the result of damage in the cochleae. The cochleae are the sensitive organs in each inner ear that convert sound waves transmitted by the three bones of the middle ear to nerve impulses which are then interpreted as sound by the brain. Damage to these organs is the most common cause of sensorineural hearing loss, more commonly known as "nerve deafness."

I do not remember any specifics about this evaluation. Nor do I recall much about the subsequent year when I went to Myklebust's clinic three times a week for intensive training in various areas. The major emphasis of the instruction was twofold: to teach me ways to maximize the use of what residual hearing I had, and to initiate comprehensive speech therapy. The clinicians also conducted periodic hearing tests to see if my loss was progressive. It was not, but it took a while for them to determine this because I refused to cooperate. They were able to get a rough estimate of my hearing loss without my cooperation, but in those days a more accurate assessment required my assistance. And that I would not provide. In fact, sometimes I outright refused to take the test. When I did consent to it, I found other ways to be difficult. For example, during the test I was instructed to either raise a finger or push a button every time I heard a sound. I would push the button or raise my finger frequently when I did not hear sounds, probably thinking that I was outwitting them and proving that I *could* hear. A couple of times I went to the opposite extreme by falling asleep during the test. Why I was so uncooperative was unclear. I never gave any reasons for my actions.

I have only two recollections of my visits to Northwestern. First, I have a clear picture in my mind of Lake Michigan, which at the time extended up to the building where my speech training was conducted. In my vision, the water appears endless and mysterious, and waves are crashing against the retaining wall I am looking over. The other memory is of stopping at Dairy Queen on the way home for a butterscotch sundae. My parents did this as a reward when I was cooperative with the training sessions. Unfortunately, it also had unforeseen consequences. My sister, who at this time was two, became jealous of the attention I received and wanted ice cream regularly too. My father recently told me he had worried at the time that her feelings of neglect would affect her personality later in life. So my parents made a special effort to ensure that she received an equal share of undivided attention from them. Their effort must have worked, because she has turned out to be a wonderful person.

In the middle of that year, my family traveled to New York as we did annually for over a decade, to visit my mother's family in the Bronx. During these vacations, we always stayed with my grandparents in their apartment on the seventh floor of a large apartment building. My sister and I loved these trips. Our grandparents doted on us, and we got to do many things we otherwise could not. So when my parents occasionally went out with friends and left my sister and me in the care of my grandparents, we did not mind at all.

Grandma and Grandpa had rapidly adjusted to the news about my hearing loss. Grandpa himself was born with deformed fingers and was acutely aware of the social stigma that could result from being different. They shared my parents' belief that my deafness should not limit my potential, and other than making sure I understood everything they said, they did not treat me any differently from their other grandchildren.

An incident occurred one day during this particular trip, when my parents had left for the afternoon and I went to use the bathroom. At that age, I never locked the door. Somehow I accidentally did this time, without realizing what I was doing (the lock was the type where one turned a wing above the doorknob). After finishing with the toilet, I tried to open the door and discovered it would not budge. I became scared and banged on the door, screaming and crying with fear. My grandparents came immediately and, yelling through the door, tried to tell me how to turn the lock. Not only could I not hear their verbal instructions, but I also had no idea they were even talking because I am unable to hear voices through doors. I cried louder, and flailed harder at the door. When they could not find a key to the door, they drew a picture of the doorknob and lock, demonstrating how to open the latter, and slipped this under the door. It did not help either. I was too panicked to think and continued my screaming and banging.

Finally, they realized that they would have to rescue me another way. After brief discussion, they decided to try the fire escape. Like many New York apartment buildings of the era, a permanent metal ladder extended along the side of the edifice from the top floor down to the ground. While Grandpa watched my sister, Grandma went out onto the fire escape and walked up half a flight. At this point, the steps crossed right under the bathroom window. Fortunately, she found the window unlocked and managed to open it fully. Then, she pulled herself over the sill and climbed through the window into the room.

It was during this same trip that Grandma also instilled in me a love—which has endured to this day—for the game of baseball. Television had been around for only a few years, but selected games of our national pastime were already being shown. And my grandmother was an avid fan of the sport. Even though she lived in New York, she was a Chicago White Sox fan. It so happened that the White Sox were playing the Yankees at that time, and the series was being televised. Although I could not understand anything the announcers said, she translated every word for me. Furthermore, she taught me many of the finer points of the game. She even "introduced" me to her favorite player, Nellie Fox, the stellar second baseman of the White Sox, who from then on was my favorite too.

It must have been difficult for my parents to cope with the news that their son had a profound hearing loss. Their decision in 1956 to go against the conventional wisdom of the time and have me attend kindergarten in a public school probably magnified their stress many times. They had two reasons for not enrolling me in a school for the deaf. First, there were no schools near where they lived; either I would have had to go to a residential school or they would have had to move closer to one of the day schools. Second, and much more important, they had investigated these schools and discovered that very few of the graduates, for whatever reason, acquired an education commensurate with that from the public schools. So they decided to "mainstream" me. In short, this meant putting me in regular classes in the public schools as they would any other child.

I was to be the first person with a profound hearing loss to be mainstreamed in the local public schools. Fortunately, both for my parents' and the educators' peace of mind as well as for my education, I would have some expert supervision. Lincolnwood, the town we lived in, was starting a special education center that would serve children with severe hearing losses from the entire north suburban area of Chicago. My parents discussed the situation with Mrs. Cutler, the teacher who had been hired for that class. She was excited about the challenge and agreed to monitor my progress and help my teachers adapt to my unique needs.

In retrospect, it was fortunate that my hearing loss was not discovered earlier. During those first few years when no one knew about it, no limitations were placed on me because of my handicap. People had the same expectations of me as they did other children. This allowed me to prove that I could do what any of my peers did. By the time my deafness was diagnosed, my parents had already realized this, and it helped support their conviction to mainstream me. Nowadays, mainstreaming is not a radical concept; in fact, it is the norm. In those days, however, it was a precocious idea, and one whose feasibility was considered unclear, especially for someone with a hearing loss as severe as mine.

Dr. Myklebust had strongly urged my parents to put me in a school for deaf children. Fortunately, my parents refused to heed this advice. Despite the educator's dire pronouncements, my mother and father insisted I have a trial period in regular classes before they would consider any alternatives. Finally, I was given a chance. And ever since, I haven't looked back. But it has not been easy. All along the way, I've had to fight similar battles over my capabilities. Even in medical school, the fight did not stop.

My parents did agree wholeheartedly, however, with Dr. Myklebust's two other recommendations: hearing aids and speech therapy. In those days, hearing aids were bulky, hard-to-use gadgets. The battery was worn in a shirt pocket, while a wire extended from it to the ear plug. Like any child, I rebelled against looking different. Besides, I did not agree with the explanations that it would help me understand others. I could communicate with others, got along well with my peers, and had lots of friends—I was happy. I certainly did not want the annoyance of a hearing aid. Furthermore, the technology itself was still quite primitive. To begin with, it did not seem to help me understand people any better. Moreover, in addition to amplifying the sounds I did not hear, the aid also amplifed those few I did. The result was unbearable. Cars, airplanes, slamming doors, and other low pitched noises became so loud that my ears hurt constantly. So I refused to use the aid.

I didn't even wear a hearing aid when I began school. Instead, I sat in the front of my classes and concentrated on reading the teachers' lips. In the lower grades, most of them did their best always to face the class when they talked, rather than the blackboard. And if they had any questions, Mrs. Cutler made herself readily available for consultation. So I had few problems. In fact, I loved school. That's not to say my hearing loss did not cause any problems. It did, but usually I could overcome them. There were times, however, when I could not.

One such time especially stands out in my mind. It happened when I was five, shortly after my family moved to our house in Lincolnwood. As part of the move, I switched to a new kindergarten midway through the year. Things went fine the first day until it was time to go home. My teacher told me which bus I was to take, but I had not understood her. Being new, I was too embarrassed to ask her to repeat herself and pretended I did understand. I followed a girl in my class who had befriended me and ended up on her bus. Each time the bus stopped, the driver would ask if that was my stop. And each time I would look for my home, then tell him no. Finally, we reached the last stop. For some reason, I got off. Perhaps I did not want to admit I had taken the wrong bus, or maybe I was confused. Either way, there I was—all of five years old and lost on a strange street.

I walked down the block a ways, looking for something familiar, but nothing was recognizable. Finally I sat on the curb and cried. Soon a lady came out from the house behind me. She found out why I was crying and invited me inside, saying she would call my mother. But I refused to go. I had been thoroughly indoctrinated by my parents never to go with strangers. So she asked what my phone number was. I was so upset I could not remember. Besides, I had been in the new house only for a few days. She then asked my name. That I told her. Then while I continued to bawl on the curb, she looked up Zazove in the phone book. There was only one listing, but it was not my parents'; it was, however, my aunt's. She knew our number, and although it was no more than ten minutes before my mother picked me up, it seemed like hours.

Other than events like this, my recollection is that being deaf did not pose significant problems for me as a youngster, especially with other kids. My speech, however, was a different story.

FOUR

I HAVE AN "ACCENT" in that I incorrectly pronounce sounds I have never heard. It was especially noticeable when I was young, and occasionally others made fun of me because I spoke differently. At times this upset me. I looked like everyone else and considered myself no different; it was hard to accept the fact I was. Fortunately, most of my peers did not care, especially after they learned to understand me. They also discovered quickly that they had to face me if they wanted me to understand what they said. So I had many friends in the neighborhood and participated in the usual childhood games. Still, my parents knew the quality of my voice would be important later on in life. Thus, as far back as I can remember, they sent me to speech therapy.

As a child, therapy was boring—extremely so. I could not hear most sounds, so I had to concentrate on learning the correct placement of my lips and tongue for each sound. This is very hard to do. I spent hours in front of a mirror, trying to get everything just right. And when I finally did, I would have no idea I was correct except that my therapist would become excited. At times, it almost seemed as impossible to me as closing one's eyes and sensing what color a crayon is. Still, little by little my speech improved.

It also became quickly apparent that maintaining this improvement would be just as difficult. The slightest change in tongue or lip position significantly changes a sound. Since I cannot hear the change, I did not realize something was in the wrong position. Certain sounds were particularly difficult to learn, and I often got these mixed up with similar-sounding ones. So my *z*'s would sound like *s*'s, my *sh*'s like *ch*'s, and my *j*'s like *g*'s.

Whenever I could, I avoided speech therapy. In first grade, I was scheduled for therapy three times a week. The special education room was in a different building, perhaps 100 yards away from my regular class. Once, after leaving my regular class, I did not go to therapy but instead spent the time playing with some friends who were having recess. My fun was short lived. Mrs. Cutler found me on the playground and I quickly learned that playing hooky from therapy was not acceptable to my parents and teachers. Still, I did not enjoy going, especially because it seemed unfair. My classmates did not have to go. Only I did. And it was so hard too. Then I learned to read.

Actually, I had learned to read a little before I started school. I always loved books, and my parents had taken me to the library regularly since I was a toddler. But it was not until first grade that I really learned to read. From then on, I was a voracious reader. It opened up a whole new world—that of language. Up until then, I knew only those words I could figure out from lipreading. Once I began to read, however, my vocabulary became almost unlimited. So I plunged into this world and, most days, for hours on end could be found with a book. I became a bookworm in the truest sense of the word. I read in the morning before getting out of bed, during the day when school was out and I was not playing baseball, and in the evening before going to bed. Even at night, when my lights were turned off, I still managed to read. Using a flashlight and shielding the beam with my pillow so my parents would not notice, I would read happily into the night. At first, despite my efforts to be secretive, my parents periodically caught me. I could not hear them coming down the hall. When we got a dog, however, things changed to my advantage. Our dog slept on my bed. Because he was not supposed to be there, he would jump off whenever he heard my mother or father walking toward the bedroom. Soon I learned to turn out my light when he did this, and thereafter rarely got caught. Others noticed my newfound infatuation; years later, my mother told me on several occasions, "You used to read so much as a kid, I thought you were going to be smart when you grew up." And at my high school's twentieth-year reunion, one of my favorite childhood playmates confided, "Philip, I always knew you were going to be a doctor. You were so smart. Every time I came over, you were reading a book."

Reading was the key to improving my speech because it allowed me to learn how words were spelled. Knowing which letters were in a word helped me pronounce it more accurately. For the first time, I began to benefit from my speech therapy lessons, although I still did not enjoy them. I continued to mispronounce words, especially those which are not spoken the same as they are spelled, a problem that persists even now. For example, it was just recently that I learned that the *ch* in Chicago is pronounced like an *sh* rather than a *ch*. Overall, though, my enunciation became much clearer. I am sure that, without reading, speaking better would have taken much longer. In fact, if I had not become literate, I probably would not have developed consistently intelligible speech.

This may be hard for most people to understand since they learn to speak and understand by the sounds they hear. But people who are deaf cannot do that. Even now, when I have trouble understanding a word, I'll ask someone to spell it. I can easily comprehend why most deaf children, when given the option, instinctively prefer signing to vocalizing. It is so much easier. And those who sign sometimes develop far superior communcation skills at an early age compared with those who are forced to "talk."

Despite years of therapy, my speech sounds "different" to this day. Many people think it is the result of my being born in another country, especially because of my unusual last name. They are often surprised to learn the reason for my unique speech. My voice also has a pronounced nasal twang to it. Although I do not hear this when I talk, surprisingly I can hear it when my voice is played back loudly on tape. I cannot, of course, understand the words, but the distinct nasal quality of my voice is readily apparent even to me. No one has been able to determine how to correct this or what the cause is. As a result, some people find it hard to understand me when we first meet. After a few minutes, however, they usually get used to my speech and it is no longer a problem.

Surprisingly, I never learned any sign language (other than the usual signs students use to talk in class behind the teacher's back). In those days, the emphasis in therapy was on talking, not signing. All my peers were hearing too. Since I did not have any contact with other deaf children, there was no one to teach me.

How can a deaf person understand people when he or she hears only the vowels and a few consonants? Simply by utilizing methods other than hearing. As do many deaf children, I taught myself to read lips automatically because I thought it was the natural way everybody "heard." Unfortunately, lipreading alone detects, at best, less than fifty percent of words being spoken. The reason for this is that many words and sounds look exactly alike. In my case, learning to read also helped by expanding my vocabulary significantly. Finally, and perhaps most importantly, I "synthesize." This is a concept experts have developed to explain how some deaf and hard of hearing people can understand speech despite not hearing most sounds (and often whole words) other people vocalize. Somehow—and no one knows exactly how—we fill in the gaps in order to understand the conversation. Sometimes our guesses are wrong. But using the context of the conversation, plus the ever-present subtle body language clues all people exhibit, we are correct more often than not.

Everyone who spends time with a deaf person quickly discovers tricks that make it easier to communicate. For example, friends and family make sure I am looking right at them when we converse. They also learn how to get my attention: either tap me if I am within striking distance or make a low-pitched noise I can hear. My wife and children are forever banging a wall or table when they want my attention; this maneuver occasionally works when I am in a different room. Our house probably sounds noisy to others.

My sister carried this to an extreme. When she was very young, she would grab my hand and talked into it like a microphone. Little did she realize that by covering her lips, she was making it harder for me to understand her. But she did accomplish her objective—to get my attention.

The 1950s were also the time when television came into its own. Programs such as "The Mickey Mouse Show," "Roy Rogers," and "Father Knows Best" were popular with many of my peers. Even the Beatles were first seen on TV in the early sixties. I remember that not because I saw them myself but because of my surprise when everyone in school was talking about them the next day. I had little interest in television because I could not understand any words, except in the rare case when the actor was looking directly at the camera. And even then I only got a few words. Sporting events were the only exception to my avoidance of TV because one can enjoy those without hearing any words. I found myself instead becoming interested in various hobbies, especially those involving collecting things. So whenever my friends went home to watch their favorite TV shows and I was tired of reading, I worked on my collections of butterflies, stamps, and coins.

My parents were extremely supportive of me from the beginning. They raised me to believe that, despite my handicap, I could do anything anyone else could. Fueled by this attitude, I was able to surmount the inherent barriers my deafness created and perform well in school and athletics. But it was not easy.

There were numerous times I did not hear things my teachers or coaches said. Sometimes, I would tell them and they would repeat themselves. But I quickly tired of asking them so often. Besides, it made me feel self-conscious too. Fortunately, I learned a few tricks which helped me get by, despite missing the teacher's instructions. One of the most helpful was the fortunate coincidence that alphabetically my name is at the end. My classes often did tasks in alphabetical order, and this turned out to be serendipitous. I would watch and learn from what the others did. By the time it was my turn, I had usually deduced exactly what I needed to do. Occasionally my guess would be way off and it would be embarrassing, but even that turned out to be a blessing in disguise. Subsequently, the teachers would remember my previous gaffes and make sure I understood their directions.

In addition, my parents were diligent about making sure I not only completed but also understood my homework. When I did not, they would review the subject with me until I did. We spent uncounted hours nights and weekends reviewing spelling words, practicing arithmetic, studying geography, and writing and rewriting reports. As I progressed through school and the amount of homework increased, my parents had to devote more time to working with me, often at the expense of other things they would rather have done. And when I had specific problems with teachers or school policies, Mrs. Cutler was an invaluable help. She would discuss the matter with the appropriate person and straighten the situation out. (I was not aware of this at the time, however, and only learned of it many years later.)

My parents helped in other ways too, although I was not always appreciative of their assistance at the time. For example, whenever we went to shows or someplace where people were lecturing, my father would orally repeat what the speaker was saying. He soon developed the ability to listen and talk simultaneously, like any good oral interpreter nowadays, and by watching his lips I would grasp as much as anyone.

Every step of the way there were barriers to overcome and battles to wage. Fortunately for me, I was not aware of many of them. At this age, my parents did much of the fighting for me. People, especially adults, do not like to deal with someone different. And I was different all right. So some of those in authority tried to keep me from many of the things others take for granted, such as school, sports, and plays. No matter how often I proved myself, people always expected me to fail the next time. Prejudices about deafness die hard.

Attitudes can be changed, however. My fifth-grade teacher was a classic example. Before the school year began, she was very upset that she was to have a deaf (to her implying really dumb, not just mute) student. She tried every tactic to have me switched to a different room. Even after classes started, she was still leery of me. By the end of the year, however, having seen my determination to succeed, she had totally reversed her position. She had become one of my biggest boosters.

In general, my childhood memories are a wonderful collage of baseball, scouting, and the other fun things young boys do. After all, that's what a childhood should be.

FIVE

"LADAWN, WHAT A PLEASURE to see you again," I smiled at her.

There was just a little giggle in response. Then she averted her eyes from me and turned her attention back to the toys.

"What seems to be the problem, Mrs. Furness?" I asked.

"LaDawn's had a problem with her nose running for a long, long time. In fact, I'm embarrassed to tell you this," she started to blush, "but it's been going on for months. I would've brought her in sooner, but her father's got the same thing. So I just figured it probably ran in the family. But lately it's gotten worse, and the smell's become so bad we can't stand it anymore. In fact, I'm embarrassed to go places with her now. Before at least, if I washed her nose, she'd be okay for a while. Now, it never goes away. There's always stuff running onto her lip. No matter how much I clean it, it runs and stinks within a few minutes. So I figured it was about time we got it taken care of."

Mrs. Furness wasn't exaggerating about the odor. You couldn't help but notice it. Otherwise, LaDawn was a normal, bouncy four-year-old. About three feet tall, she had a round, impish face and a squat nose. Her mop of floppy blondish hair never seemed to change; every time I saw her, it was frizzled and disheveled. And she loved to wear dresses. Today she had on a yellow and white sleeveless one. Perhaps most striking of all was how much she and her mother looked alike, down to the frizzled, floppy hair.

LaDawn got up and, rushing past me, jumped onto her mother's lap. Then she whispered in Mrs. Furness's ear and smiled.

"Ask him," her mother answered.

LaDawn looked at the floor and mumbled something. I couldn't see her lips to read them, so I did not know what she had said. That is a common problem deaf people have with children. Not only do children have high voices, they often speak quietly and look away, making it very difficult for us to understand them. We have to make a special effort to focus on their lips when talking to them.

I squatted to see LaDawn's face better. This embarrassed her, so she turned her head away.

"LaDawn," I called her.

She looked back at me again.

"What did you say?"

Again I couldn't see her answer. But this time she also pointed to my stethoscope, which has several tiny toy animals attached to it.

"You want to hold one of these?"

She nodded.

"Sure, go ahead and take one."

"Oh, for cute," she said as she picked a panda.

I resumed the conversation. "How long has her father had his drainage?"

"As long as I've known him," replied Mrs. Furness.

"Does it also smell?"

"No, nothing like LaDawn's. And when he blows his nose, the smell goes away for a while. That never happens with her."

"Has she ever put anything in her nose?"

"I'm sorry, I did not understand your question."

I repeated it.

"Of course not," Mrs. Furness smiled. After a short pause she nudged LaDawn and asked, "You haven't put anything in your nose, have you?"

LaDawn shook her head no vigorously.

"Are you sure?" I asked.

She nodded.

"Has she had any fever?" I continued.

"No."

"What about cold or allergy type symptoms?"

"Not that I'm aware of."

"Does the drainage come from both sides of the nose or just one?"

Mrs. Furness replied but I did not understand her answer.

"I'm sorry, what did you say?"

"I said, 'Doctor, now that you mention it, it only runs on the right side. I hadn't thought about that before, but I've never seen it from the left side.' "

With that, I was pretty sure I knew the cause of LaDawn's problem. Children frequently put things in their noses, ears, and other body orifices. Sometimes they forget, and it's only when symptoms develop that we find the objects. It's amazing what I have found in some of them: paper, small balls, Kleenex, shoelace rings, popcorn—even dog food.

"All right, LaDawn, let's see if we can figure out what's going on. Hop up here on the table and I'll take a peek in your nose."

Looking at me, LaDawn hesitated. She curled up tightly in her mother's lap.

"Go on, honey," Mrs. Furness gently encouraged her. "The doctor needs to take a look at you so we can find out why your nose keeps running and smelling."

With a little push from her mother, LaDawn slid off the lap slowly. She clambered onto the exam table and waited, obediently yet apprehensively.

First, I engaged her in small talk, in order to put her at ease.

"How old are you, LaDawn?"

"Four," she smiled, holding up four fingers.

"Wow, you're really getting big, aren't you?"

"Mm, hmm," she agreed, then proudly proclaimed, "I just had my birthday."

"You did?"

She nodded.

"I'll bet you had a nice birthday party," I half asked, half told her. "Okay, let's look in your nose now. What do you think we'll find there?"

"Potatoes," she laughed.

"Potatoes?" I played along. "In your nose? Well I hope not."

I took a nasal speculum and inserted it in her right nostril. The stench was strong but bearable. As I looked in, LaDawn started to squirm, making it hard to get a good look. The speculum was too large for her, but I found what I was looking for. Behind the foul draining pus was a greyish object.

Once it was removed, her symptoms would disappear. However, I knew that whatever it was, if it did not come out easily, I was going to have a very uncooperative child on my hands. Then I would have to use the papoose board. With this, she would be immobilized by cloth wrapped around her arms, legs, and head. I didn't want to use it unless absolutely necessary. It might make her terrified to see a physician again, and there are already enough negative aspects about doctor visits. I wanted to make her experience with me as positive as possible.

"It looks like I found the problem, LaDawn. You have something in your nose," I said.

"She what?" stuttered Mrs. Furness. "Are you for real?"

"Yes."

"What is it?" she asked, still somewhat incredulous.

"I'm not sure, but we'll soon find out. And once we get it out, all her symptoms should quickly go away."

I was smiling at LaDawn and patting her head reassuringly, when I heard a voice. I looked at her mother in time to see the words "in her nose."

"Pardon me?"

"I don't believe it. I never did see her put anything in her nose," exclaimed her mother, a little indignant.

"You'll see for yourself in a minute."

I called LeAnne Davis—my medical assistant—and asked for an alligator forceps. While waiting, I explained what they were to the Furnesses, who were becoming apprehensive about what I was planning to do. "Because kids so often put things in their noses, we've developed a special tool to remove them. Its shape allows us to remove things from the nose without our hands getting in the way. See how it opens at the end like an alligator's mouth?" I said as LeAnne returned with the instrument.

"Now, I'm going to need your help, LaDawn. You need to hold real still while I remove it, okay? It might feel a little funny coming out, but that's okay. Just hold still."

LaDawn started to fidget. She obviously was not going to cooperate. As Mrs. Furness caressed her daughter, I instructed her, "Here, hold LaDawn's arms with your hands and lean on her with your body so she can't wiggle or kick. LeAnne will hold her head."

LaDawn tried to squirm away from the two women. When she discovered she couldn't, she started to cry. Watching, I got ready to extract the object. Foreign bodies in the nose can sometimes be very difficult to remove. Every situation is different, depending on the object, how long it's been present, and the age of the child, among other things.

As soon as she was secure, I began. "Okay, LaDawn, here we go. Hold still and I'll take it out as fast as I can."

With the speculum holding her nostril open, I looked in and located the object. I inserted the forceps and inched toward it. Luck was with me! On the first try I was able to grab and extract it without breaking any pieces off. It was compressible, roundish, and yellow. Acrid pus oozed out of it. Within a few seconds the smell permeated the room.

LaDawn's mother stared at the object wide-eyed, her mouth open. She was speechless, stunned more than embarrassed. Finally, she gasped, "I don't believe it. There really was something in there." Leaning forward to see it better, she added, crinkling her nose in disgust, "It almost looks like a sponge, doesn't it?"

"I think it was a sponge at one time," I replied, holding the object at arm's length and fighting the rumbling in my stomach. "I'm sure LaDawn put it in her nose a long time ago and forgot all about it. Being in there so long sure changed its appearance, didn't it?" I opened the door to let some fresh air in.

Of course, LaDawn didn't care at all what it was. She was too busy bawling in the security of her mother's lap.

"It looks so small. I wonder where it came from?" pondered Mrs. Furness, shaking her head. "Unbelievable. My husband won't believe it. A sponge in her nose."

"Do you want to take it home and show him?" I chuckled to myself. I knew that even if she did, she would not be able to tolerate the odor long enough to get it home, let alone wait for him to return from work.

"Yech. No way," she replied, holding her nose in disgust.

As an amateur magician, I am always amused at people's reactions when I pull small balls out of childrens' pockets. Those responses, however, do not provide even close to the amusement I get when I remove something real from a body orifice, whatever it may be.

At this point I could not stand the smell anymore. I left and threw the sponge in the garbage, which was dumped immediately in the outside trash bin. Despite air fresheners, the odor lingered in the air.

I came back into the room to find LaDawn still sobbing, more from the shock of being held down than from any pain.

"That ought to solve your runny nose, LaDawn," I stated. She didn't say anything. Looking at her mother, I continued, "I don't expect any problems, Mrs. Furness. Usually the smell pretty much clears within a day or so, although sometimes it may last a week. Her nose may bleed a little too for a couple of days. If neither goes away, let me know. Okay?"

Still looking astonished, Mrs. Furness nodded.

"I do have one more recommendation," I added with a sly grin.

"What's that?"

"You said your husband had a similar drainage. Perhaps he ought to come over and let me check his nose too!"

With a sheepish smile and holding her now calming daughter, Mrs. Furness answered, "That sounds like a great idea. But I doubt if he'd ever come. Besides, he probably doesn't have anything up his nose. He's a little old for that."

Driving home that evening, I was in a good mood. Experiences like the one with LaDawn are what make the practice of medicine worthwhile. Here I had been able to really help someone. And as my practice had steadily been getting busier, despite being in existence only eight months, I was finding this satisfaction occurred more and more often. If I could help all my patients as easily, medicine would be the perfect profession.

The spring weather was delightful as the sun set behind the mountains. People were out riding their horses and chatting with neighbors. Children were zooming around on skateboards and bicycles. As I passed a McDonald's, I realized I was very thirsty and pulled into the drive-up lane. I had come here many times before but always with someone else in the car, never by myself. Suddenly, I realized what I had done and stopped before I reached the microphone. How would I order? I could not hear anything people said from the intercom. I paused a second to decide what to do. I could go directly to the pickup window and order there, but for some reason that seemed too impudent. So I elected to give the microphone a try.

I drove to it and waited. When should I talk? Had someone spoken yet? Then I thought I heard what might have been noises—it must be someone speaking. I had no idea what they said but figured it was now or never. I asked for a medium Coke and paused. I convinced myself the faint noises came again. Hmmmm. Perhaps they didn't hear me. So I repeated my order. The noises recurred, but the words themselves were a total mystery. There was no use repeating my order a third time, so I ignored the sounds and drove to the pickup window.

The girl there looked at me strangely. I smiled back and said, "How much do I owe you?"

"I told you twice, sixty-eight cents."

I gave her the change, took my Coke, and, still smiling, nodded good-bye. Then I turned my attention once again to the road and drove home, in just as good a mood as before.

SIX

AT FIRST GLANCE, becoming a teenager did not seem that different. I still had my family and friends. I was doing well in school and was the star catcher of my baseball team.

Perhaps the first indication that I was changing came when I realized my eyes were not as sharp as they had been. Other people saw things, especially objects far away, that I couldn't. At the age of ten, my mother took me to the eye doctor, who determined I was nearsighted. I would need glasses.

Suddenly, this became a very sensitive issue for me. It was bad enough being deaf. And recently, I had gotten braces on my teeth. Having already acquired the self-consciousness of teenagers, I could not bear the thought of wearing glasses in public too. So I refused to do so. Then one day, while no one I knew was looking, I tried them on just to see how things looked. I was amazed. I could hear so much better. Yes, *hear*. People's lips were now well focused, and I could read them so much easier. Before, from across the room, I would have had no idea what they were saying. Now I did. I started to wear the glasses more and more, especially when I discovered seeing better helped in sports too.

I used my new ability to see at a distance many times and in unexpected ways. In eighth grade, for instance, my class was divided into four "countries." Each was assigned a different corner of the room. For a month, we spent an hour a day there, holding elections, plotting our economies, and devising strategies for competing with the other countries. I quickly became the most valuable person in our country, for I could spy on the other countries. I would sit quietly, watching people's faces in the other corners, reading their lips. By the time they realized what I was doing and turned their chairs away from me, it was too late. My country had become the most powerful.

When I saw how much glasses helped me, I even consented to try hearing aids again, although reluctantly. But they never seemed to help much and, despite having become smaller and more technically advanced, still caused the same problems as before. In addition, having not used one before then, I found the background noise extremely distracting. Even if the problems of the discomfort from amplified low-pitched noises and the distraction of background noises had been correctable, I probably still would not have worn a hearing aid most of time. No one else I knew had one. Wearing glasses was less of a problem; many other people did that. But a hearing aid was another issue. There was no way I was going to look different.

My self-consciousness became apparent in other ways too. Up until then, I had depended on my father to orally interpret for me in situations where I could not understand what people were saying. Now, however, I began to feel embarrassed when he did this and would ask him to stop. I did not want people looking at us and would rather not understand anything than appear conspicuous.

I was not the only one who was becoming a teenager. My peers were too. This change manifested itself in numerous ways, not the least of which was the tendency to develop intolerances for people who were different. My teenage years were the only period of time when I suffered from more than the rare smattering of ridicule.

Usually only students who were insecure made fun of my speech. Either they weren't doing well in school and were envious of my success, or they were trying to gather attention to themselves by making fun of me. Even though I realized this, it still hurt. It was hard for me to ignore the derisive names or the exaggerated imitations of my speech. Several times I retorted but quickly learned that this just added fuel to the fire. The best way to stop the taunts was to ignore them. Fortunately, most of my peers also ignored the catcalls, and the perpetrators usually gave up.

Near the end of eighth grade, one of these troublemakers picked on another deaf boy. Josh and I had just met a week earlier during one of my speech therapy visits. He was tall, close to six feet already, and unlike me, was not mainstreamed; he attended the special education class full-time. He usually played alone and did not communicate well with the hearing students, in part because of his minimal contact with them. While Josh and I were talking one day, the bully went up to Josh, pointed at his hearing aids, and laughed. Josh turned and started to walk away, but the bully started pushing him, trying to get others to join "in the fun." Suddenly, things went too far. As I watched, Josh's face took on a determined look. He then swung around quickly and landed one of the hardest punches I have ever seen, square on the bully's nose. That loser never bothered either of us again.

Every summer, from age nine to fifteen, I was fortunate to attend overnight camp in northern Wisconsin for eight weeks. It was an experience that I enjoyed very much. Although there was a heavy emphasis on sports, much time was also devoted to music, drama, and the other usual camp experiences. As in school, I was the only one there with a significant hearing loss. This was not a problem insofar as the daily activites were concerned. Being athletically inclined, I easily held my own in the sports. Even the music and drama competitions were not a problem. Several other campers could not carry a tune either, and we would lip sync the songs whenever our cabins competed. Likewise, although I never had major roles in the skits and plays, I did find many other ways to contribute. I even had a couple of small speaking parts over the years.

I did miss out on a few things because of my hearing loss. My cabinmates often talked at night after the lights were out. I could never participate in this. However, this rarely bothered me, probably because I did not know what I was missing. Even if they said things to me or about me, I had no way of knowing. One night at the age of eleven, however, an event occurred in which I did feel disadvantaged. The boys in my cabin decided to raid the kitchen. We planned the heist all day, and being as excited about the plan as anyone, I felt left out because I could not be directly involved. The boys who were going to crawl through the basement window of the mess hall to get into the kitchen had to be able to communicate with each other by whispers. Counselors walked by at various times; if anyone talked out loud they could be caught. Moreover, several people had to act as lookouts to warn those in the kitchen if anyone was coming. This required the ability to hear people coming in addition to hearing whispers. There was no way I could do any of this.

The campfires and similar activities that occurred after dusk were another aspect of camp where my hearing loss interfered with my ability to participate. Consequently, I always found them boring. I never understood anything that was said because I could not see the speaker's lips. I would much rather have stayed in the cabin and read a book, but that was never an option. Everyone was required to go to the activities. So while stories of the outdoors and tales of Indians were told over crackling bonfires, I would try to pass the time by watching the wood burn, daydreaming about whatever came to mind.

There were other times like this too. Twice every summer, after all campers had gone to bed, the "Braves"—a group of older campers and counselors who previously had been campers—would come by unexpectedly banging their drums, calling everyone to attend an important powwow. The campers would get up in excitement and go to the place where the powwow was being held. During these meetings, certain campers were selected to join the "Braves." This was a prestigious honor, and all the younger campers dreamed of being chosen. One could then discover the secrets of the club, as well as gain the privileges.

During my fourth year of camp, at the age of twelve, I was one of the lucky ones picked. As the rest of the camp was ushered back to bed, the selected pledges were escorted to a campfire. Pillowcases were placed over our heads and we were positioned next to each other, side by side. Despite the pillowcase, I could barely make out the outlines of someone standing in front of us. I later found out it was the chief of the Braves, who had been explaining the initiation rites and what we should expect. During this time, he also swore the pledges to secrecy. That is everyone but me. I had no idea what he was saying. Near the end of his spiel, someone realized this and took my pillowcase off. Then, because we were right next to the fire, I was able to see the chief's lips and understood the rest of his instructions. He neglected, however, to repeat what had already been said.

Afterwards, we underwent the beginning of our initiation. It was similar to those of many fraternities, consisting of repetitive exercises and acting as servants to various members of the Braves. At no time, however, were we ever asked to do anything dangerous. In addition to this, we were forbidden to speak for two days.

The next morning, one of my cabinmates asked me what had happened the previous night. Although I knew I could not speak, I was unaware we had been sworn to secrecy about our activities. So I acted out some of the things we had done. One of the Braves happened to walk by then and immediately reprimanded me, reminding me about our vow to keep this a secret. I explained in writing that I had not heard those instructions because of the pillowcase that had been over my head. Fortunately, they realized it was their mistake and allowed me to remain in the organization.

In high school teachers were, for the most part, less intimidated by my hearing loss than my grammar school teachers had been. But it still remained a major barrier. For instance, I failed to make the sophomore basketball team because the coach felt uncomfortable having a deaf person on his team. The coach never even hinted this to me, but he did confide in one of the school counselors who mentioned it to his teenage son. That boy was not only in my grade but a good friend of mine, and he was the one who explained to me why I did not make the team.

Also, I still had the usual difficulties because I never heard the sounds everyone else used to guide their day. School bells were a good example. I had to depend on my watch, plus everyone else's actions, to know when the bell rang. Assemblies were another problem. I almost never knew what was being said unless I happened to be in the front row. And for some reason, I almost never was. The only things I ever learned about school assemblies were from comments my classmates might make.

I did not find high school any harder academically, though. There were, of course, times when I did have trouble understanding my teachers. For the most part, however, they remembered to face my direction most of the time. Still, it was almost impossible to take notes because to do so meant I had to periodically look away from the teacher. I found myself missing critical parts of lectures when I tried. I managed to obtain the information by studying the textbooks and, when appropriate, borrowing my classmates' notes. The latter was especially necessary during my junior-year honors American history class. That teacher was a fabulous lecturer, someone who constantly mesmerized his students and made history come alive. Rather than even try to take notes, I concentrated on his talk. There was one problem with this, though. Every six weeks, we had to turn in our notes to be graded on their neatness and completeness. I solved the problem by copying the notes of my best friend, who happened to be in the same class as I was. I almost always typed them; it was not only faster, but the product looked neater. Once, however, I did not get around to copying them until the night before the notes were due. It soon became apparent that I would not be able to finish that night. So, one-third of the way through, I started typing every other line, hoping the teacher would not notice. He didn't. And not only did I get an A, but my friend, who had the complete notes, got only a B because his were handwritten rather than typed!

For most people in my generation, high school was the time we first became interested in the opposite sex. I was no exception. The surge of hormones circulating through my body as I went through puberty accentuated this interest. Still, it was not until my junior year of school that I became brave enough to ask a girl out on a date. In part, this was due to the normal anxiety all teenage boys have about rejection. In my case, however, my hearing loss also played a role. I worried that girls would not want to date me because of that. The first time I asked someone out, I rehearsed my lines for two hours before calling, only to be turned down. I had no idea why she did that, but began to wonder whether any girl would ever go out with me, a deaf man. This could have been disastrous for my self-esteem. Fortunately, one of my friends fixed me up with his girlfriend's friend. Although that did not work out, it was what I needed—a boost to my self-confidence. After that, I had no more problems asking girls out than my peers.

During my junior year, I was selected as one of two students from my high school to attend Illinois Boys' State. I still remember getting off the bus in Springfield (the state capital) where the weeklong event was being held, and seeing numerous campaign signs already posted for two boys from elsewhere in the state who were running for governor. The preconvention instructions we had all received explicitly proscribed such publicity. Nevertheless, it was apparent the rule was not being enforced.

All one thousand boys were divided into ten counties, each of which was further subdivided into cities. Together, the ten counties made up the state. The program during the week was split between classes about government and blocks of free time. The purpose of the latter was to encourage us boys to intermingle and exchange ideas. As usual, I was the lone deaf person in the entire place. I did not publicly announce this, but when people asked about my speech I told them. Many boys from smaller schools had never met a peer with a significant hearing loss, and several became very curious and asked many questions.

At the end of the second day, several people in my "county" convinced me to run for governor even though others had been campaigning since they had arrived, including another individual in our county. Not having brought signs and other campaign material with me, I was at a disadvantage. Nevertheless, I agreed and plunged ahead. A boy from western Illinois in the bunk next to mine agreed to be my campaign manager and, after an evening of planning, we started the campaign in earnest the next morning. There was a store on the premises, where I purchased poster board and other supplies. We spent much of our free time that day making signs and recruiting supporters. But one thousand people is a large number to contact. It soon became obvious we would not be able to contact them all in the three days that remained. My best chance of winning would be the convention the night before the election, when the fifteen gubernatorial candidates were scheduled to speak to the entire Boy's State. When the meeting began, I learned we were to go in alphabetical order. Listening to fifteen speeches can tax anyone's patience. Since I would be last, I worried people wouldn't listen. Nevertheless, despite the fact that many in the audience had never heard me speak before, my speech received the biggest ovation of all.

Unfortunately, this was not enough. I came in fourth. Still I was satisfied with my performance. All three persons ahead of me were the only candidates in their counties (the counties, like states in presidential elections, tend to support their own), and two had brought campaign material with them. More importantly, however, this experience taught me it was possible for me to speak effectively before groups of people who were not used to hearing my speech.

I continued to succeed in school and, in fact, graduated from high school with a gold key, the highest academic honor the school awarded. I also continued to participate in interscholastic sports and made friends of all sorts.

During my senior year, I began applying to colleges. In my family, with both parents being physicians, not only were my sister and I encouraged to go to college, we were expected to. My parents had not considered any other course for us, even for me with my hearing loss. It had not been an insurmountable problem up to then, they reasoned. Why should college be any different?

My college applications, to some of the top schools in the country, raised a lot of other people's eyebrows, though. Admissions officials were not used to having deaf students on campus. And many had doubts as to whether I could compete. They believed college was much more difficult than high school because there is less structure and students are more on their own. Several schools interviewed me just to double-check that I could carry on an intelligent conversation. And at one major midwestern state university, the dean of admissions himself made special arrangements to meet me.

He could not believe someone with my degree of hearing loss could make the honor roll in a public high school. At the end of our meeting, he must have been convinced—he offered me a place on the spot. I was also accepted at several other places and had to make a decision of where to go.

My initial choice was Tulane University in New Orleans, the school furthest from home. I felt a sense of rebellion, and wanted to be entirely on my own. At the time, it seemed obvious to me that the farther away I was from my family, the more independent I would be. My parents, however, were much wiser. They wanted me to attend the best school possible, regardless of its location, and preferred Northwestern University, which had also accepted me. Over the course of several weeks, they somehow managed to convert me to their point of view. Finally, I agreed to go to Northwestern, but only under one condition: I had to live on campus. I knew the school had a housing shortage at the time and often required students from Chicago to commute from home. It took a phone call or two, but my parents arranged this. So in the fall of 1969, I began college in Evanston, Illinois.

SEVEN

In 1969, during the summer before college, I decided to try out for Northwestern's freshman football team, thinking it would be fun to play intercollegiate sports. Practice began one month before school did. I tried out as a "walk-on" and, along with two other walk-ons, made the team. I was still self-conscious about my hearing loss, though, so I never told the coaches—I worried their knowing about it would reduce my chances of playing. Looking back on it now, that decision seems foolish, but at the time it seemed logical. Some of the other players knew, but for a long time the coaches did not. It was difficult at times to understand their instructions, but I managed to survive. That is, I did until one fateful day. At the end of a short break in the middle of practice, the head coach started talking to the team. I did not realize this and said something to the player next to me. The coach stopped talking and glared at me. Fortunately, I happened to glance his way then and saw him yell, "Zazove!" He looked absolutely furious.

"Yes, coach."

"Do you have something to tell us?"

"No, coach."

"Then I don't want to ever, *ever* hear you again when I'm talking unless I'm asking you a question. Understand?"

"Yes, coach. I'm sorry." I hesitated a second, then blurted, "I didn't know you were talking."

He glowered at me. "What's the matter? You deaf?" There was a pause during which several players shifted uneasily. Finally, I answered, "Yes."

I don't know whether he believed me or not. He simply said, "Now pay attention here." One good thing did come out of that incident, though. Coach never did yell at me again. At the other guys, yes, but not at me.

Once school began three weeks later, most of my professors and many of my peers did not know about my hearing loss either. I was singled out much less than in high school, and it was a pleasure no longer being a novelty. But that did not necessarily make it easier. In fact, in some ways college was harder.

Even though Northwestern was relatively small compared to other Big Ten schools, it still had large introductory classes in several departments, especially the ones taken by freshmen. For me, the problem with these gatherings was that it was very hard, often impossible, to understand my professors. The sessions were usually held in the larger auditoriums, which were large enough that even the front row was a fair distance from the teachers, making it difficult to read their lips. One of the biggest classes of all was the general inorganic chemistry class I took in the first semester of my freshman year with hundreds of other people. The professor moved back and forth frequently, and sometimes turned away to write on the blackboard. Despite my informing him about my hearing loss and asking him to face the class when he spoke, he often did not, although whether it was from forgetfulness or indifference was unclear.

Fortunately, I had another route to the information. As a member of the football team, I had access to a special tutor hired for the players taking that class. Football players at Northwestern are different from those of many other major universities. Many major in difficult fields such as engineering and chemistry. In fact, contrary to the practice in some state universities, it is not even possible for them to major in subjects such as physical education. Because we players spent so many hours a day practicing football, the tutor was employed to help compensate for the reduced study time we had compared to other students. The particular tutor that year was excellent, a much better instructor than the professor himself. A graduate student in chemistry, he had the unique ability to make complex inorganic chemistry concepts seem elementary and easily understood. So despite my difficulties with the professor, I learned the material well.

Furthermore, the night before every test, the tutor held a special review session for any player interested in attending. Every player taking the course came. During these sessions, the tutor reviewed the various topics that had been covered in class, then gave us sample problems and explained how to solve them. After these sessions, I always found the test easy the following day. For not only had the tutor done such a superb job explaining the concepts, but also the test problems were always identical to the sample problems he had given us the night before, except for different numbers. I got a 100 every time and received an A for the semester. What amazed me most, however, was that some of my teammates barely passed, despite having attended every review session, including those the night before each test.

In smaller classes, professors were usually more willing to accommodate me. Still, some continued to face away from me, even after learning about my deafness. They either had no interest in helping me or simply kept forgetting. In those classes I had to depend almost exclusively on textbooks or classmates' notes to learn.

It was during college that I became interested in improving my speech for the first time. I had realized that the better my articulation was, the easier my communication with others would be. Since Northwestern still had one of the top speech therapy programs in the country, I started attending speech class on a regular basis. Dr. Myklebust was no longer there. Although many of the faculty members had been his students, ideas about deafness had already changed. People were beginning to realize a hearing loss was not as limiting as had once been thought. I wish Dr. Myklebust had been there. It would have been interesting to see what he thought of me, especially in view of his previous recommendations fifteen years earlier. He too would have had to admit that deafness is not insurmountable. I worked hard during therapy, and my dedication paid off. My enunciation improved and my speech became more intelligible, although it never did come close to normal. Even now, many years later, I am still benefiting from those hundreds of hours of practice.

My speech pathologists also endeavored to eliminate the nasal tone of my voice. Depsite an intensive evaluation involving several experts, however, no one could determine the reason for this tone. My voice was even analyzed by several new (for the time) electronic analyzers but nothing was ever found.

Academically, Northwestern was a challenging school for two reasons. First, all of the students had done well in high school and were interested in learning. Second, the professors expected a lot from us and challenged us with difficult concepts. Nevertheless, I flourished in my new environment, socially as well as scholastically, and received all A's and B's. Well, all except for one. In fact, I probably would never have made it to medical school if it hadn't been for that odd grade. It was a T in Latin.

I received the grade during the spring of 1970, during the third quarter of my freshman year. Among my other courses, I was taking Latin to meet Northwestern's requirement of two years of a foreign language. I had taken Latin in high school, too, because it is a written language, one that I did not have to worry about learning to lipread. Before starting college, I took the Latin proficiency exam and placed into the third (and last) quarter of the second year. At the time, I was ecstatic. I didn't enjoy the language and my placement meant I would have to suffer only one quarter of it. In retrospect, however, the placement was a mistake. I did not know Latin very well, and at best should have been in the first quarter of the second year. I had managed to fool everyone because the test had been poorly designed. It consisted of paragraphs in Latin followed by questions in English inquiring about the contents of each paragraph. I remember one of the questions being "Did Julius Caesar win the war?" Even though I had not understood most of the applicable paragraph, I did know Caesar rarely lost. In this way, I managed to answer many questions correctly and score better than I should have.

No wonder, then, that halfway through the third quarter of my freshman year, I realized the class was over my head. In fact, despite hours of studying, I was in danger of failing. The other students seemed to understand so much more. Then, a series of events occurred that prevented me from failing the course. These started with the deaths of four Kent State University students during a campus protest against the war in Vietnam. Within days, along with most other colleges in the United States, Northwestern students went on a sympathy strike. It was two weeks before things returned to normal. Fourteen days is a significant chunk of time in a ten-week quarter, especially when nobody has been studying. So the university came up with a unique one-time option. Each student could take a T grade in any subject for that quarter. We would receive automatic credit toward graduation for those courses and our grade-point averages would not be affected. In addition, there would be no record of how a student had done in a course prior to taking a T. So I took a T in Latin and preserved my excellent scholastic record.

During my second year of college, I applied for and was accepted by the Experiment in International Living, an exchange program that places students in other countries. I chose to go to Denmark the following summer. I had always been interested in visiting Denmark because the woman who cared for my sister and me for many years while my parents worked was Danish. Before leaving the country, I enrolled in the organization's ten-day intensive course in order to learn the basics of the Danish language.

Foreign languages have always been my Achilles' heel, and I suspect they are difficult to learn for anyone with a significant hearing loss. It is hard enough to understand words in one's native language when one cannot hear the sounds, and reading lips in other languages requires an understanding of the oral nuances of that language in addition to knowing the words themselves. During elementary school, from fourth to eighth grade, my school curriculum included one forty-minute period of Spanish each week. The first three years that was taught mainly via an oral method and I never learned it well. By the time the we started writing Spanish, I was so far behind I never caught up; it was the only elementary school subject I did poorly in.

I had also had to learn another language as a youngster—Hebrew—for my bar mitzvah. Fortunately, my parents were able to arrange a tutor to help me get started with this. This individualized attention enabled me to learn to read the language well. However, I never learned to understand spoken Hebrew.

Danish is a guttural language, similar to Swedish. It has extra sounds and letters not present in English, making it especially difficult to learn for English-speaking deaf or hard of hearing people. The class I took consisted of twelve people taught by two Danes. It was based on the total immersion model and was strictly oral. The teachers would read a short conversation to us in Danish and translate it. Then, we would repeat the Danish words over and over again, until we had them memorized. There was no discussion about grammar or lists of vocabulary words to learn. Instead, when we finished one conversation, we went to another.

Not knowing how words were spelled made it very difficult for me to say the words. All I heard were the vowels plus a couple of consonants. Nevertheless, at the end of the ten days, I felt I had some command of the basics of the language. When I arrived in Denmark, however, I realized this was a misconception. I could not understand anyone, or make myself understood. Fortunately, my Danish "family" spoke English fluently, and we communicated fine.

I immersed myself in the activities of the small Danish farm I lived on. Despite being surrounded by people talking Danish, I learned very little of the language. Then, two weeks into my stay, I happened to see a children's book lying on a table. I picked it up to leaf through it and found pictures of animals with the Danish name underneath. Immediately, I realized why people could not understand me, nor I them. Many words were spelled differently from what I would have guessed based on what I heard; they contained numerous sounds I was not pronouncing. So I got a stack of children's books and began studying them most evenings before going to bed. I soon found myself understanding more and more words as time went by. Just as I learned English by reading, so I learned Danish. Finally, one day during a dinner near the end of the summer, I understood a brief conversation in its entirety. It was a wonderful feeling. I felt like I had a foot in the door of a whole new world. Unfortunately, I returned to the United States shortly thereafter, before I could master that language.

Socially, my hearing loss was not a significant problem in college. I made a lot of friends in my dormitory and classes, and became fully enmeshed in the social structure of the university. I participated in intramural sports and went out with friends during evenings and weekends when we took time off from studying. None of us had cars, so we either walked or took public transportation wherever we went. If the group was large, I could not keep up with the conversation. However, I managed to understand enough to feel an integral part of the group.

I also dated intermittently during this time, although it was not until my fourth year of college that I became serious about anyone. At the beginning of that year, I met Elaine, a wonderful woman from New Jersey, via a mutual friend. She knew about my hearing loss from the beginning, but that did not bother her. We got along tremendously and dated for three years. We even traveled together in England for a week after graduating college. In fact, if it had not been for my meeting the woman who would become my wife, I suspect I would have married Elaine.

It was also during my fourth year that I began to apply to medical school, hoping to fulfill a dream I had had since entering college.

EIGHT

SPRING HAD ARRIVED. Each day, the sun stayed longer and the air became warmer. Everywhere one looked, the annual rebirth of the earth was manifest. Yes, even in Plymouth, Utah, in the middle of the desert, life burst forth. For over in the mountains, just minutes away, the snows were melting. The water flowed into streams and cascaded into the valley, where it was diverted to the sprinklers that made the land verdant. Lawns, not long ago brown, became lush again. Tall box elders, quaking aspen, and supple white birches were already covered with leaves, their canopies casting long shadows, places of relief in the hot summer to come. Lupines, lilacs, and other ubiquitous flowers of the season were starting to bloom. Even the morning glory weed, the scourge of Utah homeowners, had begun to make its annual appearance.

There was a lightness in the air that dispelled the winter blues, as if cold weather had been just a bad dream. All around Plymouth, people found themselves enticed outside. Once again, the vernal magic was working its spell.

With the arrival of my first spring in medical practice, I began to see different medical problems in the office. The colds, ear infections, and pneumonias so common during the winter were now infrequent. In their place came various injuries—sprains, scrapes, and broken bones. But from a doctor's viewpoint, as I would later learn, those were part of the annual rites of spring, and they were a welcome change from the illnesses of winter.

Late one morning, I was talking to a young, deaf woman who had brought in her hearing child with one of the last sore throats of winter. Because of my hearing loss and ability to understand sign language, many deaf and hard of hearing people have chosen me as their doctor. Some even drive over fifty miles to see me. We communicate solely with our hands, lips, and facial expressions. It's remarkable how quickly thoughts can be transmitted this way. American Sign Language, like spoken language, proceeds at a lively pace. A single facial expression can convey as much meaning as an entire spoken sentence.

Contrary to popular misconception, American Sign Language (ASL) is not a word-for-word translation of English. That system is called Signed English.

Signed English is a literal substitution of signs for English words, where the speaker uses a sign in place of every word that would ordinarily be spoken. On the other hand, ASL is a unique, complex language of its own that transmits information by gestures, signs, and visual clues rather than verbal sounds. Numerous studies have shown that it conveys complicated, abstract concepts as well as any spoken language. It differs from English not only in that it is visual but also in that it has its own grammar, syntax, idioms, and even jokes. In fact, some of the jokes are so specific to the signs or Deaf culture that they cannot be translated to spoken language.

Although the signs of ASL are not all universal, a few are; on occasion, I have been able to converse with people from other countries. Once, a friend and I were hiking in Bryce Canyon National Park when we met two deaf people, one from France and the other from Italy. Although it was difficult, the four of us managed to exchange a brief but understandable conversation.

While my patient and I were signing with each other, her daughter accidentally knocked over a chair, and it crashed into the door. I jumped involuntarily, startled by the event, seeing and feeling the bang as much as hearing it. But her mother did not bat an eyelash. For some reason, I was unusually impressed by her nonreaction. It made me realize how different I must seem to hearing people.

I thought about the boy who, earlier that day, told me excitedly about the bird he had heard chirping outside his window when he awoke that morning. Little did he know I could never fully share his experience—I have never heard a bird sing. I have never heard anyone whistle, either. Those are high-pitched sounds I cannot hear.

But my hearing loss is not as straightforward as that. In fact, it can be quite capricious. Sometimes I hear sounds I should not, whereas other times I am totally oblivious to a loud noise. I cannot hear people call my name unless they are standing right next to me. Even then, I sometimes don't notice. And, when I do, it is usually the sound of a voice that attracts my attention, not the recognition of my name. Thus, I have been accused of deliberately ignoring people. On a rare occasion, however, a woman with a high-pitched voice speaks a sentence quietly with her face turned away from me, and I somehow understand what she says. Perhaps I am just guessing correctly, using the context of the situation.

On the other hand, loud crashes have occurred right next to me and I had no idea they happened. In my second year of medical school, I lived in a rented three-floor house with four of my classmates. We took turns cooking supper, each of us responsible for a different night of the week. When dinner was ready, the cook would yell up the stairs, "Come and get it." Periodically, I would know when someone called, although I could not hear him. Somehow, I was able to sense he had called. My housemates, of course, could never understand this when it happened. After all, at other times I did not hear much louder, more obvious sounds. They would tease me about pretending to have a hearing loss. What is the reason for this inconsistency? I have no idea.

One thing I have noticed is that I am more aware of very low-pitched noises than other people are. At times, it seems I hear sounds they cannot. I may hear a car door slam and know guests have arrived long before our doorbell rings. Or I'll be the only one to hear (feel the vibrations of?) someone knocking on the door at the other end of the house. I suspect part of the reason is that these sounds are not masked by other sounds, as they are for normally hearing people. But I am also convinced that my ears have compensated for their handicap by becoming more attuned to lower-pitched sounds.

The rest of the day passed uneventfully. I left the office, felt the balmy evening breeze stir my hair, and paused to look at the mountains. The setting sun had cast a purplish glow on the Wasatch front. The effect created a stunning backdrop for the city in the valley, where lights were starting to glow. Their twinkling in the distance matched the first stars in the dusky sky. It seemed like a perfect evening, mellow and calm, the kind one spends lazily with a lover, watching the night evolve slowly.

I drove to the hospital to see my patients there. Mrs. Carradine, who had given birth to her first boy the previous evening, was sitting on her bed ogling her newborn son.

She smiled at me. "Doctor, we feel so blessed to finally have a boy. And it was such an easy delivery, wasn't it?"

"Yes, it was. Everything going okay?"

"It sure is. I feel great." She nodded at her son, adding, "And he seems fine too. He takes to my breast so well."

I watched her croon to her baby a moment, then continued, "Is your bleeding slowing down?"

"Oh for sure. It's just like my other deliveries."

"Good. Your son looked fine when I examined him this morning. Tomorrow I'll check him one more time before you go home, probably about eight in the morning."

"Okay. And Dr. Zazove?"

"Yes?"

"My husband and I decided for sure to have the circumcision. When can you do it?"

"Why don't we do that in the morning too."

Next I went down the hall to see my other hospital patient that day. Mr. Crouse had been admitted six days earlier with chest pain. Tests revealed he had had a heart attack. Fortunately, he was recovering without any complications. By now, in fact, he was chomping at the bit, eager to go home.

"Hi, Doc."

I picked up his bedside chart to review it. "You sound in good spirits tonight."

"Well, I am. I'm ready to go home as soon as you give the word."

"Any pain or shortness of breath today?"

"Not a bit," he asserted. "I spent most of the day walking around the hospital and didn't have any pain, not even a twinge."

"Mr. Crouse," I chastised him, "I told you to walk three or four times in the hall, not spend the whole day walking. You need to increase the amount of exercise you do gradually. If you push it too fast, you'll increase the chances of another heart attack."

"Aw, Doc. I'm doing fine. If it don't hurt, why can't I walk?"

Smiling at his persistence, I answered, "I think you know the answer as well as I do." I listened to his heart and lungs; they sounded fine.

Looking at me quizzically, he asked, "Doc, Mrs. Harrington told me earlier that you're deaf. Is that true?"

"Yes, it is."

"Then how can you use a stethoscope?"

"That's a good question, Mr. Crouse. People often ask me that. The answer is that I don't have an across-the-board hearing loss. Although I can't hear any high-frequency sounds, I do hear a little in the lower frequencies. Fortunately, the body sounds that doctors listen to are all in that range. And as it turns out, I'm able to hear them."

Actually, that was not the complete truth. Several body sounds are relatively high-pitched, out of the range of my hearing, but for some reason I seem to sense them too—as long as I use the right stethoscope. With one particular stethoscope, I seem to detect what every other doctor does. It is another example of the unpredictability of my hearing.

When I applied to medical school, interviewers often asked me the same question as Mr. Crouse. I had done some research into body sounds and knew that they were low-pitched. I had even tried listening to my chest with my father's stethoscope and knew I could at least hear the two main heart sounds. So I gave the interviewers the same answer that I now offered to Mr. Crouse, but the interviewers had remained skeptical. Several even suggested that if I were ever accepted, I should consider pathology or a similar specialty that did not require the use of a stethoscope. As a medical student, I experimented with different types of stethoscopes and found that only one kind seemed to work for me, although the reasons for this are unclear. I even tried amplified ones made for older physicians with mild hearing losses. These did not seem to offer any advantage; in fact, I heard worse with them, perhaps because of the constant static in the background or the decreased transmission of nonauditory clues such as vibration. So I switched back to a normal stethoscope.

After leaving Mr. Crouse, I checked the emergency room to be sure I didn't have any patients there. The last thing I wanted was to drive home only to have to come right back to the hospital.

"Oh, Dr. Zazove," the clerk exclaimed, "we've been trying to reach you. We've paged you overhead several times."

"I can't hear pages. Have you tried my vibrating beeper?"

"Oh, that's right. I'm sorry. I forgot. You are on call tonight, though, aren't you?"

"Yes, I am."

"Dr. Russell wants to talk to you. One second, let me find him."

"Philip!" the emergency room physician exclaimed as he approached me. "Just the man I'm looking for. I have a ninety-year-old gentleman here who doesn't have a doctor and needs to come into the hospital. From what I gather, he's been having trouble breathing the last few days and yesterday started coughing up blood. His lungs sound awful, and he's got a pneumonia on his chest X ray.

"His daughter told me he's been in another hospital twice in the past four months for the same thing. Both times, he stopped taking his medications as soon as he got home because he didn't think he needed them. He also got a pacemaker about a year ago, although I'm not sure exactly why. He doesn't want to be admitted, but I don't think he has any choice."

"Sounds like he's pretty sick," I said. "Which bed is he in? I'll go meet him."

"Over there. Come on. I'll introduce you to him," said Dr. Russell, leading me to the appropriate room. "Mr. Strong, this is Dr. Zazove. He's going to take care of you in the hospital."

"Okay, young man," Mr. Strong bellowed at me. "But I gotta tell ya I ain't sick bad. I do got a little cough here, but it ain't nuttin' to worry 'bout. Hey, I really don't gotta come in the hospital like this doc says, do I? Can't ya jus' gimme a penicillin shot and lemme go home? I'll be all right. Why, I usta have a doc who knew exactly what to do. When I got sick, I'd jus' go to him and git me a penicillin shot. I'd be better the next day."

Despite his protests, Mr. Strong was obviously ill. He coughed repeatedly between sentences and chucked bloody sputum as if the wastebasket were a spittoon. A lanky man, more than six feet tall despite slightly stooped shoulders, he rested on his back in a semi-reclining position, his feet dangling over the end of the bed. He had a long, weather-beaten face, prominent jutting chin, and sparse, gray hair that was slicked straight back. The most striking aspect about him was probably his voice. Dane Strong always spoke loudly, as though everyone were hard of hearing. And because it resonated like a bassoon, one could not help noticing it. Of course, for me, his voice made conversation easy. I didn't have to concentrate as much on reading his lips. It was like having all the benefits of a hearing aid without the irritation of wearing one.

"I'm afraid you do need to be in the hospital," I explained. "You're a sick man. A penicillin shot won't be enough this time. Now, I hear you have some medications another doctor gave you. Have you been taking them?"

"Naw. I got better a few days after I seen him, so I jus' stopped taking 'em. I'm ninety years old and healthy as a horse." He riveted his eyes on mine. "Besides, I gotta take care of my old lady. Now, she's a sick one, an invalid they call 'em. She can't do nuttin' without me. I feed her, dress her, and lead her 'round. Why, I even have to take her to the john to pee."

"That's probably why you keep getting sick, Mr. Strong. If you'd take your medicines, maybe you'd stay healthy."

"Somebody's gotta take care of her. And it sure as hell ain't gonna be no nursing home. Besides, I feel jus' fine, Doc. Why, last Saturday, I spent 'bout four hours planting corn in my garden. When I was done, I didn't feel a bit tired. Now that don't sound like a sick man to you, does it?"

"Have you had any fever?"

"Not that I know of, but I ain't got me no thermometer. Never did learn how to use 'em dangfangled things."

"Mr. Strong, are you having any chest pain?" I pursued his history.

"I didn't have no chest pain when I got this here pacemaker. So why d'ya think I'd have any with a little cough?"

"Let me take a look at you," I stated, pulling my stethoscope out of my pocket.

"Go 'head, young man."

That he was short of breath was manifested by his breathing forty times a minute. He also had a 101-degree temperature. I began to examine him. The pneumonia was clearly audible in both lungs. His feet and neck veins were quite swollen too, suggesting he was in heart failure. This meant his heart was not pumping adequately, resulting in a backup of fluid into his lungs and body tissues. It was this fluid, in addition to the pneumonia, that made it especially hard for Mr. Strong to breathe. His heart itself seemed normal, although its sounds were difficult to hear because they were partly obscured by the noisy respiration.

I looked at his chest X ray. It revealed just what Dr. Russell had said: pneumonia. It also showed an enlarged heart, additional evidence of heart failure. A review of his cardiogram confirmed that his pacemaker was working.

Then I checked his blood tests. He had both a high white blood count and a low oxygen level, a result of the infection and fluid in his lungs. The normal oxygen level at the altitude of Plymouth was 68 millimeters of mercury or more; his was 50.

"Jus' gimme some pills if ya don't wanna gimme a shot of penicillin. I'm telling ya, I'll be all right. I've always been healthy. Why, I've worked for both the mines and the railroad. Now that's what I call hard work. We'd start early in the morning, before the sun came up, and didn't stop till 'bout 6:00 at night. Never did miss a day, either. If a man kin make it there, then ya know he's okay." Mr. Strong sat up and started to get dressed to go.

"Wait a minute, Mr. Strong," I restrained him with a hand on his shoulder. "You need to stay here until we can get you breathing better. Remember? Now, do you recall the names of the medications the other doctor gave you?"

He pulled out a prescription bottle from his shirt pocket. "They's all in this here bottle," he shouted. "Thought you'd wanna see 'em so I brought 'em. Haven't taken none for 'bout a month, though."

I looked at the label on the bottle. The pills were digoxin, one of the more commonly used, as well as one of the oldest, heart drugs. Made from the foxglove plant, digoxin can be lethal if misused. However, it's very helpful when taken properly.

"Doc, I don't have nuttin' to wear here. I didn't bring no extra clothes with me. Jus' gimme some penicillin pills. I'll go home, and if I ain't better'n the morning, I'll git right back here and bring some clothes too."

"You're a sick man, Mr. Strong," I reiterated. "You've got pneumonia in both lungs, and your heart is failing. You need to stay here. There's no way you can go home. Don't worry about clothes; the nurses will give you something to wear.

"I'll be getting some tests on the mucus you're coughing up to find out what kind of pneumonia you have. We'll give you antibiotics for it too, as well as some oxygen and pills for your heart." After a brief pause caused by one of Mr. Strong's coughing fits, I continued, "Now listen carefully. It's very important that you cooperate with the nurses. You need to stay in bed and keep your legs up. That'll help get rid of the extra water you have both there and in your lungs. In fact, the only time you should get out of bed is to go to the bathroom."

"Well, I guess I kin stay till the morning," he snorted. "But I'll bet ya I'll be ready to go home then."

"We'll see how you're doing. But I'm glad you understand the importance of staying here. Any other questions?"

"Naw," he shook his head disgustedly.

"Fine. Then I'll be back early tomorrow morning. If you have any problems, let the nurses know, and they'll get ahold of me, okay?"

"What'd ya say your name was, Doc?"

"Dr. Philip Zazove."

"Okay, Doc Zazove. Don't ya worry. I ain't gonna have no problems. By the morning, I'll be ready to git home."

Probably the most important step in treating heart failure is bed rest. This is easily done in the hospital, where nurses make sure that patients comply. Water pills, oxygen, and salt restriction are three additional mainstays of treatment. Other drugs are also used as needed. What makes people like Mr. Strong so difficult to treat is that once they go home, they resume their old ways. They pour salt on their food, refuse to rest, and often don't take their medication. Before long, they end up back at the doctor's office, as sick as ever.

Mr. Strong is typical of some elderly people I see, people who grew up when conditions were very harsh. In those days, many of the comforts we now take for granted weren't available. Most medical problems couldn't be treated, either. People accepted suffering as a way of life and learned to just "grin and bear it." Some of these folks have maintained their stoic demeanor in the present, and often refuse treatment that could help them. Sometimes I wonder why they even bother to see me in the first place.

After writing orders and reviewing them with the nurses, I headed home, concerned about Mr. Strong. At ninety, he'd already lived longer than most people. Now he was very sick, with his third episode of pneumonia in four months. Furthermore, he had heart disease, making him an increased risk for problems such as a heart attack. His chances of surviving this illness were probably only fifty-fifty at best.

That evening, after dinner, I discussed Mr. Strong's situation with Barbara. Having a spouse who is a physician—and a family physician at that—is a distinct advantage for both of us. Our different careers complemented each other too. As a full-time faculty member at the University of Utah Medical Center, Barbara spent much time teaching and doing research and was often privy to the latest discoveries in medicine before I was. She also saw patients every week. Because this was only part-time, however, she had less practical experience than I did. So we each had skills the other did not. We sometimes discussed difficult or worrisome cases at night, and occasionally one of us thought of things the other had not.

Barbara agreed with my assessment of Mr. Strong, and reassured me that his treatment had been appropriate. Nevertheless, I slept uneasily that night. Although I had done everything possible, I still worried about him. I kept expecting the nurses to call and inform me he was worse or that his heart had suddenly stopped and they were resuscitating him. Tossing and turning, I did everything possible to fall asleep. Nothing worked. I started to debate whether to call the hospital and check on him. The next thing I knew, the bed was vibrating. My special alarm clock was going off, telling me it was 6:30 a.m. I must have finally slept. And not a call all night!

It was a rainy morning, a dreary overcast day, certainly not typical Utah weather. As I got ready for work, I found myself still thinking about Mr. Strong. Was he all right? I ate breakfast quickly and left for the hospital.

The moment I arrived there, I headed for his room. Before entering, I could see him from the hall. He was sitting in bed, dressed to go home, wearing red suspenders and a blue tie over a green checkered shirt.

" 'Bout time ya got here," Mr. Strong boomed as I walked in. Looking at his watch, he continued, "It's late, almost 7:30. Been light for an hour. What'd ya do, sleep in?"

"You're acting pretty chipper today," I commented.

"I ain't coughed up no blood since I got them antibiotics. The first one, it done clear me up real good, jus' like I told you it would, Doc. I ain't had no trouble breathin', either. Now I need to git home and take care of my old lady."

"Last night you told me you weren't feeling bad," I reminded him. "Now you're telling me you're better. So you were feeling sick last night after all, eh?"

"Aw, I was jus' havin' a little trouble clearing my lungs—nuttin' bad. What d'ya want, Doc? Ya can't expect me to be like I was as a kid. I'm ninety years old." After a pause to look me over, he commented, "Why, young man, ya can't be much older'n my grandson."

Mr. Strong did indeed look better. He breathed more easily, and his fever was gone. Furthermore, the bed rest and medication were doing their job; he had already lost five pounds of excess water.

Chuckling at his words, I examined him again. His lungs sounded clearer, although plenty of fluid still remained, and his feet were less swollen. I was amazed at how rapidly he had improved, faster than many people thirty years younger do. Despite his age, maybe he really was "tough stuff."

"Kin I go home now, Doc?" he half stated, half asked.

"No, you're not quite ready yet. I agree you're better, but you still have a ways to go. Don't forget, this is the third time in the last four months you've been in the hospital for this problem. I want to make it the last time. Let's make sure you're really better before you go home."

"C'mon, Doc, I'm strong as a horse. Jus' gimme some penicillin and send me home. I'll be okay."

"No," I shook my head. "You need to stay a little longer."

"But my wife don't wanna stay with our daughter no more," he argued. "She'd rather be home with me."

"I'm sure she would, but you're in no condition to care for her yourself. I promise that as soon as you're ready, I'll send you home."

"Aw, Doc. I gotta bunch of things I gotta do. Lemme go home. I'll be okay."

"I'm sorry, but you're not ready," I told him with a distinct tone of finality.

Despite some more objections, Mr. Strong consented to remain in the hospital. I wondered if his protests were just a show. Perhaps he needed to act tough, even though he realized he should stay.

Over the next two days, he continued to mend. The antibiotics and heart medicine did their jobs. His temperature remained normal, his lungs cleared totally, and his chest X ray improved. At this point, Dane Strong was ready to go home.

I wrote prescriptions for his medications and reviewed with him how to take them. Then I released him from the hospital.

"Do I gotta take these pills?" he argued. "I feel okay. I ain't spit up no blood since the night I came here."

"Yes, Mr. Strong, you have to take them if you want to stay well. Remember, this time we want to keep you out of the hospital."

"How long d'ya want me to take 'em?"

"The antibiotics for only another week, but the heart pills probably for the rest of your life."

"The rest of my life?" he cried. "No way. I ain't gonna be no pill taker. I got several buddies who are. They started with one, and before they knowed it, they was on a whole bunch of 'em. There's no way I'm gonna do that."

He paused a second then said, "Hey Doc, how many years d'ya think I have left? I don't wanna live too much longer, but d'ya think I'll live three more?"

"If you take your medicine, who knows? You may make it to a hundred."

"A hundred! Naw, I jus' want another three years. I don't wanna git old and have problems gitting 'round," he shouted, shaking his head.

"Now it's very important that you come to my office on Monday, after the weekend," I instructed him. "I need to check you to be sure you're still improving. In the meantime, I want you to take it easy and rest at home. That means no working in the yard or any other work until I see you Monday." I wanted to keep close tabs on him because of his recurrent episodes of heart failure and pneumonia, but was pretty sure he would not follow up. Still I did my best to persuade him to do so. For despite his crusty personality, I liked the man.

NINE

IT WAS EARLY SUMMER, and the weather was changing. The tolerable spring climate of warmish days and cool nights had become a typical desert summer—searing hot and dry. I had the weekend off and Barbara had come home that Saturday morning after a three-day trip to a medical conference. We packed a picnic lunch, gathered up the kids, and headed for the mountains to escape the heat.

A short drive from our house brought us to the trail we were to take. It was a gorgeous day up in the mountains. The temperature was in the seventies and the air smelled woodsy. We started up the dirt trail, walking alongside a rippling creek, enjoying the kaleidoscope of colors. The ground was a mosaic of various hues of leaves, strewn among the shrubs and tree trunks. Sunlight filtered through the branches, creating an artist's study of light and shade. Bunches of aspen appeared as splotches of quivering leaves amid stands of majestic green spruces, firs, and pines.

Groups of gray mountain jays played with each other, and solitary magpies sat and watched us as we passed under them. Ahead of us, we would occasionally glimpse small animals as they scattered before our noisy footsteps. Whenever we passed a large rock, my daughters insisted on climbing it and jumping off. Barbara also found them walking sticks, which were used more to bang rocks than to assist walking. And each time we stopped, they searched for stones and laughed as they threw them into the creek, delighting at each "kerplunk."

After two hours of hiking, we reached a blue-green lake and sat on nearby logs to eat our picnic lunch. The surrounding mountain peaks were reflected in the calm surface of the lake. Every so often, the flatness of the water would be broken by a fish reaching up, perhaps to catch an insect. As always, I was struck by the silence in the air. Even with my profound hearing loss, I could sense the difference from the city. Everything seemed so peaceful here, especially the lack of low-pitched mechanical noises. It never ceases to amaze me how well nature soothes. I decided this was one of the essences of nature. Unfortunately, the ever-growing miles of concrete and mortar in the cities and suburbs are reducing the amount of time people experience the solitude of nature. If people did experience it more, perhaps doctors would see fewer stress-related illnesses.

The next morning, I was awakened by someone shaking my shoulders. It was Barbara, laughing. "You're amazing," she said.

I glanced at the clock. It was 4 a.m. "You woke me at this time on Sunday morning to tell me that?"

She nodded. "You remember last Tuesday when I had my clock-radio alarm set at four so I'd wake up in time to catch the plane to Denver?"

It was my turn to nod. "That's what you told me. I never heard it, of course."

"You sure didn't. It just went off again."

I looked at her quizzically. "That means the whole time I was gone last week, it was going off at 4 a.m. every day, playing for the hour it's set for, then turning off. And you never knew."

"See, I always knew there was an advantage to being deaf."

Monday, I returned to work, invigorated and ready to go. There's something about escaping from civilization that refreshes my spirit. Checking the appointment book, I noticed the first patient of the day was Rosie Green, coming in for her six-week postpartum checkup. After being discharged from the hospital, she had managed to spend several hours with her daughter at the Children's Hospital before the infant died. Afterward, I had called Rosie to express my condolences and offer support. As usual, she had not said much. She did, however, subsequently come to the office several times for a variety of complaints: headaches, stomachaches, and constant fatigue. Despite my efforts, I couldn't find a physical cause for any of her symptoms. Gradually, I realized they were psychological, probably her way of responding to the emotional trauma that must have occurred.

I had inquired about her feelings at each visit, encouraging her to discuss what had happened. But she had always refused. Still, because of her symptoms, I knew Rosie was not as nonchalant as she appeared. For some reason, unknown to me, she didn't express her emotions. Perhaps today would be different and she would open up a little.

Anticipating her visit, I went into my office to prepare for the day ahead. Ten minutes later, my assistant, LeAnne, knocked on the opened door to get my attention. By now she had learned that calling my name out loud never attracted my attention, but the low sound of the knock usually did. When I looked up, she informed me that Rosie had arrived and would shortly be ready for me. LeAnne had worked in my office longer than anyone else. Reliable, capable, and friendly, she made my job much easier. On busy days she worked quickly without complaining; on slower days she spent extra time with patients, making them feel at ease. LeAnne cared about our patients too. She already knew most of them personally before they even came in. (Sometimes, it seemed she knew everyone in Plymouth.) And patients liked her too. They always asked about her when she had a day off. I cannot imagine a better employee.

A few minutes later, Rosie was ready. She had come alone to the exam room and acknowledged my entrance with a nod.

"Good morning, Rosie," I greeted her. "How are you feeling?"

"Okay."

"Any more problems since we last talked?"

"Naw."

"So you've been feeling better then, right?"

She didn't answer verbally but did make a slight face in response to my question.

"Has your bleeding completely stopped yet?"

"Yeah."

"When?"

"A week ago," she said softly without moving her lips. Up until now, her answers had been so brief, I had been able to figure out what she had said without really hearing or seeing them. But this time, I could not.

"What did you say?"

She repeated herself more clearly, still looking, on the surface, as nonchalant as ever. But this was where my body-language reading skills came in handy. Something about the way Rosie acted tipped me off that she was hiding a multitude of emotions. There was no doubt about it. It was as clear to me as if she had told me so herself. I decided to probe a little, to try to see if I could get her to begin to express how she really felt.

"Do you think about your baby a lot?"

She looked at me, then shrugged her shoulders.

"Rosie," I paused a second to gather my thoughts while looking at her intently. "I'd really like to know how you're feeling about your baby's death." I paused again as she turned her head and stared at the wall. "Are you coping all right?"

Although her face was in profile, I could see her lips well enough to tell she did not answer. I also saw a tear roll down the cheek closest to me.

"It must be hard," I stated quietly after another lull.

"I'm okay," she said finally.

"You know, it's normal to feel depressed after losing a baby. Often, people find it helps to talk about their feelings. I'd be more than happy to discuss them with you if you'd like," I offered. "Or, if you'd rather, I can arrange for someone else for you to talk to."

Again, there was no answer. But now she stared at me instead of the wall. I could see both eyes were wet.

"Have you talked to anyone else about it?"

She nodded.

"Who?"

"My mom."

"Good. I'm glad to hear that. Did it help?"

She shrugged her shoulders again. I waited awhile to see if she would say something. When she didn't, I asked, "Are you interested in talking about it some more?"

She looked at the floor and shook her head.

"That's fine. But remember, if you ever feel a need to do so and want someone to talk to, just give me a call. Okay?"

She agreed.

"Anything else you want to discuss? Other problems? Questions?"

She shook her head.

Rosie's examination was totally normal. I discussed contraceptive options with her, and she chose the birth control pill. She never talked about the baby after that, so I never found out what she was hiding. And as far as I know, she's never gotten pregnant again. I wonder if she ever will.

Two days later I was working in my office when Carma, my receptionist, and LeAnne ran into the room and stopped directly next to my chair, excited.

"Mrs. Altschuler just drove her van through the front of the printing shop next door!" LeAnne cried. "She may be hurt. You better go see how she's doing."

I smiled at them. Ever since I had played that April Fool's joke on them, they had been trying to get me back. "You'll get me someday but it'll have to be a better story than that."

"We're serious, Doctor," Carma pointed. "Look out your window."

I did. They were serious. No more than fifteen feet away stood a large white van, partway through the front window of the printing shop. It was Mrs. Altschuler's special van, all right. Because of a rare disease that left her unable to use her legs, her van had been engineered so she could brake with her hands, as well as enter and exit it with her wheelchair.

We ran outside, worried about her. Several other people were already there, one of whom was talking to her. Mrs. Altschuler smiled sheepishly as we approached. "I'm so embarrassed, Doctor," she began.

"Nothing to be embarrassed about. Are you hurt?"

She shook her head. "I'm okay. I wasn't concentrating on what I was doing and pulled the gas lever instead of the brake. By the time I realized what I had done, it was too late."

After a brief exam to be sure she was indeed okay, I turned to look at the damage. The facade of the building had buckled like cardboard. Fortunately, the roof remained up; otherwise, Mrs. Altschuler probably would have been injured seriously. There was broken glass and debris everywhere too. It must have been quite a crash. And if the van had hit only a few more feet to the south, it would have run into me. Yet, despite this, I hadn't heard a thing! Several people could not believe this, my employees included. But I was perhaps the most amazed of all. A car crash usually makes a loud low-pitched sound. Why had I not heard it?

I shrugged and returned to my office where I was pleasantly surprised to find Mr. Strong waiting for me. Wearing a red plaid lumber shirt, a loud green and orange tie, and baggy, gray pants held up by blue suspenders, he gave me a triumphant look. His wife sat across from him. As much as he was tall and lanky, she was short and fat. They looked like Jack Sprat and his wife. Her face, lined with deep wrinkles, projected an expression of pain and weariness. A wan smile, squinting eyes, and trembling voice supported this overwhelming impression. She seemed to have long ago passed her one-hundredth birthday.

"Quite a crash out there, eh? The old lady okay?"

I nodded.

"Hey, Doc, I'm doing fine, jus' like I told ya I would."

"You do look well, Mr. Strong."

"Course I do. There ain't nuttin' wrong with me. I ain't had no cough and am breathing jus' fine," he hollered. "I git 'round the house okay and even went for a coupla long walks with no trouble."

"Great. Sounds like you're indeed doing well. Could you take off your shirt so I can check your lungs and heart?" As he complied, I added, "By the way, that's quite a tie you've got on."

"You like it, eh? My son, he done bought me over fifty ties. I gotta do somethin' with 'em, so I wear 'em. I wear a different one every day."

"It certainly makes for an interesting look," I replied. His chest exam was normal. Likewise, his legs remained devoid of swelling.

"Everything seems fine," I told him. "Now, how many antibiotic pills do you have left?"

"Oh, 'bout ten, I imagine."

"Hmmmm. That's about right, three days' worth. Good. Go ahead and finish them. I'd also like to see you again in a week so I can be sure you're doing okay."

"Hey, Doc, I ain't havin' no trouble breathing no more. Why do I gotta take more of them pills? Ya better gimme a good reason or I ain't gonna do it."

"Because you've had this problem three times in the last four months, and because this time I want you to *stay* better," I answered authoritatively. "And remember, you'll always need to take your heart pills if you want to stay well."

"For the rest of my life? Ya want me to git hooked on 'em? I'll be jus' like them drug addicts. No way, young man."

"Mr. Strong, there's a big difference between your pills and those the drug addicts take. Yours help you. They help your heart beat stronger and kill the germs that caused the pneumonia. They're a lot different from what the drug addicts take. I'm afraid that unless you take them, you'll end up right back in the hospital. But it's up to you."

A resigned look appeared on his antique face. "All right. I'll try it awhile. Hey, you know them pharmacists? Ain't they stinking bastards? They must think I'm a sucker or somethin'."

"What do you mean?"

"I usually go to the pharmacy here on Berry Road. But when the guy told me last time that them pills you gave me would cost me 'bout twenty bucks, I thought I'd try that new place nearer my house. Well, I went in and give him the perscriptions ya wrote. He looks at 'em and says, 'That'll be sixty bucks, sir.' I looks at him in the whites of his eyes and says, 'Ya must think I'm a sucker or somethin'.' He says, 'What're ya talking 'bout?' I tells him, 'Them pills only cost me twenty bucks down the street. Whatta ya trying to do, rip me off? Ya think I'm a sucker?' The guy looks at me, then walks off. He knew he were beat. Course there's a sucker born every minute, but I sure as hell ain't one of 'em."

"No, you certainly aren't," I agreed. "So what did you do?"

"I jus' went back to the one on Berry Road and got 'em there. By the way, Doc, kin I go back to work in the morning?"

"What kind of work do you do?"

"I volunteer as a security guard. But don't worry, Doc. I don't do nuttin'. I jus' sit there and read the paper the whole time. There's another guy with me, a young one, probably 'bout the same age as you. He does mosta the work. I usually stay for 'bout four hours. They don't miss me if I don't go, but I'd go crazy if I did nuttin' all day. So I go."

"Sure, you can go to work."

He nodded his head with satisfaction. Turning to his wife, he leaned forward and, shouting, ordered, "Let's go, Mabel. The doc, he's all done with me." He stood up and started to help her get out of her chair.

"But what about this?" she protested weakly, pointing at her right upper lip.

"Oh yeah," he mumbled. "Hey, Doc," he bellowed, jerking his thumb at her lip. "She's been worried 'bout that spot on her lip ever since we got married. She wants ya to check it out for her."

"How long have you had that, Mrs. Strong?" I asked her.

"What?" she turned an ear to hear me better.

"How long have you had that sore on your lip?"

"Whaaaa?" she looked at her husband helplessly.

"She's purty deaf," he boomed at me confidentially, shaking his head in pity. "She don't hear nuttin' 'less ya talk loud to her." Putting his head next to her ear, he yelled, "Doc wanna know, how long that there thing been on your lip."

"Oh." An expression of understanding lit up her face. "About fifty years."

"Has it gotten bigger or changed size at all?" I asked loudly.

Her face resumed its helpless gaze. She looked as if she were about to cry. "What?" she finally mumbled.

"Doc said, 'Has it changed any?' "

Smiling a little at understanding the question, she shook her head.

"Does it hurt?"

"It don't hurt her none," Mr. Strong answered for her.

Looking at it, I wasn't exactly sure what it was. However, since it had been present for fifty years without changing, I doubted it was cancer or anything serious. She wasn't complaining of pain, either. It wasn't worth removing. At her age, if complications arose from having it excised, she might be worse off than she was now. And after all these years, I doubted she wanted it off for cosmetic reasons.

"I'm not sure what it is, Mrs. Strong, but I wouldn't worry about it," I told her shaking my head. "As long as it doesn't hurt or change size, I'd leave it alone." "Is it serious?" she asked, a worried look on her ancient face.

"No, I don't think so," I reassured her.

"What?"

"No, it doesn't look like that," I screamed, shaking my head.

Again not hearing my answer, she looked at her husband for help.

"It ain't cancer," he yelled in her ear.

"Oh," she smiled, visibly relaxing.

Changing the subject, I asked Mr. Strong, "Has she ever been fitted for a hearing aid?"

"Ya, she's got two of 'em at home but she won't wear 'em none. Says they hurt her ears." Turning to his wife, he bellowed, "C'mon, Mabel, let's git home now," and he helped her get up. While she waddled out with his support, I watched them, amazed at the contrast and wondering what they were like in their younger days. I suspected she wasn't so passive then. Her hearing loss probably played a role in making her that way now. In some ways, it is much more difficult for someone who has heard normally most of his or her life to cope with deafness than for someone like me, who has never heard the sounds. In my case, I am used to it. I don't miss hearing thousands of noises and have never depended on them for everyday existence. In her case, however, life in silence was probably much more frightening and, paradoxically, duller than it used to be.

Even so, I sometimes wish I could hear normally, if only for a few minutes. It must be wonderful to hear effortlessly—leaves rustling, cats purring, people talking. I can only imagine what those sounds are like, as well as other sounds of everyday life that play such a vital role in our society, such as school bells ringing. In fact, I am recurrently amazed at what most people hear. Despite all the adaptations I have made to compensate for my hearing loss, there are times when I am frustrated by it.

Take the case of running water, for instance. Although I occasionally have heard the roar of a river, especially if it is running fast, I do not hear a faucet running unless it is going full blast and I am right next to it, listening for the sound. Even if it's turned on all the way, I could walk by three feet away and not know it. Not hearing something as simple as this can lead to problems. Once I was home alone and accidentally left the kitchen faucet running into a plugged drain. Although I subsequently walked past the kitchen several times, I never realized the water was running until I actually entered the room and found a flood on the floor. Any hearing person would have heard it earlier and turned it off in plenty of time.

For the most part, however, being deaf does not bother me. Since I have never heard the sounds and never will, I don't miss them. Besides, I really have no idea what life is like as a hearing person. I can only imagine that. And what I imagine might be totally untrue.

The Strongs began to come to my office periodically, usually for checkups or medication adjustments. His pneumonia never recurred, his heart failure remained controlled, and he stayed out of the hospital. Mrs. Strong never changed a bit, either. I truly enjoyed their visits, as much for Mr. Strong's attire as for anything else.

Each time he came, he wore a different loud tie and gaudy suspenders. And neither ever matched his shirt. Although he never wanted to return for additional appointments, I was always able to persuade him to do so. I like to think that I helped him stay relatively healthy and out of the hospital. But I knew that at his age, it was only a matter of time before he had problems again.

TEN

"ARE YOU AWARE that we have at least ten applicants for every position in our first-year medical school class?"

I nodded respectfully.

"And that many of them are exceptionally well-qualified to be a member of that class?"

Again I nodded.

The interviewer leaned forward and fixed his eyes on mine. "Then tell me, sir, why should we take a chance on a deaf person like you instead of one of the other candidates who hear normally?"

"To begin with," I launched into my carefully rehearsed statement, "I would like to point out that my hearing loss has not prevented me from being quite successful, as you can tell from reading my folder. From an academic perspective, despite attending a nationally renowned university with numerous superb students, I've gotten top grades and have been involved in many activities. My test scores are also quite competitive.

"From a personal viewpoint, some of the barriers I've had to face because of my hearing loss have made me a more understanding person. This will be very useful in future doctor–patient relationships, especially when interacting with patients with various disabilities. My experiences have also strengthened my desire to go into medicine and help people who are suffering.

"Finally, my unique experiences should benefit my classmates as well. I would provide an additional dimension they would not otherwise have much contact with, which should help in their future interactions with patients. I am quite confident that if you accept me, I will contribute to both the class and medicine in general as much as anyone else."

I did not convince that man. Nor, for that matter, did I persuade anyone else that year. For despite my excellent grades and other qualifications, no medical school accepted me.

That interview, and others like it, took place in 1973, during my senior year at Northwestern University, the end of four well-rounded years there. As in all previous years, I had competed successfully with my hearing peers, excelled in academics, and participated in numerous campus activities. Despite my speech defect, I had become integrated into the social structure of the university; many people weren't aware of my hearing loss. I had even spent the previous summer in an undergraduate neurology fellowship at the University of Minnesota Medical School. Still, no one accepted me.

At first, I refused to see the writing on the wall. Instead, I convinced myself that someplace would accept me. For not only were my grades competitive, I was also on the waiting list at three schools and had several others yet to hear from. It was, I believed, only a matter of time. While waiting, I immersed myself in my classes, continued to get excellent grades, and sent periodic updates to the various medical schools. At the same time, I also concentrated on getting the most out of my final year of college. College is, after all, a unique period of time in a young man's life, a period of relative freedom that only happens once. And up until then, I had thoroughly enjoyed my years at Northwestern.

It so happened that one of the men on my dormitory floor was the son of the accountant of Charlie O. Finley (the then owner of the Oakland Athletics). Mr. Finley had given this student's father an American League pass, and he in turn had given it to his son. This allowed my friend, and anyone accompanying him, unlimited free admissions to any American League ballpark. The previous two springs, several of us in the dormitory often went with him to Chicago White Sox games. We would plan our schedule so that we had three hours available for the games, then at the designated time, took the "el" (elevated train) to Comiskey Park—where the team played before their current stadium was built.

The first year we did this, the Sox were one of the worst teams in the league and few people attended their games. So, even though we got in for free, the officials were happy just to have people there and did not mind that sometimes there were as many as ten of us. In fact, so few people showed up for some games that during batting practice, we were usually able to get as many balls as we wanted. Twice, another friend even jumped onto the field for a ball without any response from the security guards. By my senior year, however, the Sox had improved to the point of being serious contenders for the pennant, thus generating much more public interest in the team. In fact, Opening Day was sold out. This interest infected Northwestern's students too, and a large group went with my friend to the game. Now, however, with thousands of other paying folk in the park, the officials were less accepting of us. When they counted forty of us, they confiscated the American League pass, claiming my friend had abused its purpose. That spring, we attended only a couple of games; it cost too much for our relatively tight budgets to go as often as before. Instead, I found plenty of other things to do on campus, and time passed quickly.

By late spring I still had not been accepted to medical school. Finally, the reality of the situation hit me. I felt frustrated. When I learned that several classmates with lower grades and test scores had been accepted to schools that had rejected me, I also became upset. I had proven myself numerous times and was tired of having to do it repeatedly. (I had not yet come to grips with the fact that I would *always* have to do so.) What more did they want? I couldn't make myself hear. If only someone would give me a chance, I would show them. I knew I could do it.

As graduation approached, I resigned myself to the fact I was not going to be accepted to medical school and began to consider several alternative careers. Every time I contemplated the options, however, I always ended up with the same conclusion: I wasn't really interested in any of them. I wanted to be a physician. So I decided to try again the following year. It would not be the first time I had to fight for my rights. And besides, in a way I was continuing a family tradition. Both my parents had had difficulty getting into medical school too, although in their case it was because of anti-Semitism.

My mother, the daughter of Russian immigrants, grew up in a poor family. Fortunately, in those days the city colleges of New York were free, and she attended Hunter College, graduating with a degree in mathematics. After this, she decided to become a physician. At that time, not only was it difficult for a woman to be accepted to medical school, but also most American medical schools had quotas limiting the number of Jewish students. Despite her good credentials, she was not accepted by any of them. She was accepted, however, at the University of Edinburgh in Scotland. My grandparents then borrowed themselves further into debt to send my mother across the Atlantic Ocean so she could pursue her dream.

My mother spent 2½ years in Europe before she could afford to come back home and visit her family. While she was home, World War II broke out. Mom was unable to return to England because of the Nazi submarine warfare, so she was forced to relinquish her place in her class.

At first she was devastated. Gradually, she recovered from her setback, got a job working in a department store, and reapplied to American medical schools. This time, one school did accept her—the Chicago Medical School. The school was one of the few American medical institutions of the time that did not discriminate against Jews. However, it did require my mother to repeat the 2½ years she had already done. So, it took her 6½ years to become a physician. While in Chicago, she met my father, who also had a difficult time entering the medical profession.

Dad did not decide to become a doctor until he was almost finished with college. He took an extra year to complete his pre-med requirements, then applied to several medical schools. Shortly thereafter, he received an acceptance letter from the University of Illinois.

Because he wanted to go there, he withdrew his applications from the other schools. A month later, he received a letter stating that the University of Illinois had changed its mind and was no longer accepting him. The school, however, unknowingly picked on the wrong person. My grandfather was a prominent Chicago trial lawyer.

Grandpa subpoenaed the University of Illinois Medical School's admissions records and learned that the school accepted only one Jew, no more or less, each year. One to prove they weren't discriminating against Jews, but only one so there wouldn't be too many. My father had originally been that token person, but for some reason the committee decided to substitute another applicant for him. My grandfather and father then decided to sue the university.

Over the next few weeks, others hired my grandfather to represent them against the school for the same reason, and eventually he represented many people against the state of Illinois. Then, lawyers for the state threatened to have my father drafted if he didn't drop his case against them. My grandfather informed them, in no uncertain terms, that if they drafted my father, they would find themselves in even more trouble than they were currently. They never followed through with their threat.

For some reason, the Chicago Medical School owed the University of Illinois a favor at the time and it also happened to have an available spot. Thus, the problem was solved when the university arranged to have my father accepted at Chicago Medical School in return for my grandfather dropping the suit.

The year following graduation, I attended Northwestern University's graduate school of biology, hoping that if I did well, maybe that would convince the admissions committees. As the new school year began, I applied to a large number of the medical schools, not wanting to miss any place that might give me my chance. I also contacted deaf organizations, asking if they were aware of any school that might consider my application objectively. I was given the name of only one: Rutgers Medical School. It had accepted a person with a severe hearing loss two years earlier as an experiment.

So I sent an application there too. While waiting for responses, I studied hard, did well, and sent updated transcripts to the various schools.

I met many new people during my year in graduate school. It was also the time I first had to deal with the death of a friend. Halfway through the year, one of the men renting an apartment across the hall from me was killed in a car accident. That evening, my two roommates and I went over to pay our respects to his two roommates. It was a somber time, and they had turned all the lights out. We sat in the pitch-dark living room, each of us in a different chair. There was enough moonlight entering the window that I could vaguely tell the others were talking, but I could not understand a thing. I could only see the outlines of their bodies; their lips were mostly invisible. Rather than break the almost reverent mood by turning on a light, I sat mutely. They probably thought I was too overcome with emotion to speak. Finally, after almost two hours, I excused myself and left. Later, when I told my roommate why I had been so quiet, he grimaced and said, "You should have said something. We didn't even think about that."

Initially, things looked better on the medical school application front. I received more requests for interviews than I had the previous year and felt encouraged. This time around, the schools at least seemed willing to check me out.

During each interview, I stressed my solid credentials and desire to be a physician. Invariably, however, the questions eventually focused on my deafness. How would I talk to patients? (The same as I do with you.) What about lectures? How can you be sure you get it all? (I've dealt with that successfully for years, as my grades and recommendations show.) How will you be able to use a stethoscope? (Body sounds are within my hearing range.) Then I started to receive the familiar form letters. Each one was either a rejection or a waiting-list notification. Nothing seemed to have changed.

Again I found myself getting depressed. I did not want to spend my life as a biologist or some other type of professional. Although all those are excellent careers, they just were not what I wanted to do. I wanted to be a doctor, but it almost didn't seem worth the aggravation anymore. After twenty years, I was tired of the fight. I even debated whether it paid to fly to the last two schools that had requested interviews: Rutgers and Georgetown. But then, there was really no choice. I had lasted this long—I might as well finish.

I went to both schools on the same trip. While at Rutgers, I met Frank Hochman, the medical student with the severe hearing loss I had learned about earlier, and in fact ended up spending the night at his house. An older man, he had decided to be a physician later in life. We spent much of the time talking about our lives and comparing our experiences. His hearing loss was different from mine: somewhat less severe but equally spread across all frequencies. With a hearing aid, which he had used most of his life, he could hear many sounds. Still, Frank had faced many of the problems I had. We understood each other as few hearing people could.

I very much enjoyed my time with him. He was a wonderful man whose generosity and help I will never forget, especially his tips on how to convince the interviewers that I could compete. He helped in another way too. Before I arrived, he had arranged for different people to interview me than the ones who had originally been scheduled; he thought the new people would be more accepting of my hearing loss. But perhaps most important of all, meeting Dr. Hochman marked a turnaround in my willingness to persevere. It rekindled my determination to become a physician. If he had done it, so could I.

The next day I had my interview with the Rutgers admissions officials. Different from all the others, these interviewers dwelled on my record and accomplishments rather than on my hearing loss. Perhaps their experience with Frank Hochman helped. Or maybe the interviewers sensed my renewed desire to be a physician. Whatever the reason, I felt it was the first fair interview I had had.

The following day, I flew to Washington, D.C., for the Georgetown interview. While there, I met two prominent persons in the Deaf community. One was Boyce Williams, the then head of the Communicative Disorders Division of the Department of Health, Education, and Welfare (HEW); the other was Dr. Fine, a dean at Gallaudet College, the only liberal arts university for deaf students.

I did not know either of them, but when Frank Hochman told them I was coming to town, they contacted me and asked to have dinner together. All the arrangements for our meeting had been made via third parties; I had not talked to either of them. For some reason, it never occurred to me that they might be deaf too.

When I arrived at the restaurant where we were supposed to meet, I was pleasantly surprised to discover that Boyce Williams was totally deaf. I am always excited to meet other successful people who are deaf or hard of hearing. Not only do we share a lot of common experiences, it is also a pleasure to see additional proof that a hearing loss does not condemn someone to failure. The three of us had an enjoyable dinner together. Both men encouraged me to persevere in my efforts to become a physician. They also requested that I write a book about my experiences, believing it would be an example to others, both deaf and hearing, of what a person with a profound hearing loss can do.

Six weeks later I got that fateful envelope from Rutgers. It's impossible to put into words how I felt when I realized I actually was going to be a doctor. Suddenly, all the bitterness I had held toward the medical profession quickly disappeared. Instead, I became excited about my future. It now seems so long ago when all this happened—yet so recent too. I have since grown a bit wiser and less idealistic. I have also changed my perspective about many other things as well. Yet I will never forget those long-ago days when I so desperately wanted a chance to attend medical school and wondered if I would ever be a doctor. I am glad I did not give up.

ELEVEN

"JUST A COUPLE MORE STITCHES and we'll be done," I told Brian. He lay stiffly on the table, clenching his mother's hand tightly.

"It doesn't hurt, does it?" I asked while putting another one in.

He shook his head.

"You can show them to all your friends. I'll bet they'll be jealous," his mother distracted him.

Smiling at the thought, he nodded in agreement.

It was Labor Day, one of my holidays on call. I shared after-hours call with several other physicians, including my new partner who had just joined the office a month earlier. Brian was actually her patient. He had cut his hand reaching under the sofa for a toy truck, and I had met him and his mother at the office to repair it.

"There, all done," I announced.

The youngster watched with interest as I put a Snoopy Band-Aid on the repaired wound. After learning how to care for it, he and his mother left.

I wrote a note in Brian's chart, stretched drowsily, then breathed a sigh of relief. It was time to go home.

Outside the office was a beautiful morning. Although it was only 8:30, the sun had already warmed the air to the upper seventies. A deep blue sky, scattered white clouds, and a refreshing breeze made the day perfect. What more could one ask for? I inhaled deeply and felt a sense of exhilaration. Yes, this was quintessential Utah weather.

As I drove home, the dry breeze caressed my face through the open window. People were outside everywhere, enjoying the holiday. Many were loading picnic supplies into their cars or vans; the mountains would be popular today. Three children chased a dog around their yard. A lady stood by the roadside, watering her lawn, watching the traffic go by. A few houses down, in the shade of a time-worn porch, a group of older men sat in rocking chairs, conversing animatedly.

I stopped for a red light. Two joggers in shorts and T-shirts passed by, chatting as they ran. Across the street a pickup was cautiously backing out of a driveway, pushing a boat behind it. Everywhere I looked people were out. It seemed like the perfect holiday. But for me, it wasn't. I was on call.

I turned onto the street where I lived. My daughters, Katie and Rebecca, were riding their bikes on our driveway with some neighborhood children.

"Hi, Daddy," I saw Rebecca call as she got off her bike and ran to me. Picking her up, I said, "Hi, honey. Having fun?"

Before she could reply, Katie jumped on me, laughing. "Daddy, you're home," she screamed with delight.

"Yes, I am."

"Are you going back to work?"

"Not if I can help it."

We all went inside, where Barbara was baking a treat.

"Mmmmm," I said, kissing her. "Looks like I'm just in time for breakfast."

After savoring three warm cinnamon rolls and milk, I sat down to read the morning paper. Just then, the telephone rang.

"Oh boy," I thought, "Labor Day's just started and the phone's already ringing." Being on call can be very hectic, especially during holidays. One can spend many hours on the phone with patients because doctors' offices are closed.

The phone rang again with its special low-pitched sound, the result of a low-frequency bell. I can't hear the standard telephone ring. In the past, this inability was a problem, especially in my college dormitory room. I could be practically on top of the phone and wouldn't have an inkling it was ringing. This was much to everyone else's amazement; they could not understand how I could often understand people on the telephone (provided the amplifier was turned all the way up) yet could not tell when the buzzer sounded. If I expected a call, I had to keep a hand on the phone so that I could feel it vibrate when it rang. At the time, I did not use any of the special signaling gadgets available, such as lights that flash on and off when the phone rings. I am not quite sure why but back then I never felt a need for these devices. However, the result was that I missed many phone calls, some important.

For example, the summer after my junior year of college, I was awarded a summer research fellowship to study epilepsy at the University of Minnesota. While I was there, a friend from Denmark, passing through Minneapolis during a trip to this country, stopped to visit me. He had come by the dorm where I was staying and called my room. Although I was there, my roommate was out, so I did not know the phone was ringing. It was not until I found his note in my mailbox two hours later that I learned of his visit. By then, it was too late; he had already left town.

After beginning medical school, I realized it was critical to be accessible by telephone. I checked all the options that were available, including the flashing lights. But none of those seemed satisfactory for me. Finally, the phone company devised custom-made low-frequency buzzers for my phone and installed them on the wall by the phone. Using a combination of what I heard and the wall vibrations, I could tell when the phone rang. It was wonderful. I felt so free.

Still, even with these special buzzers I am more restricted than if I heard normally. If I am on call, I must refrain from going outside on the porch or even in certain rooms of the house unless someone else is home because I cannot hear or sense the buzzers there. Nevertheless, the special bells have made me much more independent than I would be otherwise.

"Hello?"

"Answering service here, Dr. Zazove."

I barely heard the voice and checked the amplifier. Someone had turned it down again. When it is turned all the way up, voices are sometimes so loud that they hurt the ears of people with normal hearing. In fact, when I am using the phone, others in my family often hear voices over the telephone better than I can, even when they are several feet away.

"Yes," I answered, hoping it was not something I would have to go back to work for.

"A Mrs. Irma Conn called. She thinks she's got pneumonia and wants to talk to you."

"Oh, no! Not Mrs. Conn," I muttered to myself. "Okay, what's her number," I inquired reluctantly. After hanging up, I paused a moment before calling. Knowing Mrs. Conn, it was not going to be a simple case of whether or not she had pneumonia.

Rrrrriiiing. Rrrrriiiing. Rrrr—"Hello?"

"Hello, Mrs. Conn, this is Dr. Zazove. I'm returning your call."

"Who's this?" she inquired. She always made me repeat my name. I suspected she didn't hear well herself, although she never admitted to that. Whatever the reason, I had come to expect that response from her.

"Dr. Zazove. I'm returning your call," I repeated a little louder, while rechecking that my phone amplifier was still turned on all the way.

"Oh yes, Doctor," she said, and as was her usual routine, continued, "let me turn down my radio. Just hang on a second please."

Several minutes later she was back. (Perhaps she had put on a hearing aid?) "Doctor?"

"Yes, I'm still here."

"Thank you for calling back. I couldn't hear you and had to turn the radio down. Doctor, I've been having a . . ."

Her voice became fainter and I could not understand her anymore.

"Mrs. Conn, could you talk louder please. I can barely hear you."

"Oh, I'm sorry Doctor. I was trying to reach some scissors and I must have moved my mouth away from the phone. Anyway, as I was saying, I've been having a bad cough and am coughing up some mucus. It's the thick green type that sticks in my throat and makes me gag. I'm worried that I may have pneumonia."

"How long have you had that?"

"It started a couple of days ago. Then I had just a cold. I decided I better take it easy since Darrell—he's my husband, you know—had plans to go fishing this weekend. So I made myself a cup of hot tea, put a little honey and whiskey in it, and sat down to read the paper. Of course, I do have to get up once in a while, but I haven't gone outside at all. Usually when I drink my cup of hot tea, it settles me right down, and in a couple of days I'm so much better. But it didn't work this time, Doctor. I've gotten worse.

"Anyway, Darrell went fishing as planned. Usually he brings back a whole bunch of nice trout. Of course, he cleans them for me. I told him I'll cook them, but I won't clean them. Doctor, do you like trout?"

"Yes, I do, Mrs. Conn," I answered, fighting the urge to read the paper as she rambled on. I did not hear a fair number of the words because of her high-pitched voice, but got enough to easily understand the gist of her monologue.

"Well, I'll be sure to bring you some next time I come see you," she offered.

"Thank you, Mrs. Conn. That's very nice of you. Now, are you having any fever?"

"I think I am, but I don't have a thermometer to take my temperature. You see, Doctor, I think I know why I may have gotten sick. I spent the whole day Thursday canning my peaches. I had picked them all on Wednesday. We got four bushels of them, you see. Oh, you ought to taste the peaches after I'm done with them. They're so delicious. You see, it all depends on how you cook them and what you put in the syrup. I put in exactly one-half cup of sugar but I also add a few herbs. Doctor, do you like peaches?"

"Yes, I do, Mrs. Conn." But before I could get in my next question, she continued.

"Good, I'll bring you some so you can taste them. But don't open the jars until you get home. You might spill some of the syrup in the car or on your clothes, and it's very hard to get the stains out. I know because I did it one time. If it happens, let me know and I'll tell you how to remove them. There's a special way, you know. Anyway, I was canning all day Thursday and I think I overdid it."

When she paused to catch her breath, I quickly asked, "Have you had any shaking or chills?"

"Yes, but I'm not sure if it's because of the fever or because it's cold in my basement. We keep it cool so we can store food there. Besides, we've been trying to save money, so we only heat half the house, even in the winter. After all, there's just the two of us, and we have such a large house. Since we don't use all of it, we closed the doors and turned off the heat to the rooms we don't use. But, Doctor, you see, sometimes I have to spend some time in the basement. You know, occasionally there's something in there that I need. Well, last night I went down in the basement and it seemed so cold. I was only there for maybe five minutes, but I think that's why I was shaking a bit yesterday. Oh yes, I told Darrell. . . ."

"Mrs. Conn," I interrupted, "perhaps I better see you, if you're having fever, shaking, and coughing up green sputum. I can meet you at the office or at the emergency room. It would be cheaper at the office, but either is fine with me."

"Dr. Zazove, Darrell is out fishing and I'm all alone. I don't drive very well. But I have an idea. Why don't you just give me some meprobamate and Seconal to last me until the morning. I'm sure that if I can relax I'd feel better. You see, I didn't sleep all night last night. I just couldn't relax. Now that isn't good for my pneumonia, is it? Darrell will be home tonight and he can take me to your office tomorrow."

"No, Mrs. Conn, I'm afraid not. If you have pneumonia, you don't need tranquilizers and sleeping pills. You need antibiotics. I'll need to see you before I can give you anything." Wondering why she asked for these drugs every time we talked, I continued quickly before she could begin anew, "We need to find out for sure if you do have pneumonia. Now, since the office is closer, I'll meet you there. How long will it take you to get there?"

"I'm not dressed, Doctor. Besides, I'm afraid to drive there myself. And when I do, I drive very slowly because you never know who might suddenly pull out in front of you. So it takes me about twenty minutes to drive to your office. Now Darrell, he's not afraid at all and can get there in about seven minutes. And besides, it'll take me at least an hour to get ready. Doctor, isn't there any way you can just give me something to relax? Right now, I have to take a couple of nightcaps every night before I go to bed. They relax me enough so I can go to sleep, but by 1:00 I'm up again, all wound up."

"Mrs. Conn, how about if I meet you at the office in an hour and a half? That ought to give you plenty of time."

"No, I think I'll wait until tomorrow, when Darrell can bring me over."

"Okay, that's up to you. Just remember, if you have pneumonia, it could be much worse by tomorrow."

"I'll be okay. But I just don't know how I'm going to sleep tonight. I'm sure a couple of meprobamate would make it much easier for me."

"No, we've already discussed many times before why I can't keep giving you tranquilizers. I guess I'll see you tomorrow then," I concluded. "But remember, if you get worse, call me back today."

"Okay, Doctor. I will. And thank you for calling me back."

I hung up and began to wonder. What on earth did Mrs. Conn get out of her extensive manipulations to obtain a small number of sedatives? I recalled another person I once knew—my landlady in graduate school, also an older woman—who launched into monologues. Once, when talking to my roommate, she went on and on for so long that he turned my telephone amplifier all the way up, placed the receiver on the floor, and lay two feet away from it, his arms folded behind his head. Then he closed his eyes and rested, every once in awhile turning to the mouthpiece and saying, "Yes, Mrs. Hendrickson."

I was eventually able to put Mrs. Conn out of my mind and turned my attention back to the newspaper. The rest of the day passed uneventfully.

"It's a lovely morning, isn't it?" I greeted Mrs. Conn the next day as I walked into the room where she was waiting.

"Hello, Dr. Zazove. I have something for you here." She gestured toward the bag she was holding, studying me closely for my reaction.

"Thank you, Mrs. Conn." I carefully remained noncommital, noting that her appearance hadn't changed since I had last seen her.

Irma Conn was in her early seventies and reminded me of the sly old lady in the movies who pretends she's naive and innocent but really is quite cunning. She was short, barely five feet tall, if that, with thin gray hair and an air of confidence. Her clothes, unlike those of many older women, were modern rather than old-fashioned, although not what some would call fashionable. Today, her weather-beaten face sported prescription sunglasses.

Still, it was her mellow voice that distinguished her from other women. Even I could tell there was something unusual about it. Because of its alluring quality, people paid attention to her. And Mrs. Conn knew this. She was very good at using her voice to disarm people in order to get what she wanted.

Mrs. Conn originally referred herself to me several months earlier, supposedly because her previous physician was too far away. When she first came, she wanted a refill of her meprobamate and Seconal, two addicting, consciousness-altering drugs. Meprobamate was one of the first tranquilizers ever made. Very few doctors prescribe it anymore now that safer drugs are available. Seconal, a "downer," is still prescribed by some physicians as a sleeping pill, even though there are less-addicting drugs for this as well. The first couple of times we met, Mrs. Conn actually succeeded in persuading me to give her a few. After that, though, I refused her requests. She continued to insist, however, despite my numerous explanations about the dangers of the pills as well as offers to arrange for someone to teach her how to relax without them. She always had a reason—or rather excuse—why she could not do so.

Although she wouldn't admit it, Mrs. Conn was addicted to the drugs. It had now been months since she had received the pills from me. She hadn't even called for a long time, and I had figured she had been trying her luck with another doctor. I sincerely believe that she wasn't abusing the drugs or selling them on the black market. She lived alone with her husband, and he was often gone on business, fishing, or hunting trips. At her age, it was understandable that, when by herself, she was afraid and unable to relax. Still, she should not be taking sedatives daily. They often cause side effects, such as drowsiness. If that happened to Mrs. Conn, she could fall and hurt herself badly.

"I'm just not feeling better," she stated, apparently deciding it was not yet time to reveal the contents of her bag.

"Looks like you have a low fever," I commented, noting the 99.4 temperature LeAnne had written in her chart. "Now, did you ever get the pneumovax? That's the shot that prevents the most common kinds of pneumonia. Remember I recommended it to you last year?"

"No, I just haven't gotten around to it. I should've come back for it, I guess, but I have so much to do. You see, we have a big garden behind our house. During the spring and summer I'm out there working on it by 6:00 a.m. I work there on and off all day long. I'm also constantly going in and out of the house doing errands. You know, I have to straighten up the house a bit. Or the phone rings and I need to answer it. Sometimes, it's one of my girlfriends, and I invite her over for a bite of lunch. We don't eat much, just a little cottage cheese, some fruit cocktail, and a cup of tea. But we do have some interesting discussions. Old ladies like to talk, you know.

"By the time dinner comes, I have to go in and fix it. Otherwise, Darrell will give me a hard time. He's not like some of you younger folks. He's still from the old school and expects me to do the cooking. But I'm not complaining. He takes good care of me. If my back hurts—and you do know I have a back problem—he tells me to sit down and he does the dishes.

"In the fall, I'm busy canning and freezing. All the fruits and vegetables from our yard need to be fixed and stored for the winter. And of course Darrell brings home fish, elk, and deer then too. I have to prepare and cook them as well. I do have a little more time in the winter, but I'm afraid of the ice. I'm scared to drive on it. Doctor, I don't ever drive in the winter unless I absolutely have to. So that's why I haven't been able to get the shot."

While she rambled, I noted she wasn't having any difficulty breathing. Her pulse was a little high at ninety, but otherwise she seemed her normal self.

As soon as she paused, I asked two more necessary questions. "Any blood in the mucus you're coughing up?"

"No, not that I've noticed, but usually I swallow it. You see, my friend—"

I interrupted her with my second question, "Any pain?"

"Not really. My chest feels heavy at times, but usually it's okay. Now, I want to tell you about how I prepare the deer Darrell brings home. What . . ."

As she talked, I proceeded to examine her and began to suspect pneumonia. Because of her age, her relatively poor compliance, and who knows what other drugs she was taking, I decided to get a chest X ray to evaluate the infection further. We then reviewed it together.

"Look here, Mrs. Conn." I pointed at the X ray on the viewbox. "See that white area over there?"

"Yes."

"That's pneumonia," I explained to her. "It's in your right lung and looks like the kind that should respond quite nicely to antibiotics."

"So I do have pneumonia. No wonder I haven't felt good. Now, if I could only get a good night's sleep, I think I'd get better a lot faster, don't you, Doctor? Oh, Dr. Zazove, I almost forgot," she exclaimed as we got back to the exam room. "I have a surprise for you. Here," she said as she reached into her bag and pulled out a plastic bag with three large pieces of venison. "Do you like deer meat?"

"I don't think I've ever tried it," I answered.

"It's good," she assured me. "You have to cook it right, however. The way I do it is to put some meat tenderizer on it and let it soak for a couple of hours before cooking. Otherwise, the meat is too tough. Then you cook it at a lower setting than you do with regular meat. That helps bring out the flavor. Now remember, don't fry it. Just broil it but put it farther from the flames so it takes longer to cook. Add a little garlic and salt, and you'll have a very nice piece of steak."

"Thank you very much, Mrs. Conn. I surely appreciate this."

"Just be sure you tell your wife to cook it like I told you and you'll enjoy it," she said, basking in her praise. "Now, Doctor, I need something to help me relax. I'm all out of meprobamate and Seconal, and I can only take so many highballs. I need a good night's sleep to help me get rid of this pneumonia. You see, when Darrell is gone, I'm afraid. You never know what might happen and I'm all alone. I lock all the doors, but I still worry and just can't relax. And lately, I've been coughing real hard at night. It keeps me up. So if you'll just give me some meprobamate and Seconal, I'll get some rest and recover from this pneumonia."

"Mrs. Conn, let's talk about your pneumonia. You aren't allergic to any medications, are you?"

"No, not that I know of."

"Okay," I immediately said as I handed her a prescription. "I want you to take these pills four times a day with food for ten days. They're called erythromycin. Most people do well with them, although a few get abdominal discomfort. If you do, let me know.

"I also want to see you next week to make sure you're improving. If you have any problems before then, such as a high fever, chest pain, difficulty breathing, or any other new symptom, don't wait till then. Call me immediately. Okay?"

She nodded, but before she could speak, I continued, "Now, I agree that a good night's rest will help you recover from the pneumonia faster, so I'll give you some cough medicine. It may make you a little drowsy, but that should help you sleep. I want you to take it only at night, though. It's important that you cough during the day—that's one of the ways your body fights the pneumonia. I won't give you any more meprobamate, though. I've already explained to you why not before."

"But, Doctor, I can't relax otherwise. And my sister is coming in a couple of weeks to stay with us for a few days. It's important that I get plenty of rest and get over this pneumonia before she comes. Just a few pills, maybe ten, would help me sleep this week and get better. I'll only take them when I really need them. After all, Doctor, I'm just a poor little old lady who's all alone this week. Please?"

"I'm afraid not, Mrs. Conn. We've talked about this many times before. If I give you some, I'd just be prolonging your dependence on them. It really is best for your health to stop them. Besides, you already told me your husband came back last night, so you're not alone anymore.

"One more thing. I don't want you to overdo it. You need to rest and take it easy. So no more canning for a few days. Okay?"

Even though Mrs. Conn did not get her drugs, I had no doubt that she would continue her efforts for them. I suspected she probably tried to get meprobamate from other doctors too. Mrs. Conn is not alone. Many people are addicted to drugs but refuse to admit it, and a large number of them are otherwise successful people. It can be difficult for physicians to tell who has the problem. It is often even more difficult to get people to stop the medications. Many of the new health plans that are spreading throughout the country would help with this problem. Mrs. Conn would have to pick one physician and would not be able to see any other doctor without his or her approval. Although these plans are not perfect, this would certainly stop her doctor hopping.

TWELVE

THE WEEK BEFORE Mrs. Conn's return passed slowly. School was back in session and as happens every year, fewer patients came to the office. No one wants to miss the first few days of school, so not many children came in sick. There were fewer injuries too, since children were in classes most of the day. Even parents seemed caught up in the excitement of a new school year; they came in less often as well. That week, I spent several hours catching up on odds and ends that I had not had time to do before.

My associate, Constance Paulos, also took advantage of the extra time. I had known Connie ever since I was chief resident on one of the hospital services and she was a medical student under my supervision. When she later finished her residency at the University of Utah Hospitals, I recruited her to join me. Although I had been in practice for almost three years by then, Connie immediately expanded the appeal of our office. Many women prefer female doctors, and despite being in practice only one year, she was already quite busy. She found herself involved in a great deal of women's health care, especially delivering babies.

Connie also made life more interesting in our office because she was single. Like most single people, she was looking for a partner, and her moods would fluctuate depending on how her search was faring. The rest of us in the office found ourselves following her quest with interest, wondering if she would ever find the right man. This possibility injected a slight element of suspense into our everyday routine.

Finally, that man came and Connie became engaged. Time had

since flown swiftly and her wedding was scheduled for the forthcoming weekend. We were all looking forward to the event—it was going to be a traditional Greek ceremony. In the meantime, however, Connie spent every spare moment on the phone, dealing with last-minute glitches in her carefully laid plans. I remembered the frantic days before my wedding and empathized with her predicament.

It was during this week, after school had let out for the day, that Mrs. Furness brought her daughter back again. This time LaDawn was complaining of her right ear hurting.

Joking, I asked, "Are you sure you didn't put anything in your ear like you did your nose?"

"No way," her mother proclaimed for her. "LaDawn's learned her lesson, haven't you?" LaDawn nodded in agreement.

"How long has it been hurting?"

"About two days."

"Any fever, cold symptoms, or drainage from her ear?"

"Not that I've seen."

"Has she had ear problems before?" I wondered.

"Only once, when she was a year old. But there've been none since."

"Okay then, let's take a look at it."

I checked her left ear first. It was normal. Then I looked in the right one. Aaaah! So that was the problem.

"Mrs. Furness, come take a look through my otoscope," I offered. "I think you'll find this interesting."

Looking in, she exclaimed, "What's that little white thing?"

"A ball."

"A ball?"

"That's right. Looks like she's done it again. Only this time she put something in her ear instead of her nose."

"Well, I'll . . ." Mrs. Furness started to stutter, then plopped in her seat, astounded and speechless. After a minute she started to laugh.

LaDawn has been the only person in whom I've seen different objects at different times in different orifices. Unlike the nose, foreign bodies in the ear canal usually don't get infected, so there was no odor this time. I removed the ball and checked her eardrum. She was fortunate that it had not been damaged. Then her mother and I examined the ball. It was small but hard. We couldn't figure out where it could have come from.

I had one more topic to address with Mrs. Furness. "Do you remember when you brought LaDawn in before for the sponge in her nose?"

"Yes," she replied.

"You mentioned then that your husband had had the same problem for as long as you've known him?"

Smiling, she answered, "Yes, I did."

"Well, I just want to know one thing. Has he complained of any ear pain too?"

Laughing, she answered, "No. And his nose hasn't changed a bit either. When I told him about the sponge, he couldn't believe it. But as soon as I suggested he come in to have his nose checked, he refused. He said he was too old to do something like that, so there was no reason for him to come in and have it checked. I doubt you'll ever see him for that."

She was right. I never did.

Two days later was the day of Connie's wedding. Barbara and I arrived early at the large, Greek Orthodox cathedral. The building, although old, has been well maintained and is one of the architectural landmarks of the city.

We walked up the stairs, entered through tall, double doors, and gazed upon the ornate interior of the chapel. A majestic dome hung over the pews, and matchless stained-glass artwork adorned the windows. The earth tones of the cushions, carpet, and altar contributed to the stately atmosphere. To the left of the altar I could see, but not hear, someone playing the piano.

An usher escorted us to seats near the front, where we sat quietly, enjoying the surroundings as we awaited the ceremony. Then, LeAnne leaned forward from the row behind, tapped my shoulder, and mouthed the words, "Can you believe she's actually going to get married?" I shook my head and then whispered as I motioned around with my hand, "Sure is a beautiful place, isn't it?"

At least, I thought I whispered, until Barbara nudged me with her elbow. "Talk more softly," she said, putting her forefinger on her lips. I nodded and stopped talking, suddenly quite conscious that several strangers around us were staring at me. My voice had been louder than I intended, which often seems to happen at the worst times. It is the result of my inability to accurately gauge the loudness of my own voice. Sometimes the reverse occurs, especially when I am wearing my hearing aid in a meeting. Then, because my voice sounds louder to me than usual, I occasionally talk so quietly that others cannot hear me.

It wasn't long before the rest of the office staff arrived. While they talked quietly, waiting for the wedding to begin, I began to reminisce about my own wedding and how my wife and I first met. . . .

It was during our third year of medical school. One Saturday morning, after working all night in the hospital, I came home at about 10:00, completely bushed, and went to sleep immediately. I had the day off and planned to arise whenever I happened to wake up. Early in the afternoon the phone rang.

"Hello."

"Hello, is Philip there?" a pleasant female voice inquired.

"Speaking."

"Hi. This is Barbara Reed."

"Who?" I have always had difficulty understanding names and numbers on the telephone, even with the amplifier. Many other words can be deduced from the context of the conversation, but names cannot.

"Barbara Reed," she repeated, "one of your classmates on pediatrics. Do you remember me?"

The connection with pediatrics helped. Despite being half-asleep, I recalled who she was. As part of our pediatric training, students were assigned to small group seminars to discuss different topics. Barbara was in my group, although not on the same floor as I. We hadn't talked very much before, except to exchange the usual pleasantries.

"Yes, I do."

"Well, my roommate, Marcy Gibbs, suggested I call you. You were on surgery with her last month, and she said you were a nice person. I'm looking for someone to see a movie with tonight and was wondering if you'd be interested in going?"

Now this was not the first time I had been asked out by a girl. However I did not really know this Barbara Reed. And I was still drowsy too. I began to think it was all part of a dream. Nevertheless, I had no plans for the evening, and it would be a good opportunity to meet someone new. In addition, I had enjoyed working with Marcy. If she had suggested that Barbara call me, perhaps Barbara would be as fun to be with as her roommate, though I knew I would not understand anything in the movie. Besides, even if it was a dream, there was certainly no harm in going.

"Sure, I'll be glad to."

"Great! There's a new one I'd like to see, called *Five Card Stud*. Is that okay with you?"

"What's the name of the movie?"

"Five Card Stud," she repeated.

I still did not comprehend the name but it really did not matter. Which movie we went to was irrelevant. Other than action films, I simply am not able to follow the dialogue. Sometimes I get an idea of what is happening from the actors' body language, but those deductions are often wrong. When the film is subtitled, on the other hand, I greatly enjoy going; then I get as much from the movie as anyone else. But I was not aware of any current movies that were subtitled. And, at this point, I did not want to explain my problem with movies.

"That's fine."

"Good. It starts at 7:30, so I'll pick you up at 7:00. Now, exactly where do you live?"

"I'll be glad to drive," I offered.

"No," she insisted firmly. "I asked, so I'll drive."

Afterwards, I lay in bed, still wondering if it was a dream. Just in case, I set the alarm before drifting back to sleep. It was 12:30 p.m.; I'd been asleep only 2½ hours. No wonder I'm hallucinating, I thought, as I curled up into a ball and fell asleep again.

The alarm went off at 6:15 p.m., shaking the bed. Blindly, I groped for the clock and shut it off. Falling back on the sheets, I tried to remember why I had set the alarm in the first place. There was nothing planned that I could remember. It was supposed to be my day off. Then I recalled why. Did she really call, or was it all a dream? I was still tired but resisted the urge to go back to sleep. If it was a dream, I could always do so later. But if it wasn't, I wanted to be ready when she came.

I trudged into the bathroom and splashed cold water on my face. The tingly sensation helped wake me up. Should I call and ask if she really was coming? I decided not to. Whatever her answer, I would feel foolish. Instead, I dressed and ate dinner in plenty of time. At 7:00 sharp, the doorbell rang. There was Barbara, on the doorstep, ready to take me to the movies.

We had a good time. While eating after the show, I asked her why she called me even though we did not really know each other.

"I had just broken up with my boyfriend and felt like going out with someone new," Barbara answered. "When Marcy told me about you, I decided to call. You don't mind, do you?"

"No, not at all," I answered truthfully.

Barbara grew up in a totally different environment from mine. Her family of seven lived in a small northern Indiana town, a place with typical rural Midwestern values. And they have been in America for centuries, contrary to my family's more recent immigration here. In fact, her father's ancestry goes back to the *Mayflower,* to a man who fell overboard on the way over. Fortunately, he was rescued. Otherwise, the course of world history, as well as my own, might have taken a different direction—this man was also an ancestor of Dwight D. Eisenhower.

Despite our different backgrounds, Barbara and I fell in love. We began to spend more and more time with each other. Through snowball fights and ice skating in the winter, canoeing and tennis in the summer, our love grew. In reality, we weren't opposites but alikes who happened to grow up in different environments.

It didn't bother her that I had a hearing loss. She could see that it had not prevented me from doing what I wanted. We had to make some adjustments, however, that most couples don't, most of which were related to entertainment. In particular, Barbara loves plays, especially musicals. For obvious reasons, I do not. If I know the story, I can tolerate going because then I have a general idea of what is occurring. But if it is a new story, it always turns out to be a boring two or three hours. At first, I went with her to the plays. After awhile, though, we both realized it was a waste of my time. So now we compromise. Although I rarely attend plays, she goes as often as she likes with some of her friends.

We both decided independently to specialize in family practice. To ensure that we would both be accepted at the same place, we applied to the various training programs as a couple. Although we had not discussed marriage at that point, we intuitively knew this would happen before our specialty training began. Still, by January 1978 we had not even become engaged, and internship was due to start in only five months. Time was running out. We arranged a weekend visit to Barbara's parents' house in Indiana for later that month. Again, there was no talk of marriage, but we both knew the reason for the visit was to announce our engagement. Hours before we left, however, it began to snow. When the time for our departure arrived, the snow had become a classic Midwestern blizzard. And this was the last weekend available for the next six weeks; we were scheduled to start time-consuming rotations the following Monday.

"It's really snowing hard. Do you think we can make it there?" I worried, looking out the window at the drifts under the lit streetlamps. "I'm afraid we'll get snowed in somewhere."

"I haven't heard anything about the roads being closed. Anyway, we need to try. This is the last weekend we can go for a long time." Just as Barbara spoke, she heard the radio announce that the highway into Indiana was being closed.

"Oh no," Barbara cried. "I can't stand the suspense any longer."

Her comment silenced us both. Then before I realized it, I blurted out, "Will you marry me?"

Barbara burst out laughing. "I can't believe you said that right now," she managed between peals of laughter.

"But I mean it," I exclaimed. "Will you marry me?"

Putting her face next to mine, she murmured, as she kissed me, "Of course I will."

Two weeks later, we somehow managed to arrange our respective schedules, escape for the weekend, and drive to Columbus, Indiana where Barbara's family lived. She wanted me to break the news about our engagement by asking her father for her hand. Although I had met her parents twice before, I did not know them well. They had always treated me nicely, but retained an air of distance. But I could understand this. I am sure I was not what they would have originally picked for a son-in-law. Not only was I of a different religion, but I was also practically deaf.

Initially, things went fine. We arrived there without difficulty late Friday evening. After an hour of talking, everyone went to sleep. I lay in bed, trying to develop a plan of attack for broaching the question to her father, but everything I thought of seemed too contrived. The next day, several situations presented themselves where Barbara and I were alone with her parents and I could have asked the question. During two of them, Barbara looked at me and nodded, encouraging me to go ahead. I procrastinated instead, rationalizing to myself why the time was not yet right.

That evening, after dinner, Barbara cornered me alone. "Time's running out."

"I know, I know. I'm just waiting for the right situation."

"How about tonight, after my brother goes to bed."

I nodded. The rest of the evening I kept searching for the perfect line, rearranging words as I tried to make them sound perfect.

After her brother went to bed at 9:00, Barbara, one of her sisters, her parents, and I remained at the kitchen table. Barbara nodded her head toward the door and said to her sister, "Patty, go upstairs for awhile."

Her sister looked at her quizzically. My heart started beating faster.

"Patty, please?"

A light of understanding flashed across Patty's face. "Sure." She got up and left the room as the tempo of my heartbeat increased to a pounding. Barbara's father took a sip of his martini and her mother worked on the sweater she was knitting. I looked at Barbara and she raised her eyebrows to encourage me.

I tried to remember the words I had chosen for this occasion but my mind was a blank. I knew that was no excuse, however. I had to do it. I took a deep breath, looked at her father, and spoke the first thing that came to my mind.

"I would like to ask you for your daughter's hand."

He did not answer, but instead sat awhile before getting up and refilling his glass. Meanwhile, it seemed to me that her mother was knitting faster.

I wondered whether he heard me. I am never quite sure what hearing people should and should not hear. And the last thing I wanted to do was to repeat the request if he had heard. He came back to the table, sat down again, and took a long swallow.

I looked at Barbara. Tears were starting to form in her eyes. I looked back at her parents. Just as I had decided to repeat the question, Barbara's mother spoke. "You can always elope if you want to."

At that, Barbara ran upstairs crying, leaving me alone with her parents. Now the silence was real, even to me. The three of us sat at that table without speaking. One, two, five minutes went by. Not a word was spoken. I understood where her parents were coming from and how my request had probably shocked them. Still, I wanted to get away from there. Seven, ten, fifteen minutes. I began summoning up the courage to leave. Just as I was about to rise, Barbara returned.

"Philip and I don't want to elope," she told her parents. "We want to have a wedding." She went on to explain in detail how we felt about that. As soon as I could, I excused myself and went up to the guest bedroom. Later, Barbara came in and explained. Her parents had been taken completely by surprise. They had not realized how serious our relationship was, and had worried that Barbara was merely having an infatuation with me that would eventually pass. Once they realized it was more than an infatuation, however, they were very supportive of our decision. They have since treated me wonderfully, and have included me in the family doings in every which way.

We were married four months later, two days after graduating from medical school. It was perfect timing; both our families were in town for the graduation, and our medical-school friends were able to remain in town for the wedding.

The music in the Greek Orthodox chapel stopped and Barbara nudged my arm, bringing me back to the present, Connie's wedding. As if on cue, an air of anticipation permeated the room. Then the wedding procession began. As the bridesmaids passed, we recognized Julia, Connie's nurse, and waved at her. She smiled back. Soon Connie herself appeared, resplendent in a white gown, a veil over her face, and a long train behind her. She looked simply magnificent. The ceremony was also lovely. It was a typical Greek Orthodox ceremony, including the customary three processions around the altar by the bride and groom. Afterwards, as they walked out arm in arm, Connie's happiness was evident for all to see.

I have been to weddings of many different cultures and religions; they're all beautiful and unique. But there is also a common theme that binds them all—the consecration of marriage, the union of man and woman. And this wedding upheld that tradition. It reaffirmed my belief that despite all the dissimilarities among mankind, there is even more that we have in common.

The reception in the Greek Cultural Center next door was lively, loud, and fattening. People laughed and talked. Tray upon tray of delectable Greek pastries were laid out on the table. Barbara and I went over to sample them. As fast as the food appeared, it was gobbled up and washed down with one of the numerous types of drinks available.

"Aren't these great?" Carma, my receptionist, said. It was harder than usual to understand her because the music drowned out the few sounds I heard. Fortunately, I could see her lips and did not have to ask her to repeat herself too often.

"They sure are, especially the baklava," I noted. "Those are my favorite."

"I've never seen so many pastries at a wedding before," LeAnne added.

"You ain't seen nothing yet," said a middle-aged Greek man who overheard our conversation. "The night's just starting."

"What do you mean? Is there more?"

"You bet there is. We'll be drinking, eating, and dancing all night. It's a custom that goes back to the old country." He took a swig of his drink and then continued. "I remember some of the weddings there when I was a younger man. Boy, were they something. When we Greeks have a wedding, you can bet we're going to have a good time. After all, it doesn't happen every day, does it?"

"No," we agreed.

"So we drink and enjoy." He gestured at me with his glass of wine, "Tasted this?"

I did not understand his words but did his gesture. "I've had some," I told him. "It's good."

"The best," he smacked his lips with pleasure. "Made in Greece."

He turned to Carma. "Ever seen any Greek dances?"

"Not really."

"They're starting to dance now in there." He began to walk in the direction he had pointed. "Come on, follow me. I'll show you."

We followed him to the next room where a band was playing. Crowds of people were gathered around the dance floor. Barbara tapped my shoulder and, pointing, said, "Look." I followed the direction of her finger and saw Connie and her family leading a group through a traditional Greek dance. Several people from our office were among the dancers. Barbara and I joined in, learning the steps on the spot. (Actually, although I could hear or sense the underlying beat of the music, being able to do so is not an absolute prerequisite for dancing; a sense of rhythm is enough). The hours floated by until it was time to leave.

The following Monday, Mrs. Conn showed up as scheduled. As she went back to an exam room, she winked at me and gestured toward the bag she was carrying. LeAnne came out of the room and, smiling slyly, informed me that Mrs. Conn did indeed have something for me.

I walked in while she was cleaning her glasses with a piece of Kleenex. "Hello, Doctor," she said as she greeted me with a smile. "I feel a lot better than I did last week. Thank you so much for helping me. I've been coughing less, and seem to have more energy. I'm still awfully nervous in the day, though. You see, there's so much to do. After I get up in the morning, I get the paper. Then I fix myself—and Darrell, if he's home—a nice cup of coffee. Sometimes I put a shot of whiskey in it. We sit at the table and read the paper from front to back. We don't usually finish that till about 10:30. Lately I've been straightening out my storage room. I've been working on it all week. Now, that's a lot of work, Doctor. And I remember you told me to rest a bit. So I've been taking it easy doing that. Whenever I get the least bit tired, I fix myself a cup of hot tea and sit down for a while. But I just can't totally relax. I think I'm going to need something to help me do that."

"Are you still coughing up the green sputum?"

"Yes, a little, though not nearly as much as before. It's mostly at night when I lie down in bed. Darrell tells me that if I don't stop coughing he's going to start sleeping on the couch."

I listened to her lungs. They were much clearer. Moreover, she no longer had a fever and her pulse was down to seventy.

"I agree with you, Mrs. Conn. You are improving. I still want you to finish the last few days of the antibiotics, though, for a total of ten days. After that, you should do fine. A slight cough may linger on for a couple of weeks but it shouldn't bother you much. If it does, let me know. Okay?"

"Yes, Doctor, I understand. I am feeling a lot better. By the way, have you ever eaten mountain trout?"

"Yes, I have." I had a gut feeling what she was leading up to.

"Do you like it?"

"As a matter-of-fact, it's my favorite type of fish."

"Well, I have a surprise for you. Darrell caught a whole bunch of rainbow and cutthroat trout over the weekend, and I thought I'd bring some over for you." Pulling three fish out of her bag and handing them to me, she continued, "I breaded them for you so they'd taste just right. The two on the bottom are rainbow trout, and the other is a cutthroat trout. I make my breading in a certain way. I soak it in beer before I put it on the trout. It tastes better that way. Now be sure you bake it for 25 minutes at 375 degrees. And don't forget to defrost them first. I take mine out of the freezer the night before to give them enough time to defrost." With piercing eagle eyes, she watched closely for my reaction to her gift.

"Thank you very much, Mrs. Conn," I voiced my appreciation sincerely. "This is very kind of you. I'm sure my wife will enjoy them too."

Apparently satisfied with my response, she became visibly more relaxed. "Doctor, I can tell by your speech you have a hearing loss. My grandson has one too, and he talks like you. How long have you had yours?"

"I was born with it."

"Oh really? Now, Danny got his from meningitis when he was two years old. He's eleven now. They have him in a special class for deaf people. He wears a hearing aid in both ears because otherwise he can't hear a thing. But let me tell you. He's smart, smarter than any of my other grandkids. I know because he spends a lot of time at our house. Sometimes, I almost feel like he's one of our own. We've worked with him as much as possible, trying to get him to talk better. We take him places and encourage him to talk to us. Darrell even took him hunting this year. But he still communicates mostly in sign language."

"Perhaps that's the way it should be. Maybe it would be easier instead for everyone else in the family to learn sign language than to try to make him talk."

"I agree with you totally, Doctor. I learned it myself and use it with him all the time." She shook her head. "But my daughter and her husband, they refuse to even consider learning it. They want him to speak more. I tried convincing them otherwise, but they think they're doing the right thing." She shrugged. "That's up to them. Doctor, when you were younger, were you in special classes?"

"No. I went to the same school everyone else did."

"I see. You know, Danny's had problems with some of the kids in the neighborhood making fun of him. He's been real upset over it. Kids just don't realize how cruel they can sometimes be. That's why he doesn't want to go to the public school. It's probably just as well anyway because they can't understand him. At least in the deaf school he's made friends. Did you have that problem too?"

"With a few people, yes. But I quickly learned to avoid them and played with the other children. In many ways it was some of the teachers, rather than the kids, who were the problem. They didn't want anything to do with me because I was different. For some, it was because they found me difficult to understand. Others because they had to change their usual routine. With a few, well . . . I wouldn't say they thought I was dumb; let's just say they thought I was less intelligent. But for the most part though, people were very supportive."

"Did you speak sign language when you were in school?" she asked me with her hands.

"No. It wasn't until medical school that I learned how to sign."

"That's interesting. You know, in so many ways, Danny's like you. Besides being deaf, he's also tall and has dark hair. If you don't mind, I think I'll have him come by and meet you. He'd like it."

"I'd love to meet him too."

"Good. By the way," she lifted her eyebrows, "how did you like the deer meat?"

We hadn't, but I didn't have the heart to tell her. So, I avoided answering her question directly by reassuring her that it had been well prepared.

"Darrell will be going hunting again in October. Since he always gets his elk, I'll bring you over a couple of steaks when we get them." After the slightest pause, she continued with the inevitable, "And, Doctor, I'll need some more Seconal and meprobamate. I'm out of the ones I had before. When Darrell goes away, I need something so I can rest and sleep a little bit. Otherwise, I just can't relax. And hunting season is coming up soon too. Darrell's usually gone the whole time.

"You know, sometimes I think about going back to work. I used to be a masseuse. A darn good one too. They tell me I was the best around. I know how to really give a massage and get all the soreness out of the muscles. Here, let me show you," she said, grabbing my arm. She massaged my forearm vigorously a minute and asked, "What did you think of that?"

"That's quite a rub," I said admiringly.

"See, I still have the strength and know-how to be a good masseuse, but I'm too nervous. I need something to calm me down. Maybe a few meprobamate will do the trick and get me to relax a little. Then I can think about going back to work."

Sighing silently, I answered, "I'm sorry, Mrs. Conn, things haven't changed. I won't be able to give you any, for the reasons we've talked about before. Taking those pills is not good for your health. There are better ways to relax. As far as your pneumonia is concerned, you're doing much better, and won't need to come back again for that. And one more thing. I suggest you get that pneumovax shot now."

"I won't take the pills every day, Doctor, I promise. I'll only take them when I'm really nervous. But I need a few to keep on hand. Otherwise, how am I going to be able to rest like you told me to?"

"I'll be glad to give you the names of people who can help you with that. They can teach you how to relax so you won't need medication anymore. It's totally safe, too, and more effective than taking pills."

"But, Doctor, I don't drive well and it's hard to get around to see someone else," she whined. "Please, just a few meprobamate. I'll only take them when I really need them."

"I'm sorry, Mrs. Conn." I got up and walked toward the door. Turning, I added, "I'll have LeAnne come in and give you your shot. If there's any other way I can help you, please let me know. And thanks again for the trout." Smiling at her as I left the room, I knew it wouldn't be the last time I'd hear from her.

THIRTEEN

THE SUMMER AFTER GRADUATE SCHOOL I got a job in the outpatient laboratory of Edgewater Hospital, in the northeastern part of Chicago. It was interesting work and I learned a lot about how hospital laboratories function, but I was anxious to begin medical school. Therefore, despite my good job, time passed slowly that summer, and each week seemed to last forever. Finally, September arrived and it was time to go to the east coast.

My parents drove across the country with me. We left on a Friday morning, three days before school started. First, we stopped at Ann Arbor, to drop my sister off at the University of Michigan where she was beginning her third year of college. The following morning, after making sure she was settled, we left for New Jersey. Slightly less than halfway there, however, in the middle of Ohio, the car suddenly died. Because it was Saturday, we had a difficult time finding someone to do the emergency repairs. I worried that we would not arrive at our destination on time. After all the difficulty getting into medical school, I did not want to be late for the first day. Finally, we managed to locate a mechanic only to learn that the car needed a part he did not have. And no other automotive shop in town had it either. Fortunately, the local junkyard did have the parts and the car was repaired. So we were able to reach New Brunswick in time.

Initially, I was anxious about my upcoming adventure, despite my strong desire to become a physician. I knew that like all medical schools, Rutgers had the luxury of being very discerning in its selection process. All my classmates would be top students, people who had excelled in their respective colleges. Although confident of my ability, I still wondered what it would be like to mingle with such a select group. Orientation started with a meeting of the entire class. At first, it was slightly awkward. No one knew anyone else, and most people sat quietly in their seats. A few speakers gave brief talks—at least half of which I did not hear—about the school and upcoming courses. After we filled out various administrative forms, the class was divided into six smaller groups. This helped break the formality and people began to open up. By the end of the day a definite camaraderie had begun to develop. I quickly discovered that despite their academic excellence, my classmates were individually as diverse as my college friends had been. I also learned that there were few other out-of-state students, not surprising considering Rutgers Medical School is a state-supported institution. It was in the small groups that I first began informing people of my hearing loss. Most were surprised, although no one seemed upset.

Classes started the following day. In those days, the first year of medical school was solely lecture- and laboratory-based; there was no patient contact. The second year provided only a little interaction with patients. I found the first two years of medical school, although much more intense and time consuming, not that much different from college. The lectures were held in an auditorium just big enough for the 110 persons in the class, and much smaller than the large ones at Northwestern. Nevertheless, the lectern was still far enough from the front row that I had a hard time understanding many of the professors. At first, I was able to compensate by borrowing notes from several classmates and studying from textbooks. This became more difficult with time, however, because as the date of the first examination approached, people were less willing to lend their notes; they were too busy perusing them themselves. I found myself trying to juggle my schedule, borrowing notes from whomever possible. It was a difficult situation.

Then the day came for the anatomy examination. It was a hard one, and over a quarter of the class failed. Immediately afterwards, several of these students organized a note-taking service, in which every lecture in each class would be taped and transcribed verbatim.

Each person who participated in the service would be responsible for producing the transcripts for their share of the lectures and distributing copies to all participating students. The organizers hoped this would enable everyone to do better on future tests. Although I had passed the test with room to spare, I willingly participated in the service as did almost all my classmates. From then on, I did not have to worry about missing important information in lectures—it was always in the transcript. Furthermore, I was no longer concerned about being able to hold my own with a group of top-notch students. I did well during my years at Rutgers, scoring in the top ten percent of my class, thus vindicating the admissions committee's decision to give me a chance.

Initially, as did several of my classmates, I lived in a dormitory on the undergraduate campus about a mile from the medical school. Within a day, it became apparent to most of us that this would not be feasible. There was a group of college students who not only played their stereos full blast almost twenty-four hours a day, but also refused to turn them down when requested. This interfered with our sleeping and studying. Even I could hear the boom-boom of the underlying rhythm whereas normally I cannot hear any sounds from other people's stereos when I am in a different room. What's more, I could also feel the tremendous vibrations being produced by the bass line of the music. Since the other dormitories were full and there was no separate dormitory just for medical students, we all began to look for places to move to. Fortunately, a second-year medical student had an extra room in his apartment, which he offered to me. Even though it was tiny, not much bigger than a large closet, I was happy to move there and escape the dorm. Most of my colleagues in that dormitory also relocated by the end of the second week.

The rest of the year went smoothly, and the summer after my first year I set about starting to fulfill an oath I had made back in high school. I had promised someone who worked with deaf and hard of hearing persons that if I ever got into medical school, I would learn sign language. A medical school friend and I started to attend the meetings of a local deaf club to begin this process. My friend went simply because he was interested, not because of any personal or family experiences with deafness. The members of the club were wonderful. They were excited that we were willing to devote time to such a pursuit and went out of their way to teach us. So every Tuesday, the two of us went to the weekly gatherings and began to slowly acquire the basics of the language. First, we learned how to fingerspell the alphabet. Once we mastered that, we spent our time on learning the more commonly used signs. The rest of the week, we practiced with each other. By the end of the summer, we both had developed some fluency in Signed English; at that point, however, neither of us could communicate in American Sign Language.

My second year, four other men in my class and I rented a house from a professor who had left on sabbatical for a year. We had a wonderful year together. Not only were we all going through the same pressures, but we also enjoyed each other socially. It was during the second half of this year that we had our first direct contact with patients. It was in an introduction to psychiatry course where all the students were assigned to interview patients in the presence of a faculty member. Everyone was excited. After a year and a half of courses, we were finally going to deal with patients—just like real doctors. I recalled several of my medical school interviews when the interviewers had expressed concern over whether I would be able to communicate with patients. Still, I was not worried. Up until that point I had been able to communicate with all types of people. I did not see why it would be any different with patients.

I was right. Although not specifically by design, I somehow ended up not telling any of the patients about my hearing loss. It did not seem appropriate to me at the time in the context of the situation. None of the patients I interviewed that spring asked about my speech either. Perhaps this set the stage for the rest of my career, because since then I have not gone out of my way to explicitly inform every patient about my hearing loss; when I have trouble hearing them, or if they ask, I tell them. It never seems be a problem when they find out, either. On occasion I have specifically asked people if it bothered them. The answer has always been some variation of the following: if I was able to graduate from medical school, then I must be capable of doing what I do.

Although I had a wonderful experience at Rutgers and developed close relationships with some of my classmates, at that time the medical school did not have enough places in the last two years to accommodate the whole class and required that some students transfer to other institutions. Early in my second year, it became readily apparent there was discontent among the clinical faculty, for reasons that were unclear. Several professors moved elsewhere, and we heard threats that many others might do the same. Because these people were responsible for teaching the last two years, many of my colleagues decided to transfer rather than take a chance that things might deteriorate. In fact, so many of us left that Rutgers had to recruit people from elsewhere to fill all the positions. Although several schools had openings for transfer students in their third year, I decided to apply to Washington University, one of the country's top medical institutions, via their "early decision" program.

In November 1975, I flew to St. Louis to interview at that school. I was immediately impressed by the size of the medical center, with its skyscraper hospitals and well-equipped research wings, in addition to the prominent faculty. Because Washington University is so highly regarded, it is very difficult to get accepted there. Nevertheless, I felt confident of my chances. Not only did I have excellent grades, I had also been elected by my classmates as the second-year-class student member of the Rutgers Admissions Committee. Thus, I was familiar with what medical schools looked for in applicants, and knew I was quite competitive.

My first meeting of the day was with the assistant dean. Everything seemed to go well until, after a few minutes, he did a most amazing thing. He stood up, walked to the other side of the room, and covered his lips with his hand. Then he said something to me.

"I'm sorry, sir, but I can't understand you when you cover your lips."

Still holding his hand over his lips, I deduced he was speaking again.

What was I to do? "Sir, I still can't understand you."

This time he dropped his hand and started whispering to me.

I strained to read his lips. The area he was in was darker than the rest of the room, and his lips were hard to see. Fortunately, he enunciated well. I was able to make out several words, but still could not understand what he said.

"Pardon?"

He repeated himself, again whispering the words. This time I managed to read a few more words, enough to understand the gist of his sentence.

"Yes, I can understand what you're saying."

Then he walked back to his desk and finished his interview, never asking me directly about my hearing loss.

The next meeting, with a psychiatry professor, was more reasonable. Because my encounter with the dean made me realize the faculty were concerned about my hearing loss, however, I decided to find out from the interviewer if he thought it would be a problem.

"Will my hearing loss play any role in your decision whether or not to accept me?"

"Well, it certainly won't help."

"You know, it hasn't been a problem at all. I've not found medical school any more difficult than my classmates."

"But that's in the classroom. You haven't had to deal with patients yet," he countered. "That's what happens the last two years of medical school, and that's what we're concerned about."

"I've had some contact with patients already, and it was not a problem." I told him about the introduction to psychiatry class. Nevertheless, he did not seem totally reassured.

I will never know how much of a role my deafness did play, but Washington University accepted me one month later. And that was providential in an unforeseen way. It enabled me to meet Barbara, during my pediatrics rotation.

FOURTEEN

"I WANT TO PET the goats again," pleaded my daughter Rebecca.

"Me too," her sister Katie chimed in.

"All right," I agreed. "One more time. But then we have to go home because I need to get ready for work this afternoon."

Laughing, the two girls skipped ahead to the children's petting zoo. The bare trees and leaf-covered ground presaged the fast-approaching winter. A blanket of grayish clouds covered the skies, and there was a definite nip in the air.

I had the morning off, and my daughters had wanted to visit the zoo. Because of the cool weather, few other people were there. Many of the animals, however, were still outside, roaming their enclosures. I felt sorry for them, confined to small spaces for the rest of their lives, but Katie and Rebecca were too young to appreciate the wretched state of these creatures. To my daughters, it was exciting to see the animals, and especially to touch the domesticated ones.

I devote much of my time off to my two girls. We do all kinds of activities together and have become very close. As with most doctors, though, my life is a juggling act, trying to spend time with my children and still be available for my patients. Fortunately, most people understand my desire to be with my family and are willing, when necessary, to see the doctors who cover for me.

We walked into the petting area.

"Let's go pet this one," Katie yelled to Rebecca and ran toward a gray goat. Ignoring her, Rebecca caressed an old black one. They quickly realized the miniature animals were mainly interested in those kids offering food.

"Here, Rebecca, pick up these crackers on the ground and feed them to the goats," ordered Katie who, being older, often tries to boss her sister around.

This time Rebecca agreed.

I have never had difficulty understanding my daughters, even when they were toddlers, an age when it is often particularly hard for me to read lips. Probably they discovered two things early on: first, I did not respond to their questions unless they were facing me and I was looking at them when they spoke; second, they had to enunciate clearly for me to understand them. Now, they get my attention by hitting a table, banging on the closest wall, or touching me before speaking. For the most part, they are comfortable with their "deaf Daddy." Occasionally, however, it bothers them.

After fifteen minutes with the goats, it was time to go. We walked to the car, talking about the animals we'd seen. Suddenly, Katie said, "Daddy?"

"Yes?"

"Why do you talk so funny?"

"Because of my hearing loss. You know that."

"I know, I know, but it sounds like you have something stuck in your throat."

"Honey, the problem is that it's impossible for me to say sounds I can't hear."

"All my friends say you talk funny. It embarrasses me." She paused a second, then ordered, "Swallow."

First I warned, "We've been through this before. That's not going to make a difference in my speech." Then I swallowed while she watched me.

"Swallow harder."

I complied again.

We walked a little more, then she instructed, "Okay, now say *sounds*." She overenunciated the word.

"Sounds?"

She nodded.

I repeated the word.

"No, listen to me closely. *Sounds.*" She again overemphasized the pronunciation.

"Are you talking about the *s* and *z* sounds?"

She nodded.

"I can't hear them. So I can't tell when I say them right."

"Oh."

After we got home, I changed clothes quickly and ate lunch. After kissing my daughters good-bye, I drove to my office, watching the dark clouds with interest. The threat of rain in Utah is unusual because of the desert climate. When it does rain, it can be exciting, especially a classic desert storm. In a short time span, clouds rush in from the west, pour a torrent of rain over the valley, then disappear behind the mountains to the east, leaving behind blue skies again. Thunderstorms, in particular, provoke a lot of interest. Many people in Plymouth sit on their porches and watch them, delighting in each bolt of lightning and clap of thunder.

I stopped at the drive-in window at the bank to get some money. Although the two outer lanes were not occupied, I pulled behind the car in the inner lane and waited. That window was the only one where I would have a possible chance to read the teller's lips. The two outlying islands were too far away, and I could never understand the intercom the rare times they used it. (Though it sometimes means waiting awhile, I always use the inner window if I am too lazy to walk inside the bank.)

Shortly thereafter, I reached the office and parked on the far side of the lot, leaving the closer spaces for patients. It still had not rained, but the air seemed cooler than it had that morning. Did the nimbus clouds covering the sky contain the first snowstorm of winter? Only time would tell. I walked in, anticipating the day ahead. A glance at my schedule revealed that it would be the usual busy one.

Five minutes later, LeAnne signaled with her fingers that my first patient—a new one—was ready. On the table in the exam room sat a frail, older man who must have been in his seventies. He stood five feet six inches in his shoes. He had a long, heavily wrinkled face, hanging jowls, and a prominent, hawkish nose that was knobby at the tip. The skin of his squat neck was thickened from sun exposure. Dark eyes, short graying hair on the sides, and an almost bald scalp made his appearance commensurate with his age. His hands were in constant motion, especially when they rested in his lap, where his thumb and forefinger moved as if they were rolling a ball. A middle-aged, heavyset woman sat primly in a chair, facing him.

Looking at the name on the chart, I said, "You must be Rico Gatto."

"Yes, that's me all right." His gruff voice had a thick Italian accent, and he didn't enunciate well, tending to slur his words. I had to concentrate hard to understand him.

I consider myself an expert lipreader. Like many persons who are deaf, I can read most people's lips. In fact, we can read the lips of people who are in profile or even upside down. Part of our success is due to our ability to correlate the lip movements with our observations of the speaker's facial expressions and body language. The two together are much more effective than either alone. Even the best lipreaders in the world can only understand about twenty-five percent of the words spoken; the rest of the words are inferred from other clues, such as body language and whatever sounds the person does hear.

Actually, there are certain persons I can often understand better than hearing persons. These are individuals who barely utter any sounds, such as a person who is hoarse or someone who is debilitated and can't put much voice into his or her words.

More common, however, is that sizable group of people I have particular difficulty understanding, usually because they do not move their lips. I am told that their speech sounds perfectly distinct. Nevertheless, I can't understand them; all I hear are scattered noises, and what I see makes no sense. It can be a frustrating experience. I have to concentrate intently on their lips and expressions, often asking the person to repeat themselves several times. This task rapidly becomes exhausting. Try it for a minute. Plug your ears and have a friend talk without moving his or her lips; you will be surprised how quickly you get tired.

People with thick accents are also hard to understand (I suspect, in part, because they move their lips differently). Similarly, anyone with a beard or mustache that covers the lips is particularly difficult for deaf and hard of hearing people to lip-read. These persons also often have to repeat themselves many times.

"I'm his daughter," the red-haired lady in the chair volunteered. "My father's been visiting me from Florida for two weeks now, and the whole time he's had problems urinating. He's always going. Sometimes he doesn't even make it to the bathroom, and he wets his pants. I'll say he probably goes through three or four pairs of them a day. He never did that before. Doctor, there's definitely something wrong."

I looked at Mr. Gatto again. "Let's start at the beginning. How long has this been going on?"

Mr. Gatto glanced at his daughter, as if checking something with her, then answered my question. "Oh, about three weeks, I think."

"Have you ever had prostate problems in the past?"

"Naw. I had it . . ."

I did not understand anything he said. "I'm sorry. I didn't catch that. What did you say?" I concentrated hard on his lips.

"No, I haven't. I had it checka the last time I saw the doc, about four months ago. They told me everything was fine. But I had no problems then. Now I just can't control it. And if I cough or sneeze, I leaka in my pants."

I managed to get most of that. "Are you getting up at night to go to the bathroom?"

There was a pause as he thought for a few seconds. "Yeah. I never used to do that, but the past few months I've been getting up several times a night. Lately, I can't even sleep because I gotta go every half hour or so."

"Have you been losing weight or feeling tired?" I asked.

"Naw, I've weighed the same long as I can remember." He shook his head. It was getting easier for me to understand him as time went on. I was getting the hang of reading his lips, despite his accent.

"Mr. Gatto, have there been any changes in your life in the past three or four weeks? For example, did you start taking any new medications?"

"Now that you mention it, Doc, I did starta on a new pill about two or three days before this began."

Aha, I thought. The key to the whole problem. "What's the name of the pill?"

"The doc in Florida, he tolda me I had Parkinson's and gave'a me a pill for it. I don't remember the name of them." Turning to his daughter, he asked, "Did you bring them pills with you?"

"Yes, Papa, I did," she answered, rummaging through her purse for them. When she found the bottle, she handed it to me.

The label read: Sinemet 10/100. "These pills might be the problem," I said. "First, though, let's examine you to be sure we don't find any other cause." I started to walk toward him, then stopped. "One more question. Do you have any other medical problems or take any other drugs?"

"Well, I got some pills for high blood pressure. But I don't take'a them every day because I forget them." Again he turned to his daughter. As she handed the rest of his drugs over to me, he continued. "I also take'a a nerve pill for when I get upset, but I've been taking those for a long time with no problems."

I inspected the bottles his daughter gave me. He was taking a diuretic for his hypertension, and his tranquilizer was Librium; neither sounded like the cause of his symptoms.

I stood next to the exam table where Mr. Gatto sat stiffly. He appeared somewhat rigid, despite his continuous hand movements. I looked in his throat, checked his lymph nodes, and examined his lungs, heart, and back. All were normal.

Then I came to his abdomen. It seemed a little bloated, particularly in the lower half. I started to examine it, then stopped, a little startled. Something was there that I had not expected: a large mass occupying most of his belly below the navel. Then I realized what it probably was—his bladder, markedly distended. Mr. Gatto most likely had a large prostate.

"Mr. Gatto, I'll need to check your prostate next." Turning to his daughter, I continued, "Could you step out of the room for a minute?"

"Sure," she agreed, slightly embarrassed.

I was right: his prostate was immense. But it was also irregular, and the right side was rock hard. These findings made me worry about cancer. The addition of the new medication, on top of his huge prostate, had effectively dammed his bladder. Since his kidneys continued to work, the bladder had gradually filled with urine until it reached his navel.

After his daughter returned, I sat down to discuss my findings with them. "Mr. Gatto, you have a prostate problem. As you may know, this is quite common in older men. What happens is that the prostate slowly gets bigger over the years. Sometimes, it becomes so big that it blocks the urine from leaving the bladder. That's what yours did about three weeks ago. As a result, your bladder filled up with urine, just like a balloon fills with air. The reason you keep wetting your pants is that the pressure inside the bladder sometimes gets so great, a little urine is squirted past the prostate. Unfortunately, you have no control over that.

"I suggest you go into the hospital, where we can empty your bladder with a catheter. We'll have to leave that in awhile since it'll take time for your bladder to regain its ability to function. I'd also recommend you have a prostate operation to prevent this from happening again in the future."

"The hospital!" he protested angrily. "I don't want to go to the hospital, Doc. And I don't want no operation. Can't you fixa me up here and senda me home?"

"I'm afraid not, Mr. Gatto. Remember, we need to leave the catheter in a few days. If we didn't, you'd be right back where you are now. After a few days, we'll take it out and see how you do. But if you still can't urinate, you'll have no choice. They'll have to operate."

He frowned and looked at his daughter ruefully. "What d'ya thinka all this nonsense, Judy? I thinka I'll wait till I get back home to Florida. I'll see my doc there, see if he can't fixa me up, eh?"

"Papa, if you're going to be in the hospital, I want you here so I can be with you. In Florida, you'll be all alone. Let's go ahead and get this taken care of now."

Grumbling and upset, he eventually agreed to go. "How long will I be there?" he asked, glaring at me.

"However long it takes to get you urinating again. Hopefully, not too long, but we'll have to see."

His daughter drove him over to the hospital immediately. The nurses passed a catheter into his bladder and removed over two liters of urine—much more than most people ever have at one time. And because of his rock-hard prostate, I ordered some blood tests and X rays to look for evidence of cancer.

After office hours, I went to see him. It was now 6:00 p.m., and Mr. Gatto had been in the hospital eight hours. He was lying on the bed wearing a blue velour bathrobe over his hospital pajamas. The head of the bed was inclined slightly upward and he seemed comfortable. Just before I walked into the room, he saw me.

"Doc, when are you gonna take'a this thing outa me?" he pointed to the catheter. "It hurts like hell, and I can't stand it no more."

"It'll be at least two days before we can do that."

"Two days? Awwwww. I feel fine now. Look, my stomach doesn't stick out anymore. Let's take'a it out now."

"Mr. Gatto, if we did that, you'd fill right back up. Even if we waited until the morning, we'd probably have to replace it. Your bladder's been distended for so long, it's completely lost its muscle tone. It'll take several days before that comes back. Until it does, you won't be able to urinate on your own."

"You know, Doc, I never had no problems before this except with my eyes. I had a physical in Florida, about a year ago. They tolda me then that I was okay. But even if they'd a tolda me I wasn't, it don't matter. I don't do nothing there. Hey, Doc, where are you from, anyway?"

"I grew up in Chicago."

"Chicago, eh?" He made his right hand into the shape of a gun. "Bang, bang," he smiled. "I remember the days of Al Capone. Every day we hearda something new about him. They sure don't make'a them like him anymore, do they? But where are you from originally? You have an accent."

I smiled. "That's because of my hearing loss. I was born in America."

"Oh." He looked at my ears. "But you don't wear a hearing aid?"

"No, I don't, except in certain situations. They don't work well for me."

"Hmmmm, I see. Anyway, as I was saying, it don't matter if I stay in the hospital. I don't do nothing at home. There ain't nothing to do."

"What do you mean?" I asked, not sure exactly what he meant.

"Well, it's so hot there, I don't want to do nothing. I just sit on the porch all day watching TV and talking with the guys. Sometimes, we go in the pool and sit there with the water up to our necks. That ain't no fun. I worka all those years so I can retire and for what? To sit in the pool?"

"How long have you lived in Florida?"

"Oh, about six years, I reckon. I was born in Italy and came over here when I was sixteen. We went to New York. I spent the resta my life there until I retired. I used to do all kinds of work, mostly union work, you see. Boy, those were some days. I lived in Brooklyn mosta the time. Used to go to work at six in the morning and wouldn't come home at night till seven. Used to loada trucks with the other union boys. I was a good union man, paida my dues, I did. Without that, I wouldn't have got a good day's pay. After work, I often went to see them old Brooklyn Dodgers play. Boy, that Ebbetts Field, it were one hell of a place to go to a ball game. I'd go with my buddies. We'd drinka beer and watcha them Dodgers play baseball the way it should be played.

"Then I retired and moved to Florida. There ain't nothing to do down there, I'm telling you. I don't have family there. Nothing there but old people, just sitting around waiting for the end. My buddies from New York, mosta them died. My daughter and her family are here. Of course, she's been mighty good to me, seeing as I didn't see her much as I should have when she was growing up. For a woman, she ain't bad. Most women are rotten, though. This world could do better without them."

"Now, wait a minute," I interjected. "What about your wife? Are you saying she was bad too?"

"She sure was, the damn bitch. I founda out early on that she played around on me while I was busting my ass working. I dropped her mighty quick. Ain't had nothing to do with her since."

"Have you thought about moving out here, if you like it better?"

Mr. Gatto gave me a hard stare with this question, making me wonder if I was prying too much. "Doc, I like'a it up here but I don't want to move. It would be too hard."

"You mean the weather's too cold here during the winter?" I guessed.

"Naw. I'd love that. I'm tired of the damn hot weather in Florida."

"Then why don't you move here?"

"Well, it would be too hard on my daughter. She's got her own family to take'a care of. And besides, she'd just want to take'a over my life too."

I looked at my watch. It was almost 6:45. Late for dinner again.

"Okay, Mr. Gatto. I'll see you in the morning. Have a good night and we'll look at taking out your catheter in two days."

"All right. And Doc?"

"Yes?"

"Don't get lost going home," he guffawed. I'm not sure why he made that joke, but he did it every day in the hospital, and each time he seemed to get a big kick out of it.

Leaving his room, I paused to check his lab results. They were all normal except for the acid phosphatase, a chemical produced by the prostate. His was sky high, indicative of prostate cancer, especially one that has spread. I felt my spirits drop. Just then, his daughter arrived and inquired about her father's condition. I mentioned the possibility of cancer but emphasized we were still doing tests to find out.

Driving home, the brilliant sunset lighting the way, I mused at the contrast between the everlasting beauty of the valley and the finite life of man. On the one hand was Mr. Gatto, who could very well die soon, depressed, alone, and unhappy with life. On the other was the natural splendor of the landscape, present for eons past and for centuries yet to come. Confronting death is difficult for anyone. As doctors must, I've learned to accept its inevitability, yet it's still hard to deal with. It's a time when my own mortality becomes apparent, and the limitations of modern medicine become starkly obvious. All that remains, then, is hope. And I hoped that Mr. Gatto did not have cancer.

FIFTEEN

THE NEXT MORNING, when I saw Mr. Gatto, it almost seemed as if a night had not passed. He lay in the same position, his robe still on.

"I'm all ready to get this damn thing outa me," he snorted.

"Mr. Gatto, I wish I could do that, but it's been only one day. You'll need to wait at least twenty-four more hours. And if we give it longer than that, you'll have an even better chance of keeping the catheter out."

"I don't want to wait another day. Take'a it out now."

"No, it's too soon. I don't blame you for wanting it out, but we'll have to leave it in today."

The following morning he was even more insistent.

"It's been two days, long enough. Get the damn thing outa me right now. It hurts like hell."

"All right," I agreed. "But if you don't urinate within six hours, I'll have to put it back in."

"No problem, Doc," he assured me. "And if I go, I go home, right?"

"If you can go all day without problems, I'll send you home," I promised him.

Unfortunately, and not to my surprise, he was unable to void and the catheter was replaced. At that point, I also started him on medication to help his bladder contract. However, the subsequent day he did not do any better. Mr. Gatto was going to have no choice—he needed surgery. I had a urologist see him; he agreed with my diagnosis and recommended that a TURP be done.

TURP is the acronym for Transurethral Resection of the Prostate, an operation where the center of the prostate is opened, thus allowing urine to pass through unimpeded again. It is a relatively safe procedure, and the success rate is high. The tissue removed is sent to the lab and analyzed for cancer.

After the urologist left, I talked with Mr. Gatto and his daughter to be sure they understood his recommendations.

"Do I gotta have the operation?"

"No, but if you don't you'll need the catheter in you the rest of your life," I informed him.

"No way! Well, if I have it, will I get this tube outa me after the surgery?"

"Yes, you will, but not for a couple of days."

"Damn," he swore. "I'll bet you never had a tube like this in you, Doc."

"You're right. But remember, you have one because you need it, not because we want it there."

"Well, if I gotta have it, I gotta. But I'm telling you, when I get back to Florida, now I'm gonna be happy to just sit in that pool and do nothing all day."

The surgery was successful. The urologist went on vacation the morning after and left the postoperative care to me. Two days later, the biopsy report came back.

I read it carefully, crestfallen at the results. It was not as I had hoped, but it was what I had suspected. Mr. Gatto had prostate cancer. Moreover, an X ray of his bones revealed it had spread beyond the prostate gland itself.

I felt that it was only fair to inform him about his diagnosis. I hate telling anyone he or she has cancer. So many people fear it dreadfully, and rightfully so, since it's the second leading cause of death in America. But I felt that Mr. Gatto should know as soon as possible. If I had a cancer that was going to kill me, I would want to know so I could make plans for the time that was left. I believe in giving my patients the same courtesy. But that didn't make my task any easier.

I walked into his room and sat on the edge of his bed where he was, as usual, lying in his blue robe. He was reading a book while his attentive daughter knitted in a chair by his side. The lights were turned down, and Rico Gatto appeared relaxed, almost content.

"Hi Doc," he said cheerfully.

"How are you feeling this evening?" I procrastinated, reluctant to shatter the serenity in the room.

"Great, since they took out my tube two hours ago."

"I'm glad that you're feeling so well, " I told him slowly.

"You know, Doc, I feel better than I have for a couple of months. You shoulda had the guy fixa me up the first day."

Over the years, I have learned the hard way that to beat around the bush is not the way to inform patients they have cancer. Moreover, it seems that most of them suspect it long before I tell them or even know for sure myself. Coming across directly may be a shock, but revealing the news slowly is a different form of torture that is worse for both the patient and me. Thus I take the direct approach, always trying to put the situation in the best light possible.

"Mr. Gatto," I began cautiously, gathering up my courage. "We need to talk about the pathology report that came back from your surgery." I hesitated for a second, then plunged ahead. "You have prostate cancer."

There was another split-second pause before he answered. "Well, I gotta die sometime. I ain't surprised, Doc. Everyone in my family has died o' cancer so I've known it was coming. I guess it's about time I die. I'm old and useless and don't do anything worthwhile anyway."

"Now wait a minute," I broke in. "I didn't say anything about dying. There are all different kinds of prostate cancer. It does seem that yours has spread to the bones in your back, but that doesn't necessarily mean you'll die. There are treatments available even for those cancers that have spread. Let's keep our hopes up."

His daughter, who at first had been stunned, also spoke up supportively, "Papa, you can stay with me. I'll take care of you, and we'll do whatever we have to to lick this thing."

He continued to talk to me, ignoring his daughter's statement. "You may be right Doc, but I've been tired the last month or two and I thought I had some kinda cancer. Like'a I said, most of the people in my family that died have died o' cancer. That's okay. There ain't nothing left for me anyway."

He didn't seem to be crushed or upset, maybe only a little sad. Outwardly at least, he accepted the diagnosis fairly well. I'm never quite sure how people truly feel inside when they appear to be unaffected. Was he ready to accept death? Or was he struggling fiercely with his emotions?

"One thing Doc. And Judy, I want you to hear this too. I don't want none of them cancer drugs. If I'm gonna die, I'm gonna die."

"But Papa—"

"No Judy, I don't want none of them cancer drugs."

"Then let's concentrate on getting you out of here now," I spoke up. "When the urologist comes back to town next week, we can see what he'd recommend next."

"Okay, Doc. Just so long as I don't have no cancer drugs. And no more tubes either. They're pure hell."

"That's fine, Mr. Gatto, I won't give you any cancer drugs. Whether you'll need another catheter, that depends on if you can urinate. If you can, I'll send you home first thing in the morning."

"All right," he assented. "Don't you worry. I won't have any more problems. And Doc?"

"Yes?"

"Don't get lost going home!"

Rico Gatto wasn't able to void that day and the catheter was replaced, much to his chagrin. I decided to send him home with the catheter, until he saw the urologist. That would give his bladder plenty of time to regain its ability to void again. His reaction was easy to predict.

"You mean I gotta have this damn thing in me at home?" he shouted.

"I'm afraid so," I confirmed quietly.

"What're you trying to do? Make'a my life miserable? I won't even be able to walka outside because people'll laugh at me."

"No one will know. Just keep the urine bag under your jacket and no one will even see it."

"Hell, no way. I ain't going nowhere with the tube in me," he declared.

"That's up to you. But you should keep taking the new pills. They'll help your bladder regain its strength. And remember, the urologist needs to check you in one week. At that time, the two of you can decide which way to go."

"Okay, Doc. I'll stay here with Judy for that long. But then I'm going back to Florida. The doc there can take'a care of me."

"Whatever you want. If there's anything else I can do in the meantime, let me know."

I went outside, feeling disheartened. Dealing with cancer is always depressing. Even heart disease, the leading killer in this country, does not produce the extent of anxiety that cancer does. I suspect this is probably due to several factors. First, cancer is mysterious. Not only don't we know what causes it, we often cannot cure it. Second, it results in a slow, lingering death that is frequently painful. Finally, all ages are affected.

The ground was covered with a thin layer of snow that had fallen earlier that morning. The sun was just rising. As it rose over the Wasatch front, there was a split-second blinding glare, and then the winter panorama was illuminated in the pellucid air. The mountains, completely covered with snow, were pristine white. A thick mist hovered near both mountain ranges, hugging the bases of the peaks. Taking in the uplifting scenery and a deep breath of the cool air, I felt my despair lessen a bit.

The traffic was lighter than usual. Children waiting for their school buses threw snowballs at each other by the road. Their youthfulness was a stark contrast with the terminal condition of Mr. Gatto. They had their whole future ahead of them. He had little. Thoughts about my own mortality began to surface. I tried to suppress them. I don't like thinking about death, especially mine. I have too many things to do yet. But the thoughts wouldn't stay away. How long would I live? What would I die of? If I died soon, had all the correct arrangements been made for my family? I dwelled on my life, on the goals I hadn't yet realized, on the desire to see my kids grow up. These are thoughts everyone has at various times.

People ask me how doctors take death so calmly. I don't think most of us do. We may appear calm, but inside we're suffering like everyone else, coping with the situation in our private way. Doctors, facing death and disability every day, maintain their sanity by distancing themselves from the emotions of this issue. Periodically, however, our defenses break down, and we too have to confront the inevitable. This is particularly true for family physicians, because the people who die are often those we have gotten to know well. Sometimes it is impossible not to become emotionally involved. When that happens, we suffer too, along with the family.

I walked into the office, feeling melancholy again. My first patient's problem, teenage acne, seemed so trivial compared with Mr. Gatto's illness. Forcing myself to concentrate on the present, I entered the room to try to help her.

SIXTEEN

MY LAST DAY at Rutgers Medical School was during the second week of June, two weeks before the July 1 date for starting my clinical rotations at Washington University. Despite my success during the two years at Rutgers, I was just as apprehensive entering my third year of medical school as I had been when traveling across the country to start my first. To begin with, I was again going to a new school in a city I had never lived in. Not only would I have to adjust to the differences of the clinical years, I would also have to start anew in meeting people and learning my way around St. Louis. Moreover, I wondered how I would fare when thrust into a medical center staffed by some of the top students, residents, and physicians in the world. Would the training I had received at Rutgers be sufficient to allow me to compete on an even keel with my new classmates?

My first rotation was on the internal medicine ward of Barnes Hospital, the massive structure that serves as the main teaching hospital for Washington University. It quickly became apparent that the psychiatrist who had interviewed me had been right about one thing. The last two years of medical school were indeed a drastic change from the first two. Instead of classrooms, students spent all their time in the institution's various hospitals. It was more fun too because of the constant human contact, both with patients and teachers. Fortunately, it did not take long for me to adjust. It turned out that my training at Rutgers had been excellent and I kept pace easily with the other students. Moreover, I discovered that my new classmates were not any brighter than my previous colleagues had been. The clinical opportunities at Washington University, however, were vastly greater and the intellectual stimulation was likewise immense. We all found ourselves assimilating huge amounts of information in short periods of time.

The psychiatrist who had interviewed me, however, had been wrong in his concern about my ability to communicate with patients. For the most part I was able to converse with everyone I came in contact with, just as I had always done. There were, of course, the usual number of people I had difficulty understanding. These were most often those whose lips were difficult to read—either they did not enunciate well or were obscured by facial hair. Likewise, there were individuals who had difficulty understanding me. After being together awhile, however, both of us would usually find it easier to carry on a conversation. I would acquire the knack of reading that person's lips, and they would find it easier to understand my speech. As had been my previous experience, patients rarely asked why my speech was imprecise. And when they did find out about my hearing loss, it never seemed to bother them.

I even discovered two types of situations where I actually understood patients better than my colleagues. One was the occasional patient who used sign language. Hearing persons often feel uncomfortable communicating with deaf people, even when an interpreter is present, an unfortunate reality well known to the Deaf community. The second were patients who were so debilitated that they barely uttered any sound when they spoke. If they were able to move their lips, however, I could often make sense of what they said, whereas hearing persons were unable to do so.

It was not patients whom I had the most problems understanding during my clinical years. It was certain members of the faculty. In fact, my first attending physician on the internal medicine rotation was one of those people who manage to speak without moving their lips. My hearing peers, as well as the intern and resident, had no trouble understanding him, but I sure did. Even after meeting for ninety minutes, three times a week for several weeks, I did not find it easier to read his lips. Needless to say, because I could not understand many of his questions, I received a poor evaluation from him. Fortunately, I received much better ones from other people.

Once a week, all the students on the internal medicine rotation at Barnes Hospital met with the chief of the service for "Professor's Rounds." One student was chosen ahead of time to present the case of a complicated patient. Afterwards, the professor would spontaneously quiz us about various aspects of the case. The physician in charge when I was on the rotation enjoyed intimidating the students, and we always entered the conference with a fear of being embarrassed in front of our colleagues because we did not know the answer to one of his questions. I was more worried than most. There were usually about twenty of us in the room during these conferences. When the professor asked his questions, he usually kept the conversation jumping round the room, making it impossible for me to keep up with the dialogue. Fortunately, for some reason he rarely put me on the spot, and I managed to avoid committing any faux pas.

After completing the required three months of internal medicine, I switched to the surgery ward. This required more specific adjustments in my day-to-day activities, especially in the operating room where I could not understand anything that was said because of the facial masks people wore. I tried wearing a hearing aid again for the first time since grammar school, and found that with it I could understand an occasional word here and there. By considering the context in which the conversation was taking place, I could even rarely guess correctly what someone had said. Still, those times were few and far between, and almost all the conversations in the operating rooms escaped me. In addition, because I had to turn the volume up all the way, sounds would sometimes ricochet inside the aid and emit a shrill whistle that annoyed everyone else. Loud as it was, the noise was also high-pitched and I could not hear it; it was only when everyone began to look around quizzically that I knew what had happened. And if it occurred during a surgery I had scrubbed in on, I could not turn down the volume myself because my hands were sterile. Instead, I was put in the embarrassing position of having to ask a nurse to do this. Because they were usually not familiar with hearing aids, it often took them awhile to figure out where to make the adjustments. When they finally did, they often turned the volume too low. After a couple of weeks of this, I finally figured out exactly how high I could turn the volume control of the hearing aid without causing any whistling. Still, most conversations remained unintelligible.

The inability to understand these conversations in the operating room was a hindrance to my education, as well as being frustrating. Most of the surgeons, as well as some of the residents, discussed various aspects of the operation with the students during the surgery and often pointed out specific findings as they occurred. I missed all of these. To compensate for this, I carefully noted what everything looked like and, after the surgery was over, asked the resident or intern to review what had been found.

By the time I finished surgery, my third year at Washington University was half over. By now, I had become acclimated to my new surroundings. I was even beginning to feel part of the class as well as feel more at home in St. Louis. It was not until I met Barbara later in the year, however, that I really felt I belonged. Through her, I got to know many other classmates outside of the hospital, which in turn resulted in my becoming integrated into their social network.

My next rotation was pediatrics. While on the floors of the Children's Hospital, I noted that it was harder for me to understand younger children, especially toddlers, than it was for hearing persons. Children at this age often enunciate poorly and move their head while talking. Moreover, because they tend to have high-pitched voices, I frequently could not even hear the vowels. I tried to compensate for this in several ways. I would attempt to engage the children's attention with toys while talking to them so that they were more likely to face me. I would also repeat their answers periodically to confirm what they said. Finally, I would get as much history as I could from their parents before talking to the child. This gave me a context in which to better understand the child. By doing all of these things, I found I was able to acquire all the information I needed.

I did not fare as well in pediatric grand rounds. But then I had just as much trouble with medicine and surgery grand rounds too. These are weekly conferences that each specialty has, where a particularly unusual or interesting case is discussed. Because there was frequently a robust discussion among the faculty during these meetings, I had no chance of being able to read people's lips. Nevertheless, I tried to obtain as much information as I could, usually by focusing on the main speaker and attempting to understand as much as I could from that person.

My obstetrics and gynecology experience in many ways was similar to surgery because in those days people still wore masks in the delivery room. However, I was fortunate to do part of my rotation in the county hospital. Most patients there were indigent and did not have a private physician. Consequently, students were allowed to do much more than they were at Barnes Hospital. Moreover, my supervising resident was especially interested in teaching medical students. He spent a good deal of time teaching me the important points about obstetrics, including extensive reviews of how to do deliveries. I even got to deliver several patients all by myself, under his close supervision. So despite the barriers inherent in the use of facial masks, I managed to learn a lot and acquire much valuable experience.

During these clinical rotations, as well as the subsequent ones in subspecialties such as neurology and ophthalmology, I quickly realized that whereas most other students and physicians were infatuated with the scientific aspects of diagnosing and treating patients, I most enjoyed the patients themselves. I loved talking to them about their lives. Of course, it was satisfying to treat their diseases too, especially when we could help them. But I found patients' personalities the most enjoyable aspect of being a doctor. In fact, my main regret was the lack of continuity. Because students move to a different rotation every six weeks, I never saw the same patients again. It was disappointing not to know what happened to them.

It was at the end of my third year of medical school, that I made a firm decision to select family practice as my specialty. I had been considering this field ever since beginning medical school, and my years in training clinched my decision. I enjoyed all the areas of medicine I was exposed to. Each had its own inducements: obstetrics, with its happy mothers and babies; pediatrics, with its innocent children; internal medicine, with its profound depth of knowledge; surgery, with all its drama.

What I really wanted, however, was to be a "real doctor." Like the old country doctor who took care of the whole family, made house calls, knew everyone personally, and was respected and trusted, I too wanted to care for families, with all the compassion of the old days but with the knowledge of modern medicine. Furthermore, I wanted to help people stay healthy, not merely treat their diseases. The glamour and expertise of other specialties were appealing, but they each had limitations. Only family practice would allow me to be a complete doctor. Only family practice fit my dreams.

I had other motives for wanting to be a family doctor. Following in my parents' footsteps was one, although not a major one. My hearing loss, however, was a significant reason. Deafness has made me more attuned to "the person" in each of the people I deal with. Because I miss much of conversations, I partly compensate by using other clues, such as body language. This ability has proven handy numerous times. In fact, body signs not only often convey what a person is trying to say better than their words do, it sometimes also reveals emotions their words do not disclose. This has made me realize how important people's feelings are.

The obstacles I've faced in my life because of my hearing loss also played a role. At times, it is downright difficult being different. Living through these experiences has made me sensitive to the feelings of others, and this sensitivity has, over time, fostered an interest in getting to know and help people. And what better field to do so than family practice?

My medical school professors, however, disagreed. They were convinced I was making a mistake. At that time, family practice was a relatively new specialty, and they believed it would turn out to be a passing fad. Nevertheless, for the reasons given previously, and probably others, I did not change my mind. I wanted to be a family doctor. Barbara chose family practice too. So during our fourth year, we determined which family practice programs in the country were the best and investigated thirteen of these; eleven were in the Southeast and the remaining two were in the West. We interviewed at each one. Even though all were considered top programs, we found a significant variation in their quality. Five clearly stood above the rest.

We ranked these programs in the order of our preference and turned the list into the central matching consortium, the method used by almost all medical students and residency programs for determining who goes where. Through the consortium, each student lists every program he or she is considering in order of preference; likewise, each residency program ranks the students. A central computer matches the two lists so that all students get the highest choice on their list that corresponds to a program that also listed them. A few variables can be added to the equation, and we used one of them—we applied as a couple. This way, we guaranteed that both of us would be accepted into the same program. We ended up matching with our second choice, the University of Utah. So two weeks after graduating from medical school, we returned from our honeymoon, loaded our cars and, pulling two U-Hauls, headed west across the plains to our new home by the Wasatch front.

SEVENTEEN

"WHICH IS WORSE, being blind or being deaf?" Helen Keller was supposedly once asked during an interview. Contrary to what most hearing people would have predicted, her answer was, "There's no doubt about it. Deafness is worse because it prevents people from communicating."

To people who are deaf or hard of hearing, this answer is no surprise. We confront the communication barrier numerous times every day. Others, however, seem to have a more difficult time accepting the logic behind this statement.

But think about it a minute. To begin with, what is the one thing that differentiates human beings from all other species? It is not that we walk on two legs (birds do that), have an opposable thumb (monkeys do too), or even have the biggest brain (elephants' are larger). As one of my psychiatric colleagues points out, the one thing that makes us different is our ability to communicate at will with each other about any topic—including abstract concepts—and to pass our knowledge to succeeding generations. We are the sole creatures on earth with that capability.

All humans have this aptitude at birth. And from the time we are born, it is nurtured and developed. Parents coo and talk to their babies many times daily. Most of them hear this and learn to distinguish different sounds and bond to their loved ones' voices. They also learn that by crying and making other sounds, they can elicit a response from other people.

As they get older, children learn to communicate more directly. First they merely babble. Eventually, they begin to imitate sounds they hear. By becoming excited about this, parents encourage their children to continue this mimicry and to repeat certain sounds again and again. Soon, these sounds become associated with specific objects and actions. So the child learns to say *ma* for mother, *da* for father, *ba* for ball, and so on. Similarly, the baby hears other people talking and begins to connect different sounds with the appropriate objects. The basis for speech as communication has been laid.

With time, the children expand their language skills. Two words, then three, are strung together. Sentences follow. From here on, the ability to communicate effectively develops at astounding speed. By age three, most children already understand and use correctly most of the grammatical rules and syntax of their native language.

The child hears other sounds in the environment too, and learns to associate them with certain things. The noise of the furnace is followed by a warm flow of air, and the ringing of the doorbell by people coming into the house. Dogs barking, cats purring, cars roaring by, and numerous other sounds are likewise categorized. All these are additional stimuli to the psychological and emotional development of the hearing child.

But this wondrous process of spoken-language acquisition does not happen to children who are deaf. Early on, they make the same sounds as all children. However, because they do not hear these sounds nor their parents' responses, they fail to get the same reinforcing feedback that hearing children do. Although children who are deaf also see their mothers and fathers get excited when they make certain sounds, they cannot correlate this with specific sounds, and soon the noises cease to be made. Neither do children who are deaf benefit from hearing other noises. Their world is a silent one. Consequently, they focus instead on their vision and become keenly aware of movement, much more so than other children. Unless someone is teaching them sign language, however, this awareness does not translate into an ability to communicate. Of course, you might say, the child can always learn to sign later in life. But there is a critical limitation we have not yet mentioned.

It is well accepted, as research done at the Salk Institute has shown, that although we are born with the innate capacity to master a language, this process must begin within the first three to four years of life. A child who has not been exposed to language within this time period loses part of this inborn ability. Thus, although he or she may subsequently learn a language, it will not be with the proficiency of someone who learned it during those first crucial years.

And that is what often happens to people who are deaf. The average age at which deafness is diagnosed is approximately three years. By the time their hearing loss is detected, many of these children have no skill in communicating. Even if they subsequently receive intensive training, it may be too late. If the golden time for language acquisition has passed, these people will never develop the communication skills they could have.

There is another way children who are deaf can communicate besides sign. They can lipread, as I learned to do, especially if they have some residual hearing. But lipreading alone is a notoriously inexact science. Moreover, learning to do it early is possible only if one has the right caretakers—people who are easy to lip-read and who spend time with their children. And even if one learns to lipread, there is still the issue of how to express one's thoughts to other people. The most common ways of doing this are sign language and speech through intensive oral training.

Because most hearing persons cannot understand ASL, many believed it to be an inferior language, merely a series of pantomimes. In the past twenty years, however, numerous studies have dispelled this misconception. It has been shown that deaf children who learn sign as infants develop the same capacity for communication as hearing children, including the same ability to grasp abstract concepts. ASL is now considered a language the equal of any spoken one.

Nevertheless, those who use ASL face another problem when interacting with the hearing world because ASL's unique sentence structure is quite different from English. Consequently, many deaf people have a hard time reading and understanding written English. Some even have problems with Signed English. As a result, the average deaf person reads only at a sixth-grade level—not because of inferior mental capacity, but because of being used to a different language structure. Over the centuries, this inability of deaf people to communicate with hearing people, plus deaf people's difficulty with reading and writing, has led to the misconception that deaf people are less intelligent. Consequently, all decisions about what was best for deaf people were traditionally made by hearing people.

Only recently has the Deaf community begun to express its desires to the rest of the world. The Deaf community is composed mainly of persons who have a profound or total hearing loss and who communicate with each other in ASL. Over the years, like any other culture, it has developed its own customs and traditions. In the past, the Deaf community allowed hearing persons to make decisions for them. Recently, however, they have learned the importance of both fighting for their rights and needs as well as how to do so. This newfound assertiveness has led to an array of impressive gains, the most notable being the inauguration of the first deaf president of Gallaudet University and the passage of the Americans with Disabilities Act.

Whether children who are deaf should be taught oral communication or sign language remains a major controversy in deaf education. This battle has raged for more than a century without any solution in sight. There are pros and cons to both sides, and ardent proponents of each method. The main advantage of the oral method is that persons who learn to read lips and speak intelligibly are able to get around in society. Because hearing persons have traditionally, and still do, control the education of deaf children, this method has been the predominant one most of this century.

One problem with stressing oral communication, however, is that it is extremely difficult to teach someone who cannot hear sounds how to say them, even with hours of practice and the use of the most modern techniques of speech therapy. It is almost as hard as a blind person trying to identify colors by feeling them. Yet, many hearing people have trouble understanding this.

Sign language, on the other hand, is easily learned by deaf people, almost rapturously so since it is much easier and provides an expressive and a comprehensive method of communication. Yet, as noted before, signing has limitations: it cannot be used with the rest of society. Currently, the emphasis in many programs is the so-called total communication approach, where both methods are used. Although this may be the best approach, it will probably be years before we determine its success.

The difficulty in communication between people who are deaf and people who hear erects barriers to the successful integration of the two communities. The same psychiatrist who points out the uniqueness of human language, also gives a great example of the way these barriers affect deaf people. Picture yourself in a room at a party. Suddenly, a blind person comes into the room, obviously unsure of where she is heading. What is your instinctive reaction? If you are like most people, it is to walk over and offer to help her get where she is going.

Now put yourself in the same room, but this time a deaf person walks in. What happens now? Chances are, you don't even know he is deaf. And even if you did, you probably would not have the desire to help, in large part because you know you would have trouble communicating with him.

Over the years, many professionals who work with deaf people have expressed amazement at what I have accomplished despite my handicap. They usually end up attributing it to exceptional intelligence. I would like to believe this is true, but I think it is much more likely a combination of fortuitous circumstances. I was lucky enough to be born with enough hearing to hear the vowels and a couple of consonants. I was also the first-born; there were no siblings to compete for my parents' attention during most of my language-formation years. Perhaps most important, my parents were fully supportive of me and committed to my success. They have very easy-to-read lips, spent much time with me, and encouraged me to do anything I wanted. And last, but not least, I have had much support from numerous other persons during my lifetime.

Like Robert Frost's poem "The Road Not Taken," about coming

to a fork in the road, taking one direction, and later wondering where the other path would have led, I too sometimes wonder what would have happened if I had found myself in a situation where the above circumstances had not been present. I have not reached any definite conclusions. But those circumstances did occur and they have certainly made my life much easier. It is hard to believe I would have had done as well on any other path.

EIGHTEEN

Although it wasn't official yet, winter had arrived. Snow fell on the mountaintops, and the snow line moved down the slopes daily. The ski resorts, eagerly touting every inch of powder, had opened early this year, hoping this auspicious beginning augured a prosperous winter. West of the Wasatch front, the valley remained dry. But the weather was nasty there too. Freezing temperatures and biting winds made it unpleasant to be outside.

With the arrival of the first cold snap, the annual onslaught of winter illnesses began. It happens every year, as all family doctors will attest. For reasons that are unclear, humans are more susceptible to infections during these frigid months. So we saw them in our office, these sick people, one after another, with their winter diseases; ear infections, pneumonias, sore throats, and influenzas arrived in a never-ending stream. At times, I was so occupied with patients that it seemed I didn't have time for anything else. Even lunch was sometimes a forgotten luxury. But then, surprises happen when one least expects them.

It had been a particularly busy day, a Tuesday before Thanksgiving, and at 3:00 p.m. we finally had a brief lull. Checking the phone messages on my desk, I noticed one from Peter Rutherford, the urologist. I called him first. Put on hold for a minute, I began checking my mail. I was surprised to find a letter from my alma mater, Northwestern University. It was an announcement of my class's fifteen-year reunion.

Boy, does time fly, I thought to myself, I'm getting older than—

"Hello, Dr. Rutherford here."

"Peter? Philip Zazove. I had a message that you called."

"Yes, I did, and thanks for calling back. I wanted to chat about Mr. Gatto who was in my office earlier today. Do you remember him? He's the nice gentleman you referred to me a while back for prostate cancer."

"I remember him well."

"Well, I'm afraid it's spread to involve most of his pelvis. Fortunately, he's actually feeling pretty good, so I wouldn't do anything about it until he starts feeling sick again. At that time, I'd recommend removing his testicles."

Removing the testicles eliminates the male hormones that seem to stimulate prostate cancer. Interestingly, it seems that no matter when in the course of the disease the surgery is done, the resulting benefit lasts for the same amount of time. That's why doctors wait until the patient actually develops symptoms.

Peter continued, "The other option is chemotherapy, but as you know he won't have that. He wouldn't even consider surgery when I first discussed it with him, but his daughter persuaded him to try that when the time comes. They are aware, though, that it won't cure him and may only make him feel better for a few months. Anyway, for now, I asked them to follow up with you in two weeks or sooner if he has any other problems."

"Thanks. You know, when I last talked to him he was going back to Florida," I mused out loud. "In fact, I thought he'd already gone because I hadn't heard from him since he left the hospital."

"His daughter convinced him to stay here with her," Peter explained. "He didn't follow up with either of us after I removed his catheter because he'd been feeling so good. Then yesterday, he had some abdominal pain and came to see me this morning because he thought it was due to the surgery."

"Oh. Well, I'll be happy to see Mr. Gatto again," I concluded the conversation. "And thanks for your help."

LeAnne, who had been waiting for my attention, informed me with a sign that my next patient was ready. Over the years, we developed ways of communicating silently that enable us to work together efficiently, despite my hearing loss. These include, among other things, our own unique group of signs. With just one hand motion, for example, LeAnne can not only indicate a patient is waiting, but also which room that patient is in. Moreover, using these signs she can communicate faster than if she told me the same information verbally.

I picked up the chart. LeAnne's note indicated that the patient had a rash. Oh good, I thought, a relatively easy problem.

A tall, thin, nine-year-old, Lindy Bloomer had long, blondish-red hair and a sparkle in her hazel eyes. She looked the picture of health, with a freckle-covered face and bright, white teeth. Her mother, who was also tall, thin, and redheaded, sat casually in a chair next to the desk. Other family members had come in previously for various illnesses, but this was Lindy's first time.

Smiling, I welcomed her and held out my hand. She grinned shyly, blushed slightly, and glanced at her mom. Then gathering her courage, she shook it.

Mrs. Bloomer nodded a friendly greeting and wasted no time getting to the point, "Dr. Zazove, Lindy's had a rash on her legs for two days. It doesn't seem to bother her, but it's been spreading. And she's been complaining about her ankles hurting. Yesterday the right one was swollen. That's better today, but now the left ankle's starting to swell. I'm worried about her."

"Are any of your other joints hurting?" I asked.

"No, I don't think so," she answered in a soft, feminine voice, the kind people with severe hearing losses hate, as she questioned her mother with her eyes. Mrs. Bloomer shook her head in agreement.

"Hmmmm," I murmured. "Any fever?"

"No, not that we've noticed," her mother answered.

Since Lindy had partially undressed already, I was able to scrutinize the rash. There were numerous irregular purplish blotches, mainly on her shins and calves, but some on her upper legs too. In addition, as her mother had noted, her left ankle was swollen.

I had been wrong. This was not going to be an easy problem to solve, for this was not just another rash. No, it was definitely something unusual. Straining hard to remember the different causes for skin lesions associated with swollen joints, I finished taking my history. It didn't turn up any further clues.

I noted the blotches didn't blanch when I touched them. In fact, they looked like multiple bruises. For a second the possibility of child abuse came to mind, but they didn't look like that.

I examined Lindy's ankles closely and discovered the left one was slightly tender and warm. However, she was able to move it with only minimal discomfort. Her other joints were fine. Likewise, the rest of her skin was also unaffected.

"Have you had a sore throat recently?" I asked as I stood up to examine it.

"No."

With Lindy sitting calmly on the exam table, I looked for significant lymph nodes, listened to her heart, and checked her abdomen. Everything was normal.

The more I thought about it, the more I began to suspect Lindy had a rare disease called Henoch-Schoenlein purpura. I had seen only one patient with it before, during medical school. Struggling to recall all I could from that time nine years earlier, I remembered it is an untreatable disease of unknown cause that is often self-limiting. Sometimes, however, abdominal pains or serious kidney problems develop. The latter are detected by a urine test and, if present, can be serious. Although doctors often try administering steroids, this complication can be very difficult to treat. Therefore, those who develop it are usually referred to a pediatric kidney specialist; the closest one to us was at the University of Utah hospital.

I was concerned. Lindy's symptoms had started only two days ago, and she already had a significant rash and swelling of both ankles.

"Lindy, I need to check your urine. Could you get some in a cup for me?"

As is often the case with children, she could not. During the next fifteen minutes, she drank several cups of water, trying to develop the urge to urinate. Meanwhile, I pulled the new pediatric textbook I had bought to see whether there was any new information about the disease. There was not. Then other thoughts began to rise in my mind. I found myself becoming a little anxious, worried about the possibility of Lindy's urine being abnormal. I thought of my own two daughters. If either of them developed this condition, I would be extremely worried. After all, Lindy was, until yesterday, a normal prepubescent child. Then suddenly she had this disease. Who could say my girls wouldn't acquire some similar illness? As a doctor, I probably worry too much about incurable diseases occurring in my family.

At least I did not have to worry about my children being deaf. During both of my wife's pregnancies, I was particularly concerned about this. Even though no one else on either side of the family has hearing problems, the fact that I am deaf made my children slightly more likely to be so. And I did not want my children to have to go through the same difficulties I did. Still, I knew there was no way to tell until after they were born. Even if there had been a way, nothing could be done about it while they were fetuses.

After each daughter was born, Barbara and I paid close attention to how she responded to noises. From the very beginning, both seemed to hear. By the time each was eight months old, we had no doubt. The hearing tests merely confirmed our impressions. Yet, if one of our daughters had been deaf, we would have been able to address it early. And I could have taught her many things too. Far more important than their hearing, however, was that both children were healthy. For unlike Lindy's disease, deafness is never fatal.

As a physician, I am faced with many situations where people are dying. It's probably the hardest aspect of the profession to deal with. Death at any time is sad. Sure, sometimes in an old person who's totally incapacitated or in a person with severely painful cancer, death is a blessing of sorts. But it's still sad. It is especially depressing when a child is involved. The dreams that will remain unfulfilled, the profound pain the family feels, the loss to society of years of productive life, and the seeming unfairness of it, all combine to make the death of a child heartrending.

During my rotations as an intern and resident at the Children's Hospital, I saw many children die. Usually these deaths were unexpected: children hit by drunk drivers, accidental drug overdoses, crib death, meningitis, or drowning. Whatever the reason, it always deeply hurt both the families and the doctors. As physicians in charge, we would often prolong resuscitation efforts past the point of no return, partly because of vague hopes for a miracle but also, I suspect, as an expression of our frustration at the sudden death of a healthy child. Often, too numbed by the loss to cry ourselves, we then had to inform the family of their child's death and console them as best we could. Yes, the finality of death is definitely one of the worst aspects of practicing medicine.

"The urine is spun down and ready for you to look at," LeAnne interrupted my thoughts. I hesitated a minute, then checked the tests LeAnne had performed on the urine. No protein! I immediately felt relieved. Protein in the urine is one of the first signs of kidney disease. I then examined the specimen under the microscope myself. Everything was normal there too.

Much more at ease, I returned to the exam room and began to discuss my findings with Lindy and her mother. "I think Lindy has a disease called Henoch–Schoenlein purpura," I began.

"What's that?" interrupted her mother, looking alarmed at such a strange-sounding name.

"It's an illness that usually occurs in children and causes a purplish rash and swollen joints, just like Lindy has. Those often go away by themselves within a couple of weeks. However, certain other problems may arise, such as severe abdominal pain and kidney disease. If the kidneys are involved, it can be serious. Fortunately, Lindy has no evidence of either of these at the present time. Still, the kidney disease can occur up to a year later, so we'll need to keep a close eye on her."

"What causes it?"

"That's a very good question," I answered. "There are many different theories, but no one really knows."

"Well, what can I expect?" asked Mrs. Bloomer anxiously. "I mean, what do I look out for? Is there anything I can do to help her?"

"There's no treatment available at this point, but there are several things you can watch for. For one, Lindy may get more swollen joints, especially in her legs. The rash may also spread further up her legs. So far she's been lucky in that she hasn't felt sick. That too may happen. She may also develop abdominal pain, blood in her urine, trouble urinating, or swelling of her eyelids, hands, or feet. If any of those happen, call me immediately."

"Doctor, do you think Lindy will get the kidney problems?"

"I hope not, but there's no way to predict who will. Only time will tell," I explained, wishing I could provide more specific details. I didn't blame Mrs. Bloomer for wanting information about her daughter's prognosis. I would, too, if Lindy were my daughter. It was frustrating not being able to give an answer, but there was just no way to know.

"Lindy, we'll need to get some blood tests," I told her. "It'll hurt a little bit, but we need them to help us figure out how to make you better. Okay?" Turning to her mother, I added, "I'd like to see her Monday. And if she gets worse, call immediately."

Lindy, unlike her mother, was not upset about her illness. Instead, she was scared of the needle that would be used to get the blood. "I don't want the blood tests, Mommy," she started to cry.

"I know you don't, honey, but they have to be done. Dr. Zazove needs them to find out how you're doing."

"But I don't want to," she fought.

"I'm sorry, Lindy, but we have to do it. Now if you're good and lie still while they draw the blood, we'll go get some ice cream. Okay? Don't move your arm now. It'll be over before you know it."

After some difficulty, we obtained the blood. I wasn't as concerned waiting for those results as I had been for the urine test. I felt pretty sure they would be normal, and they were.

Thanksgiving arrived two days later. It has always been one of my favorite holidays. Almost every year, my parents and sister's family fly to Utah for the long weekend so we can celebrate it together. This year was no exception. Everyone enjoyed themselves as we ate the traditional turkey dinner, skied, reminisced, and relaxed. My kids played with their cousins continuously.

Periodically, during this time, I thought of Lindy and wondered how she was doing. Was she okay? I had not heard anything from Mrs. Bloomer, but then I had arranged for Connie to cover for me over the weekend so I could spend it with my family. Thus, if there were problems, she would be handling them. Still, thinking about her got me into the spirit of the holiday. I was thankful that everyone in my family was healthy and hoped they would always remain that way.

On Monday, Lindy returned for her appointment. She leaned back on the table, supporting herself on her elbows, and smiled. Before I could greet her, she piped up cheerily, "My rash is much better. Look, you can hardly see it," she pointed at her legs.

"Great!" I said. Then I noticed her ankle was still swollen. "Seems like your ankle hasn't changed much though."

"Oh, that was all gone for a couple of days before it came back yesterday. But it doesn't hurt anymore," she reassured me.

Lindy did look improved. Her rash had faded, although it was still visible, and her ankle, despite the swelling, was no longer warm or tender.

"Any other problems? Aching joints? Other rash? Fever? Abdominal pain?"

"Nope, I feel good."

"Okay, let's check your urine again. Do you think you can give us some now?"

"You bet," she replied. This time, she was expecting me to ask for that and had no trouble. And the results were normal.

"Lindy, you're right. You're definitely much better," I told her. "And there's no evidence of any complications. I'd like to check you again in a week."

"Do you think she'll be okay?" inquired Mrs. Bloomer hopefully.

"So far, so good. But remember, kidney problems may develop up to a year later. We'll just have to wait and hope."

"She does seem to feel better. You know, she's really been a wonderful daughter. She rarely causes problems or complains. Even when she was sick last week, she didn't complain much. I just pray that nothing happens, Doctor. She's so young and full of life. And she has so much to look forward to," her mother thought out loud.

"I hope she stays well too."

Two days later, the rash vanished completely, never to return. Within a week, the swelling in Lindy's joints also disappeared.

Over the next year, I saw her periodically. She remained as vivacious as ever, showing no sign of recurrence of her illness. After twelve months, I pronounced her cured.

"For real?" she chimed.

"Yes, for real."

"Oh, for neat," she cried. Lindy and her mom practically skipped out of the office, huge smiles on their faces.

I'm sure that someday, people will not fear Henoch–Schoenlein purpura because it will be better understood. The cause will be known and a treatment available. But when Lindy Bloomer was sick, such was not the case.

Although it is not well realized by the public, doctors make most of their diagnoses from a patient's history. A good physical exam is essential, of course. Properly chosen tests also help. But the history is still the most important tool a physician has. Even then, a diagnosis can't always be reached. And when one can be made, the disease may be untreatable.

Many years ago, untreatable diseases were a much more common problem. Physicians would care for their patients as best they could, using the limited medical knowledge available at that time. Often patients didn't respond. Still, a doctor was viewed as someone who tried his or her best to help sick people rather than as a person to sue if things didn't go well.

Today, we can do so much more than we could years ago. From preventive practices through antibiotics to intensive care units, medicine has come a long way. There are, however, many illnesses that remain untreatable.

One example is the common cold. The treatment for this is the same as it has always been: plenty of rest, fluids, common sense, and time. Nerve deafness, the kind I have, has been another, although less prevalent, example. Deafness of this sort has up to this point also been incurable, only partially compensated for by amplification aids. In the future, as the cochlear implant—the artificial ear—becomes more sophisticated, doctors may be able to cure nerve deafness (although many members of the Deaf community are very much against cochlear implants; they feel that this surgery, which enables previously deaf persons to hear some sounds, is unethical, especially when performed on children, because it changes the essence of those persons). Other diseases likewise illustrate the limitations of modern medicine. Doctors can often identify these illnesses and explain them to patients, but we can't offer cures. So we just hope, along with the afflicted patient, that all turns out well.

Some people do not understand this. With all the publicity about medical miracles, they expect physicians to be almost supermen and superwomen. They want an answer to every question and a quick cure for every disease. These people are astounded to discover that many illnesses exist that doctors don't even begin to understand, let alone have a treatment for.

This misconception probably plays a role in the rising number of malpractice suits that are filed today. Certainly there are situations where there is true malpractice by physicians. In these cases, the patient is entitled to fair damages. However, in most cases, treatment is appropriate. It is the expectation of perfection from doctors—mere human beings—that underlies many of these suits.

I have been lucky. Most of my patients appreciate my efforts to help them and understand I try my best. They may show their gratitude in unusual ways, but they are grateful nonetheless. In situations such as Lindy's, I explain the limitations of modern medicine. Then, together, we do our best to cope with the illness.

Lindy has returned periodically to my office since. She is growing up to be a beautiful, charming young lady. Whenever we meet, I am reminded of the fear we all felt at the diagnosis of her disease and our happiness at her uneventful recovery. And once again I am conscious of how, even in modern times, nature often does more than doctors to help people heal.

NINETEEN

IF ANYONE HAD TOLD ME while I was growing up in the Midwest that I would one day live in Utah, I would not have believed it. The idea had never entered my mind. In fact, I knew only two things about the Beehive state: Salt Lake City is its capital, and the Great Salt Lake is located there. Neither sounded like a good reason to live there. The idea would have been as foreign to my wife in her younger days too. So, as did most of our fellow interns, Barbara and I planned to stay in Utah only for the duration of our training and then move elsewhere.

But we were not aware at the time of the powerful allure of those mountains. The towering Wasatch front juts up east of Salt Lake City with nary a foothill along most of its span. The western boundary of the city is formed by the Oquirrh mountains, which would be significant mountains in their own right had it not been for the presence of their cross-valley cousins. Snow-covered peaks are visible most of the year, and countless miles of virgin terrain are available for exploration and skiing within thirty minutes drive of the city.

Our trip from the Midwest to Utah was uneventful, and we arrived a few days early to allow us time to do all the numerous things that must be done when one moves to a new place. So, when we weren't unpacking and settling into the four-room apartment we had rented near the University, we were doing those necessary jobs, things such as establishing checking accounts, finding the local grocery stores, and learning our way around the city. As it often does, my deafness ended up complicating matters. It happened when I applied for a Utah driver's license.

I went to the downtown license office, where the clerk had me fill out an application for a license. Then, I took a required test on Utah's driving laws, and passed it with flying colors. This did not surprise me. After all, I had a ten-year history of safe driving and had never been in any accidents. Finally, they took my picture, then asked me to wait while they processed the paperwork. Everything seemed fine until they handed me the license. I looked at it and saw two codes in the restrictions box. I looked up the codes. One was that I wore glasses while driving, and the other was that I have a side-view mirror on the passenger side. This took me by surprise because in the 1970s, unlike now, this feature was not standard. Also, my previous license had no such stipulation.

So I asked a woman behind the desk why I had this restriction. She replied it was because of my hearing loss. Utah required that any car driven by a person with a profound hearing loss have side-view mirrors on the passenger's as well as the driver's side. I did not see the logic behind this rule. Why should people with hearing losses be singled out, especially considering the good driving record many of us have?

At first I protested the limitation. But the woman stated she did not have the authority to drop the restriction. Her manager also stated he could not make the change. It quickly became apparent that it would require a lot of time, perhaps weeks, to eliminate the restriction. Internship orientation began in two days, followed immediately by internship itself. I would have little leisure time once it began, and did not wish to spend this trying to convince the state to change their rule. So, I reluctantly took my car in to a dealer and had the mirror installed.

Barbara and I were very excited about our orientation, which lasted two days. We met our fellow interns, attended numerous meetings, and began to learn our way around the hospital. At the end of this time, we were eager to start despite our awareness of what was to come.

The job of interns and residents, collectively known as "housestaff," can be extremely demanding, both physically and emotionally. Although it is much easier now than it was years ago when housestaff often did not sleep for days, the pressures can still be great, especially during internship (the first year of post-medical school training). Interns are the front-line physicians in a teaching hospital. They manage the patients, complete the paperwork, and handle all the phone calls from the nurses. By doing this, they acquire the experience necessary to become competent physicians. To ensure that patients are properly cared for, these duties are done under the supervision of a resident (who is likewise supervised by an attending physician); however, the everyday responsibility for patient care remains the intern's.

Housestaff spend long hours in the hospital, often with critically ill patients and frequently far from home. It is not uncommon for them to have little social support. Even when family or friends do live nearby, they often do not understand the immense stresses the physicians-in-training are undergoing. In our case, we were lucky. Barbara and I benefited from having a spouse who was also going through internship. In fact, because we were in the same residency program we understood precisely the demands being placed on each other. Still, life as an intern was hard.

Even during our subsequent two years as residents, there were many times when we worked long hours. During one month, for example, I was on the high-risk obstetrics rotation at the University of Utah hospital while Barbara was working in the Newborn Intensive Care Unit. Because my schedule was mostly nights with days off and hers was the reverse, we saw each other only five days the entire month.

As a member of the hospital housestaff, communication with patients was never a major issue for me. There were, of course, situations when I had to deal with people who had a strong accent, enunicated poorly, or spoke softly with a high-pitched voice. In those cases, the patients often had to repeat themselves several times. Conversely, some patients had difficulty understanding me. I am amazed, however, that despite the degree to which my speech is typical of a person who is profoundly deaf, most people rapidly learn to understand me.

It was in the other than face-to-face situations that communication was more of a major issue during these years. One problem was figuring out how the hospital staff could reach me when they needed to. Normally, the staff has two ways to contact an intern or resident. One is by overhead paging and the other is by beeper. Neither worked for me. I have never been able to understand loudspeakers. In fact, I rarely even hear any sounds from indoor ones, the exception being when I am near a speaker that happens to be particularly loud. When I started my internship, I informed everyone that I could not hear overhead pages. Nevertheless, people tried reaching me with it, probably because they forgot about my warning. After all, no one had ever met a deaf doctor before. It did not take long for them to learn I really did not hear the overhead page. Within a week, it seemed that everyone in the hospital had suddenly become aware of this and tried to inform me when I was paged. It was not unusual for someone to come up to me ten or fifteen minutes after the fact and say, "You got paged a few minutes ago, did you know that?"

Beepers were not any better. When I first began my internship, I decided to try and use one, even though I was pretty sure it was not practical. At the time, I was reluctant to appear different by requesting special arrangements, especially at the beginning of my internship. So when the beepers were issued to all the interns, I took mine and did not say a word about my concerns. Within a day, my suspicions were confirmed. My first night on call was almost a disaster, for in addition to missing my overhead pages, I could not understand the voices coming from the beeper. Moreover, I did not even know when that little gadget on my belt beeped. In those days, beepers lacked the capability of vibrating or displaying phone numbers; they only rang and transmitted by voice a phone number to call.

So the whole time that long night, I was at the mercy of that small machine. I would be talking to a patient, writing at the nurses' station, or even just walking in the hall when the beeper would go off and a voice said something. I would blithely continue my activity, unaware of this event until someone came up to me and said, "Aren't you going to answer your page?" Eventually, I learned that whenever people around me looked at me for seemingly no reason at all, that meant my beeper had gone off. Because that realization did not occur for another week, I spent much of that first night constantly contacting the nurses on the various floors to ensure they had not been trying to reach me.

On top of this, none of the hospital phones were amplified. Unlike now, public institutions were not required then to provide telephone access for people with hearing loss. To compound matters, the telephone switch on my hearing aid did not work well with the hospital phones. So even when I did know someone had called me, it was difficult to call them. After a few unsuccessful attempts to use the phones, I found myself walking to the pertinent location to discuss each situation face-to-face with the appropriate people.

When morning finally came, I went to the communications department of the hospital and explained my inability to hear the beeper.

"No problem," the man said. "We can make the sound louder."

He made some adjustments while I waited, then gave it back to me. "Let's see if that's better."

He dialed my beeper number and it went off. I heard nothing.

"I'll turn it all the way up, as loud as it gets. That should take care of the problem," he reassured me. The man took apart the machine and fiddled with it awhile. When he was done, we tried it again. I still heard nothing but when the machine beeped this time, he jerked his head back in discomfort.

"You can't hear that?" he asked incredulously.

"No. It must be too high-pitched. Can you lower it?"

He discussed the situation with two of his colleagues. After much manipulation, they managed to lower the sound as low as was technically possible then. Even though I still did not usually hear the beep, at least I could now occasionally feel the vibration.

The rest of my years in training, I wore that same beeper. At first, people in the hospital were startled whenever it went off. In fact, the sound was so loud, it was sometimes disruptive. It was even embarrassing at times, especially when someone beeped me in the middle of a conference and I had no idea until everyone looked at me and someone said, "Your beeper just went off." After a while, however, people got used to it and were no longer distracted by it.

I also had a problem with the telephone. I tried portable amplifiers that hooked on the telephones but these did not work well. At no time did anyone offer to put amplified telephones in the hospital. Perhaps I should have more strongly requested them, but I didn't. Over time, though, I found a few phones scattered throughout the hospital that generated connections that were consistently louder than the others. Whenever I used these phones, I found that calls which originated from within the hospital were frequently loud enough that I could manage to hear enough of the conversation to understand its essence. But calls from outside were another matter entirely.

One of the duties of the intern or resident on call for the Family Practice Service was to attend to all phone calls from clinic patients of the faculty or other residents. The purpose of this was to provide experience for the housestaff in handling these types of phone calls. The calls would be for various reasons, ranging from parents concerned about their sick children to requests for prescription refills. A senior resident or faculty person was always available to discuss any phone calls the intern or resident did not know how to handle. For most housestaff, these calls were a significant burden only when numerous phone calls came in at once. For me, however, it was a nightmare.

To begin with, the calls originated from outside the hospital, making the connections more difficult to hear, especially without amplified phones. In addition, all calls were routed through the hospital operator, making the voices softer than they otherwise would have been. Finally, some patients were too sick to speak loudly. So most of the time, I was unable to understand the caller. It was frustrating, not only for me but also, I am sure, for the patients. I found myself often meeting patients in the hospital lobby and talking to them there. Surprisingly, most of them were not upset at having to come to the hospital; many were even grateful to be seen by a physician for free.

Another recurring problem was what to do at night, when I did manage to finish my work and go to the call room to sleep. As an intern, it was imperative I be accessible when the nurses called me. But how was I to "hear" the phone ring? I solved this problem by sleeping with the phone, the receiver taped securely to its cradle with adhesive tape so I would not knock it off as I slept. This way, I could feel the vibrations when it rang. Still, I never got much sleep that way; I found myself waking up all through the night to check that I hadn't somehow accidentally knocked the receiver off the cradle. Furthermore, when the phone did ring, it sometimes took me a while before I could tear off the tightly applied tape and answer the phone. Although no one ever said anything to me, I'm sure the nurses and other callers must have wondered what the cause of the ripping sounds were. The only time answering the phone was not a problem was on rotations when other interns or medical students slept in the same room. Then I could depend on them to answer the phone and, if it was for me, wake me.

When I became a resident, however, talking to patients on the telephone was no longer a problem. I usually had a fourth-year medical student with me during my nights on call. So I would have him or her answer all the phone calls, then report back to me on each one so I could determine that the appropriate care was being rendered.

Another time that my inability to talk on the phone was a problem was when I flew on a Life Flight transport. This was the helicopter/plane service used to travel to various towns in the intermountain west area and bring sick patients back to the university hospital for evaluation and treatment. Outlying physicians usually called Life Flight when their patients were very sick and needed to be cared for at the university hospital. Nowadays, specially trained nurses and physicians staff the Life Flights. In those days, however, it was the interns and residents on call who went with a nurse to stabilize patients before they were transported back to Salt Lake

City. After arriving at the particular town and evaluating the patient, the housestaff often called their supervising resident at the university hospital to discuss the patient's status with them.

For me, the usual difficulties with the phone were magnified by the loss of intensity in the sound due to the fact that the calls were long-distance. One time in particular sticks in my mind. It was during the fall of my first year as a resident, when I was one of physicians on call during a pediatric rotation at Primary Children's Hospital, the major children's hospital in the intermountain area. A call came in from a small town about sixty miles west of Salt Lake City requesting a transfer of a six-month-old child who was having severe respiratory distress. I was chosen as the physician to transport him and, because the town was relatively close, was flown there in a helicopter rather than one of the Life Flight airplanes. After initially evaluating the child, it was apparent that he had a case of croup. Because of its severity, however, I wondered whether to place a tube in his windpipe before we transported him, in case he stopped breathing on the way. The helicopter was so small that patients were placed under the pilot's seat; there was barely enough room in the back for the physician and nurse to sit. If the infant should stop breathing during the flight, it would be almost impossible to put the tube in then because of the lack of room to maneuver. I decided to call the supervising resident to discuss it with her. Then I discovered I had forgotten my hearing aid, so the nurse had to act as an interpreter. The phone we used at the emergency room desk was no more than ten feet from the patient. The parents, who were with their baby, saw the whole process. Imagine how they felt. Here I was, the rescuing physician, and I couldn't even talk on the phone!

The resident agreed with my inclination to intubate the child. Unfortunately, the hospital did not have the right-size equipment available and I had to try another size that was not optimal. In addition, for some unknown reason the procedure was more difficult than usual, and I had a hard time seeing the vocal cords. I noticed the parents becoming progressively more nervous. Finally, I decided that because the helicopter could get us back to Children's Hospital in twenty minutes, it would be better to get the child there than to waste more time trying to place the tube.

As we loaded the child in the helicopter and took off, the parents got in their car and drove toward Salt Lake City. By this time, a dense fog had fallen and totally obscured the view of the terrain from the air. On the way back, the helicopter got lost. Whether it was due to an inexperienced pilot, malfunctioning radar, or some other reason, I have no idea because I could not understand what the pilot was saying. I could see he was talking on the radio the whole time, as if he were trying to get directions from the control tower. Periodically, he came down under the fog, as if to check where he was and change his course accordingly. As time passed, my concern for the infant increased. If he stopped breathing, there was nothing we could do. Fortunately, the monitor attached to the baby showed that he continued to breathe.

About forty minutes after leaving the small hospital, the pilot descended again. As I looked out the window, I shuddered at the sight. We were within two feet of hitting electrical lines. We were also near enough to a street light that I could see the nurse's lips. She told me the pilot said that we were in Sandy, a town about fifteen miles south of the hospital. Now I started to worry about myself as well as the baby. Primary Children's Hospital is above the city, snuggled into the side of the Wasatch front. A slight miscalculation by the pilot, and we could easily crash into one of the mountain peaks. And I would have the least warning of all because the one sense I depended on the most, my vision, was useless. If a crash were imminent, the others might know from the radar or radio and could at least brace themselves. Fortunately, at this point the fog lifted a little and we could all see the lights of Children's Hospital. We arrived there minutes later. When we got out and brought the child inside, we found the parents already there, waiting for us. They had beaten us with time to spare. Fortunately, the baby was fine. As is often the case with croup, the cold night air, despite several wraps of blankets around the infant, had reduced the swelling in the child's windpipe and he was actually breathing better than when we had left his home town.

One advantage to being deaf and having some understanding of sign language is that I can communicate better with other deaf people. During my years as a member of the housestaff, however, it was hard for these persons to make appointments to see me. Although I did see patients in a clinic, most of my time was spent in the hospital. On the other hand, if a deaf person was hospitalized I was often called to care for these persons or to interpret, especially when a qualified interpreter could not be found. Nevertheless, it was not until after I started my medical practice that I began to see deaf patients regularly.

TWENTY

CARMA CAUGHT ME as I finished seeing one patient and started to enter the adjoining room to see my next one. "Mrs. Sanchez just called about Maria who's had diarrhea for two days. She's worried the baby may be dehydrated and wants to bring her in. But there's no room to put her."

She held out my appointment book and I looked at it. It was only 9:10 in the morning, yet we had already booked in several extra patients for that day. We didn't even have any room in the book to write in another name. There was simply no way I could squeeze Maria in today. It would not be fair to make everyone else wait that much longer.

"You're right. Could you explain that to her and have her see Dr. Paulos today?"

"She can't do it either. Not only is she as booked as you are, she also has a patient in labor."

I sighed. "Well, in that case, have her come at the end of the morning. I'll see her during lunch. But let her know she may have to wait a little."

This is becoming a problem, I thought as I watched Carma walk off. It was the second time that week, and it had been occurring more and more frequently even though Dr. Paulos and I each worked one night a week and alternated Saturday mornings. Moreover, we were finding we did not have as much time to spend with each patient as we wanted to. This pace could not continue long or we would both burn out. We had to make a decision—either close our practices or recruit another physician.

It did not take us long to make the decision to recruit a third doctor. In fact, we did it within days because we had already been discussing this choice for several months. We knew this would mean expanding the office, as our existing setup did not have space for a third physician to practice. Nevertheless, despite the cost and inconvenience of this, neither of us wanted to stop accepting new patients. We wanted to be available for whoever needed help.

We drafted a letter describing the details of our practice and distributed this widely. In addition, we contacted various residency programs and and other pertinent people we knew, and informed them we were looking for a third physician. Despite finding ourselves in the middle of the intense nationwide recruiting competition for board-certified family doctors, we were lucky. Three qualified candidates were interested in joining us. After interviewing each one, we finally selected Doug Johansen. Originally from the East Coast, he had come to the University of Utah for his internship and residency in family practice. Not only were his credentials impeccable, he also shared our philosophy of medical care. Finally, because Doug still had six months of training left, we had time to expand our space to accommodate him.

It was a busy six months. We hired an architect and designed a layout that would expand our space almost fifty percent. Then, for the next two months, we saw our patients admidst the hubbub of construction. Nevertheless, things went relatively smoothly and everything was completed before Dr. Johansen started.

Almost immediately, Connie and I saw a lightening of our schedules. Now that Doug was available to see the emergencies, we no longer felt so harried and could once again spend as much time with patients as we desired.

One day, a month after we became a threesome, Connie and I were in the lunch room consulting with each other about a couple of patients with complaints that were difficult to diagnose. "I got this interesting phone call—" Connie began but stopped when Doug walked in the room.

"It's been a month since you've been here," I noted as he sat down at the table. "What do you think so far?"

"I like it. It's a lot different than being a resident."

"In what way?" Connie wondered.

"For one, I feel like this is my own practice, whereas before I felt like I was working for the university. And second, even though I've only been here a short time, I already feel like I'm getting to know some of my patients."

"Good." I turned to Connie. "You were going to say something when Doug walked in?"

She nodded. "Yes, about a phone call I got yesterday. I guess people sometimes don't think before they call. Last night, this lady called about a rash that had started a couple of days earlier. She said it itched, was red, and was all over her body. She also said that it seemed to come and go. Because she has a lot of allergies, I figured it was probably hives. But I couldn't tell for sure without seeing it, and I couldn't do that over the phone.

"I remember once during my training, another doctor became exasperated with patients asking him to diagnose rashes over the phone. Finally, he started telling these people to put the phone next to the rash so he could take a closer look at it! They quickly got the message."

"Yes, I've had that happen too," Doug noted. "But you know what bothers me the most? When someone calls for a sick adult, doesn't know the answers to any of your questions, and won't put the ill person on the phone. They insist on being the intermediary, so everything has to go through them. It's so frustrating and so much harder to handle than talking directly to the patient."

Connie and I agreed with him. All doctors periodically have the same problem.

He continued, "Last week I had a call like that which I'll never forget. The conversation went something like this." Doug went into a routine that would make any stand-up comic jealous:

"I'm calling for my wife. She's been having stomach pain for the past four hours."

"Can I talk to her, please?"

"She's in bed. She's hurting too much to come to the phone."

"What part of the abdomen is the pain located in? Above her belly button? Below? On the side?"

"Just a minute, Doctor. Honeeeeey! The doctor wants to know what part of your stomach is the pain?" There was a brief pause, and then, "She says it's on the left side below the belly button."

"Has she had any diarrhea, constipation, or blood in her stools?"

"Just a minute, Doctor. Honeeeeey. The doctor wants to know if you've had any diarrhea, constipation, or blood in your stool?" Another pause before, "She said she hasn't."

"Let me talk to her directly. It would be a lot easier."

"I don't think she wants to come to the phone, Doc. I can tell you what she says."

Doug shook his head before continuing. "How old is she?"

"Just a minute, Doctor. Honeeeeey. The doctor wants to know how old you are. . . . Twenty-eight."

"When was her last period?"

"Honeeeeey. The doctor wants to know, when was your last period? . . . She said one month ago and that she's due for another one any day."

"Are you using birth control?"

"Just a minute. Honeeeeey. Are we using birth control? . . . She said we are."

"What kind?"

"Let me ask her, Doc. Honeeeeey. The doctor wants to know what kind of birth control we're using? . . . She said condoms."

After we finished laughing, Connie asked Doug, "So what finally happened?"

"I finally persuaded him to put her on the phone and ended up sending her to the emergency room. It turned out she had a pelvic infection."

Later that afternoon, I was seeing patients in the office when Carma informed me that a man had fallen and hurt himself in the parking lot in front of the grocery store around the corner from our office. I excused myself from the patient I was with and hurried out. There, in the middle of a small crowd of people, was an elderly man sitting on the sidewalk, appearing slightly dazed. I recognized him as the husband of one of my patients. Bending over him, massaging his leg, was Irma Conn. As I approached, I could read her lips long before her voice was audible. She was giving him some instructions.

"Just relax, sir. You'll be okay. I'm not a doctor, but I know a little about these things. Now don't move, or you might cause some damage. While we wait for some help, I'll take a look at you and see if.... Oh, Dr. Zazove. Am I glad to see you! I saw the whole thing happen because I was right behind him. This gentleman was walking to the store when he tripped on that curb over there and fell forward. He hit his head first and then rolled over on his side. By the time I got here, a few seconds later, he was already sitting up. Now, I took first aid when I was in high school and know what to do. I saw that cut on his head. It's not bleeding so I know it's not serious. I was just starting to check the rest of him to make sure he was okay when you came. Shall I go ahead and finish, Doctor? I know—"

"I think we'll be okay, Mrs. Conn. Thanks for your help." I had examined the man quickly while Mrs. Conn had been talking. He was basically unharmed except for the one-inch laceration on his forehead.

"Okay, Doctor. Now, I haven't checked his right foot yet. I wanted you to know that because he did bang it against the curb and he might have broken it, you know."

I acknowledged her statement and then helped the man up so we could go to my office and repair the injury. Mrs. Conn started addressing the others in the crowd about the incident, relishing their close attention.

"I saw exactly how it happened," her familiar voice expounded. "You see, he was walking over there . . ."

Leaving them behind, I found myself amazed at how she managed to appear so often at events like this. Mrs. Conn certainly got out a lot for a woman who didn't like to leave the house and drive. As I walked into the office with the wounded man, I wondered where I would bump into her next.

TWENTY-ONE

"SO YOU'VE HAD THE CHEST PAIN on and off for ten hours," I summarized. "It feels tight, like something is squeezing you, but doesn't radiate into your neck, arms, shoulders, or back. Right?"

"Yes, and it seems to come and go," signed Mrs. Allred.

"Exactly where is the pain?"

She made a fist with her right hand and placed it on the left side of her chest.

Elthora Allred is deaf. She communicates by using signs, mouthing the words as she converses. Although I am not fluent in American Sign Language (ASL)—one of the most commonly used languages in the United States—I understood her easily. And because she reads lips well, she had no difficulty understanding me either, despite my occasional mistakes with my hands. In fact, she has always enjoyed correcting these mistakes and teaching me new words.

Her husband, Jared Allred, cannot hear either. Since they are both totally deaf, neither wears a hearing aid. Thus, at first glance they look like everyone else. It is only when one starts talking to them that their deafness become apparent. But it doesn't hold them back. They hold steady jobs (he as an engineer and she as a quality control inspector), own a house, and support their three normally hearing children.

"Tell me," I signed with both hands while speaking so she could read my lips, "when do you get the pain?"

"What do you mean?" she asked, a quizzical look on her face. Since ASL is a visual language, facial expressions and body movements play a key role in signing. Signing using just hand signals is much worse than speaking using just one flat tone of voice. It is more like speaking only every other word of a sentence.

"Well, do you get it when you eat? With exercise? At certain times of the day?"

"No, it usually happens when I'm sitting. When it came on last night, I was just watching TV. Usually it goes away in ten minutes, but this time, it lasted four hours. So I thought I'd better come in and have you check it out."

"How long have you been getting the pain?"

"Oh, since about Labor Day, maybe four months."

An overweight woman in her forties, Mrs. Allred dressed professionally. She wore a forest green wool suit, a white blouse, and black low-heeled shoes. Her jet black hair had several streaks of gray and was shaped in a sedate style. A few wrinkles on her forehead added to the maturity of her countenance. She watched my lips and hands intently, so that she would not miss anything I said.

"Have you ever had rheumatic fever or other heart problems before?"

"No, not that I know of."

"Anyone in your family had a heart attack?"

"Yes, my father died of one when he was forty-eight years old."

The rest of my questions did not elicit much other pertinent information except to remind me about her previously diagnosed high cholesterol level. Neither did a careful physical exam. In particular, her lungs, heart, and abdomen were all normal. Since I wasn't sure what was causing her pain, I ordered a cardiogram and a chest X ray. These were likewise normal.

I reviewed all the findings. Mrs. Allred did have two major risk factors for having a heart attack: a father who had had one and her high cholesterol level. Perhaps she was having angina, a precursor to a heart attack. But her story didn't sound like that. Any one of a number of other things was more likely causing the pain.

"So far, Mrs. Allred, everything looks okay," I explained with my signs. "I'm not sure why you're having the pain, but I don't think it's your heart. It may be from the pancreatitis you had a month ago, or it may be something else totally different. What I'd recommend is to get some blood tests and see if they give us any clues. Depending on the results, we can decide what to do next."

"How long will it take to find out?" she wondered.

"I hope to have them back by tomorrow."

She shook her head as she imitated my sign. "That's not how you say tomorrow. It's like this. Move your hand forward more."

"Tomorrow," I signed, this time correctly. She nodded with satisfaction.

"Okay," she signed, then shrugged. "But I'm confused by it all. I don't understand why I have the pain." Her dramatic gestures and expressions left no doubt that she felt frustrated. I'm not surprised that the Deaf community has developed superb theater groups. Deaf people are, for the most part, experts at using body language to express their emotions. It's unfortunate that most people do not understand sign language and thus cannot appreciate the full beauty of their performances.

That evening, shortly after supper, I received a phone call at home. "Dr. Zazove, this is the lab. I'm calling about the cardiac enzymes on a patient of yours, Elthora Allred."

"Yes?"

"The CPK is 432, the LDH is 198, and the SGOT is 81. Since they're elevated, I thought you'd like to know tonight."

"Thanks for calling," I told him. Suddenly, I felt scared. The tests were indeed abnormal. Cardiac enzymes measure chemicals present in heart muscle. If a heart attack occurs, they are usually released into the bloodstream in a typical pattern. First, the CPK becomes elevated within twelve hours. It remains high for up to forty-eight hours. Then a day later, the SGOT rises for a few days, often with a day or so overlap between the two. The LDH, although the last to rise, stays up the longest—about two weeks. In Mrs. Allred's case, her CPK and SGOT were both elevated, whereas the LDH was normal. The results definitely suggested a recent heart attack.

Mrs. Allred needed to be in the hospital. If she had indeed had a heart attack, she could develop sudden complications and drop dead at any time. Therefore, close observation was required. I needed to reach her but didn't have a TTY, a device that allows deaf people to use the phone, at my home. It was at my office.

Quickly explaining the situation to Barbara, I dashed over there and called. The line was busy. A couple of minutes later, I tried again. Still busy. Over the next twenty minutes I kept trying and kept getting a busy signal.

Then I looked up her address. The Allreds lived way out in the country, in Mountain View. Still, because I couldn't reach her on the phone, I decided to drive out to her home. I jumped in my car and headed for the country.

A full moon lit the way. Initially I drove past a few subdivisions, but then the scenery became small farms and open spaces. The wintry fields were bereft of life except for an occasional evergreen. Every so often, a gust of wind blew a bunch of tumbleweeds across the road in front of me. Otherwise, nothing moved on the bare ground, not even other cars on the road. I made good time.

The Allred house, surrounded by open fields, was a modest ranch home. All the windows were dark, and there was not a sign of anyone present. "That's funny," I thought. "I hope they didn't go out while I drove here."

I knocked on the door. No answer. Wondering if they didn't hear me, I banged as loudly as I could. No answer. There was no response to the doorbell either. Then I tapped the windows sharply, hoping they might feel the vibrations. Still no answer. I stood still and listened carefully, to see if I could hear any low sounds, but there was only silence.

I was just about to give up when I heard a very low-pitched sound that seemed to come from the house. I had no idea what it was, but there definitely had been a noise. I waited patiently in front of the door, but no one appeared. I started to feel slightly nervous. Then I heard the noise again.

"Maybe they think I'm a burglar," I wondered. "Maybe they're getting a gun to shoot me with." Scared at this thought, I started backing up toward the car, all the time watching the house carefully. Suddenly the lights went on over the porch. Then the door opened a crack.

Feeling my heart pounding, I wasn't sure whether to run for the car or not.

"I'm Dr. Zazove." I managed to sound calm. "I'm sorry to bother you this late at night, but I'm looking for Elthora Allred."

I thought I heard a voice answer but wasn't sure. "I'm looking for Elthora Allred," I repeated, as I cautiously walked closer. This time I was sure someone had answered but still couldn't understand anything. I got close enough to see a woman's face, then closer still to read her lips. "I'm sorry, I didn't hear you. What did you say?"

"What's the matter with you? Are you deaf or something? I've been shouting at the top of my lungs. I said Elthora Allred moved out of this house six months ago. She don't live here no more."

"She did? Do you know where she lives now?"

"It's here in Mountain View, but I don't know where," she grumbled, starting to close the door.

"Do you happen to know her new phone number?"

"No, I don't, but it's the same damn one she had before."

"Thank you. I'm sorry I bothered you," I apologized again as the door slammed shut.

I drove back to the office and called the Allred number again. It was still busy. I called the phone company. The operator confirmed that her phone was off the hook. I looked through her chart again, to see if we had a new address written down anywhere. No such luck.

At this point, I didn't know what else to do. It was imperative that I get hold of her: her life could depend on it. In desperation I called Carma, who knew the Allreds personally. Did she know the new address? She did not, but voluntarily came in to help me track it down.

Carma made several calls trying to get the information. Finally, she contacted Mrs. Allred's insurance company, a prepaid health plan that maintained a twenty-four-hour phone service. They had it!

First confirming the line was still busy, I drove to the new house, agonizingly close to their old one. I arrived there (by now it was 11:30) and noticed lights shining through the blinds. "Aha!" I thought. "They're home."

I rang the bell. No one answered. I banged on the door and tapped on the windows. Still no response. "Oh no, not again," I lamented.

Finally, I decided I had done everything possible. For over four hours I had endeavored to reach her. I wrote a note telling Mrs. Allred her blood tests suggested she may be having a heart attack and that she needed to go to the hospital immediately. Opening the screen door to leave the memo between the doors, I noted the inner door was slightly ajar.

"Should I open it?" I wondered, pausing to reflect on that. I considered it briefly, then decided not to. In Utah, especially out in the country, not only do many people have guns, they don't hesitate to use them. Because the Allreds would not hear me calling to them, they might think I was a burglar. If so, they very well could shoot first and ask questions later. Afraid to take the chance, I stuck the note on the door and drove home. After contacting the emergency room and asking them to notify me the moment Mrs. Allred arrived there, I went to sleep, expecting to hear from the hospital later that night.

Instead, I awoke the next morning, surprised the night had passed without interruption. I worried about Mrs. Allred even more. Perhaps she had died, and that's why no one had called. A sense of guilt arose inside me. If only I had put her in the hospital when she was in the office the day before, she would still be alive. Or if I had asked the police to contact her the night before, she might have been saved. Feeling despondent, I drove to work slowly, wondering how I was going to face her family. Upon arriving at the office, I forced myself to call the Allreds again on the TTY.

This time her son answered. He was not very friendly. Yes, the phone had been off the hook. Yes, they got the note, but his mother had been feeling okay, so she didn't go. No, she hadn't planned on going to the hospital this morning. Yes, he'd tell her I called. No, he didn't want to wake her up because she would be grumpy. I emphasized the importance of doing so and asked him to rouse her and send her to the hospital at once. He finally agreed to do so.

Resolving to call back in an hour if I had not heard from them,

I began to see patients. The first two were regular, well-child checks. The third was not so routine. A morose, wasted, elderly man whom I barely recognized as Mr. Gatto was waiting for me. His concerned daughter was with him as before.

"Dr. Zazove," she spoke immediately. "My father is getting really depressed. He just doesn't want to do anything. I can't get him to eat, talk, or even get out of bed. He needs something for his depression so he can feel better."

I looked at the old man. There was quite a change from when I had last seen him. His once proud face was now gaunt, his cheekbones much more prominent, and his eyes vacant. His arms and legs had become bony sticks too. He slouched precariously over the exam table, staring at the floor. I knew that his problem wasn't depression. He was dying of cancer.

"Mr. Gatto?"

He didn't answer, continuing to gaze emptily off into space.

I laid my hand on his right shoulder as I repeated my greeting, a little louder. "Mr. Gatto?"

"Yes," he spoke so softly I didn't hear a sound.

"Are you in pain?"

"No."

"You've lost twenty-one pounds since I last saw you. Have you been eating?"

"I'm not hungry," I saw him say.

"He needs some pills for his depression," his daughter firmly tried to instruct me. "He's getting worse because he's given up."

I asked her to step into the hallway with me. There I explained the situation. "Mrs. Harding, your father's dying from his prostate cancer. Unfortunately, this is how people with cancer die; they waste away. They often get depressed too, but the underlying reason is the cancer."

"If you just give him some pills for his depression, I'm sure he'll do okay," she insisted. "If he'd only eat, he'd feel better. He can't be dying of cancer."

I looked at her, trying to decide the best way to discuss the matter. "I know it's hard to deal with your father dying. It's normal to refuse to accept it, and I wish I could do something for him. But this is what happens. People with cancer lose their appetites and they sometimes lose interest in life," I explained. "At this point, it's more than depression. He's dying from the cancer." After a pause, I continued. "If you want to try antidepressants, they won't hurt and I'm willing to do so. But I recommend your father have the surgery the urologist recommended as soon as possible. That should make your father feel better for a few months."

"Okay, I'll take him over today, but I want the pills too."

After we returned to the exam room, I said, "Mr. Gatto, you'll be seeing the urologist again, okay?"

"I don't care," he whispered.

"See, I told you, he's just depressed," his daughter interjected triumphantly.

Ignoring her comment, I continued, "I think you'll feel better after he treats you. It may even prolong your life some."

"For what?" he replied.

"Papa, the doctor's going to give you some pills to help your depression. Once you get feeling better, you'll be glad you took them."

I understood why she refused to admit her father was dying. Denial is a common response. Cancer patients and their families often deny that death is imminent even though they know it is. Over time, as they begin to accept it, they may feel anger and grief before finally acknowledging the inevitable. It was going to take a while, but Mr. Gatto's daughter would eventually accept the situation. She had no choice.

I gave her a prescription and watched them leave the room. Almost immediately, Carma informed me that Mrs. Allred had finally shown up at the hospital. I called, admitted her to the intensive care unit, and went over to see her as soon as I could get away.

"When did you get that note I left on your door last night?" I asked in sign language.

"My son found it about 1:30 in the morning. I'm so sorry you had to come all the way out there. I wish I'd known you were there. You should've come in. The door was open, and I was sleeping on the living room floor. I wasn't feeling too well, so I just lay down there. You really should've just come in."

"Well, I was afraid someone would think I was a thief or something and shoot me. After all, you weren't expecting me. Besides, if I'd seen you lying on the floor, I would've been really worried about you. But why didn't you come in last night when you got the note?"

"I felt too sick to go. When I woke up about two, and saw the note, I didn't want to bother anyone that late, so I went to bed. The pain's mostly gone this morning."

"Since you're doing fine, I think you'll be okay. But you really should've come here last night when you got the note."

"Doctor, I feel so bad about your coming out like that. Really, you should have come in." Then she asked, almost as an afterthought, "So you think I had a heart attack?"

"Well, I'm not sure. Your blood tests suggested that might be why you had the prolonged attack of pain. Let me explain," I went on, " what to expect here in the hospital. There will be daily cardiograms, which are tracings of the electrical activity of the heart. And there'll also be frequent blood tests. You'll be on a heart monitor and will be breathing oxygen. By tomorrow, we should know for sure if you've had a heart attack.

"For the time being, we'll treat you as if you have. If you have any pain at all, don't be brave and bear it; tell the nurse. That's what she's here for. She'll give you something for it. This is very important because pain can aggravate a heart attack. Okay?"

Fortunately, all the tests came back negative. The elevated blood tests were found to be from a source other than her heart. A treadmill heart test was likewise normal. When she remained pain free, I sent her home.

So I had done all that worrying and driving for nothing. But that didn't bother me. I would do it all again just on the chance that it would make a difference.

TWENTY-TWO

It was 1981, the last year of our residency, when Barbara and I made the momentous decision to make Utah our home despite its great distance from our families. After living there for over two years, we had fallen in love with it. The spectacular natural beauty, the open spaces, the clean, uncongested towns, and the friendly people were all attractive inducements to live in the state. From the rugged peaks of the north to the red-rock country of the south, from the searing deserts of the west to the plateaus of the east, natural splendor of some type is always near.

Salt Lake City was a satisfying place to be, too. The upstanding citizenry, the strong family values, and the relatively inexpensive cost of living were appealing. Moreover, as the major city between Denver and California, it had more cultural attractions and professional sports than many other metropolises its size.

Barbara elected to go into academics and accepted an offer to join the faculty at the University of Utah Medical School. This would enable her to pursue her strong interest in conducting research. She would also continue seeing patients part-time at the same clinic she had worked at during her residency. I chose private practice. Having made the decision to remain in Utah, we searched along the Wasatch front, looking for a place to live. We wanted a family-oriented community where neighbors were friendly, children were welcome, and crime was low. We also desired a rustic area with open spaces and a sense of freedom—a place that wasn't one subdivision after another or teeming with business, industry, traffic, and smog. Yet at the same time, we wanted to live close enough to take advantage of Salt Lake City's cultural offerings. And finally, we wanted a place where the people needed family doctors.

It was almost by accident that we found Plymouth. While looking for a community, we had driven farther out than previously and happened to wander through it. Plymouth is a mixture of a suburb and a rural town. Although it radiates the atmosphere of a large farm community, its downtown contains modern shopping plazas. As one drives away from its center, well-maintained houses of all types and ages are interspersed with open fields, many with horses in them. Driving a few minutes farther brings one into farm country. The farms are not large but are also well maintained: cows, sheep, and horses roam their pastures, and verdant fields of grain are commonly seen.

But there is more to Plymouth than this. As Barbara and I scouted the area, we saw many different types of people. This melting pot appealed to us. We wanted a community with an interesting mix of people, not just the wealthy or the poor.

The more we looked, the more we liked it. Making the decision to locate in Plymouth turned out to be easy. Finding a place where I could practice, however, did not. There were two small medical buildings in the area, and they were not what I had in mind. One was hidden from the road and would be hard for some people to find. The other required one to go up steps to get into the building—there was no handicapped access—and steps are a problem for some people.

I called the only family physician listed in the Plymouth phone book, but he said he was not interested in an associate. (Later, I found out he had been actively looking for someone but had turned me down because, due to my speech, he thought that I was foreign. Years later, he confessed he wished he had met me back then.) It appeared that if I were to practice in Plymouth, I would have to open my own office.

So we went home and did some research about Plymouth. About 40,000 people, a population that was easily large enough to support another physician, lived in the area surrounding the city. The economy was stable and fairly well diversified, too. We returned a few days later and drove around the fields and subdivisions, looking for a suitable location where I could open a practice. The only satisfactory place available was a small shopping center a little south of the center of town. Not only would the grocery store at one end provide a lot of free exposure for an office, but it was also fairly close to the site where there were eventual plans to build a hospital. We deliberated about the shopping center office for several days, although deep inside we both knew it was the place. And a week later, we made our decision official.

The next three months, Barbara and I spent eight hours a day, six days a week—literally hundreds of hours—getting ready for the opening of my practice. Our training up to that point had been only in medicine, and we knew little about business. But we learned fast. We talked to other doctors, read up on various topics, and utilized a consultant for a while. It's unbelievable how many things go into opening a doctor's office. Slowly but surely, we put it all together. From minor things such as ordering the various paper supplies and choosing an appointment system, to major things such as deciding the office layout and which equipment to purchase, we plodded our way through the tasks. And we managed to fit it all within our budget.

Then, we hit a roadblock—the banks. They were surprisingly cautious about lending me the funds. Our credit was impeccable and our financial status stable, but still they hesitated. Was it my hearing loss? Perhaps. But no one intimated so. Instead, the bankers claimed they were that cautious with everyone.

I became worried. I was about to sign a lease for the space and wanted to start construction as soon as possible. After all, there was no other reason to delay the start of my practice. So, frustrated as I was, I forged ahead. I went to every bank in town, one by one, filled out their papers and answered their questions. I even hired a management consultant to answer the banks' concerns about the finances of the practice. Whatever the reason was for their hesitation, there had be to some way to assuage their concerns. Finally, one bank agreed to lend me money. Although the amount did not cover all the expenses, it would be enough because Barbara was able to borrow the rest through a group that lends to doctors.

Construction began, and the office started to take shape. It was exciting seeing all our planning approach fruition. Meanwhile, we purchased equipment, obtained licenses, and hired Carma, my first employee. Then, when the office was half-built, we received some stunning news: the landlord had declared bankruptcy. The contractor immediately stopped building and gave me a choice: pay the landlord's share of the construction costs myself or forget the office.

At this point, despite my eagerness to be a family doctor, I began to experience second thoughts about opening my own practice. I did not want to be overburdened with debt. Moreover, it was the human aspect of medicine that interested me, not the business part. I worried that the financial demands would overwhelm my practice. After two days reviewing the figures, we decided it would still work out. The extra amount Barbara had been able to borrow would be just barely enough. I plunged ahead.

The contractor finished on time and we started organizing the office. We had just begun this when the newly installed telephone rang. It was a patient, calling to make an appointment. I was so eager to start that I elected to see him anyway, despite the boxes stacked all over. We scheduled an appointment for later that day, and I rehearsed with Carma again and again what to do in the various areas of a doctor's office, since she had never worked in one before. The time came and we waited expectantly, a little excited. Five, ten, fifteen minutes went by. No one appeared. We called the number he had given us—it was no longer in service. So I can honestly say that my first patient in private practice was a "no-show"!

One week later, on September 28, 1981, the office officially opened. I saw two patients that day, one of whom I had seen previously during my residency training. Subsequently, the practice grew slowly. There were even some days when not a single patient came. Being new, I was not known in the area, and in those days doctors did not advertise or promote their practices as they do now.

I passed the hours reading medical journals and talking with Carma.

As the months went by, the number of patients rose steadily. And I am happy to say, many deaf people came to see me too. For not only was there no other doctor in Utah with a profound hearing loss, there was only one other who knew sign language (a liver specialist at the medical school). I also saw patients outside the office, both at the hospital (which was finally built) as well as in the homes of people who were physically unable to come see me.

My patients turned out to be all I had dreamed of and more. They are down-to-earth, interesting, friendly people of all ages, creeds, and personalities. Over the years, I've come to know some of them well. These patients have made my practice a reality. They have also allowed me to do what I had always dreamed of: to be able to provide the best medical care in the most caring way possible.

TWENTY-THREE

THE BED SHOOK as the alarm went off, rousing me from a sound sleep. I found myself wishing it weren't so foolproof. When it was first rigged up, I thought it was so clever—a motor attached to a bed frame that vibrates the bed when a set time arrives. It gave me a lot more independence too. But now I cursed it. Just once, I wished I could sleep through an alarm.

I knew I was lucky to have the alarm, especially since the bed also vibrates when the phone rings. That way I know when someone is calling me while I'm sleeping. But connecting both the bedside alarm and telephone to the same vibrator was not easy; the alarm uses normal household current, whereas the telephone uses a much lower voltage. An electrician rigged an ingenious system that managed to do this. However, there was one problem: all the connections had to be in a certain alignment, which meant that the plugs had to be turned just so. Otherwise, an electrical short would occur. The first time this happened, we labeled each connection so that we knew how to reconnect them correctly. But this did not prevent Katie from almost getting electrocuted.

She was fifteen months old and, like many toddlers, interested in exploring everything in her environment. One evening, while Barbara and I were both in our bedroom, we saw Katie walk over to the plug in the wall. Before we realized what was happening, she pulled the plug out, turned it ninety degrees, and reinserted it in the outlet. Sparks flew, and the lights went out. We rushed over to her, just as she started to bawl. Fortunately, she was okay. The plug, however, was not. One of the prongs had melted from the heat of the reaction. Barbara immediately bought a cover and put this over the outlet containing the plug until I could get another vibrator. Now there are two separate systems attached to the bed—one for the phone and one for the alarm—and we no longer have to worry about causing a short.

This particular morning, I felt dead tired, having spent the night delivering a baby and getting home just before dawn. It seemed as though I had barely fallen asleep when the clock shook at 6:30.

My body felt torpid and did not want to move. Even my thoughts seemed sluggish. I lay quietly, eyes closed, trying to convince myself I could get up. Several minutes passed before I finally forced myself to roll out of bed. While I ate breakfast, Katie got up. She has always seemed to need less rest than many children her age. Although in bed by 9:00, she often doesn't fall asleep for two hours and usually awakens by seven, if not earlier.

"Daddy," she said, after pounding on the counter to get my attention, "will you get me some breakfast?"

"Okay, what do you want today?"

"Let me look and see."

Just as I put her bowl of Cheerios and a glass of milk on the table, Rebecca trotted into the kitchen.

"I want cereal too," she proclaimed. She also had to review the choices and chose Quaker's Maple-and-Brown-Sugar-flavored instant oatmeal.

I joined them shortly afterward with my own bowl of cereal. Two minutes later, Katie frowned at me and said, "Daddy, you're smacking again."

"Sorry," I said. "I didn't realize I was."

I don't know whether other people who are deaf have the same problem but apparently I often smack while eating. It's due to letting my mouth open ever so slightly while chewing my food, thus letting the sounds escape. Because I can't hear it, I don't realize I am doing it. Unfortunately, it sometimes bothers my family. When we have company or if I am eating out with others, I have to consciously think about keeping my mouth closed while chewing.

After breakfast, I drove to the hospital to make rounds on the four patients I had there. The first two were a mother and the baby boy she had delivered a few hours earlier. The woman had decided to go home after twelve hours, to save money. Since everything was going well, I agreed. More and more women leave the hospital soon after a normal delivery, in contrast to years ago, when patients remained for several days to "recuperate." Interestingly enough, those who go home earlier often recover faster than those who stay.

The third patient, a fifty-three-year-old man with a kidney stone, was being treated with a rapid infusion of intravenous fluids. Although his pain had disappeared twelve hours earlier, he still had not passed the stone. I decided to watch him a little longer. Until it came out, his pain could return suddenly, as severe as ever.

I then saw the teenager who had been admitted two days earlier with a severe arm infection. It was rapidly improving with intravenous antibiotics. I changed this to medication by mouth and decided to send him home the following morning if he continued to improve.

It was now past 8:30. My first patient in the office was scheduled at 9:00. Stopping in the medical records room to pick up copies of my previous dictations, I found three more charts that needed to be done, quickly finished them, and then drove the mile to my office. A look at the day's schedule confirmed it was going to be a typical Friday—busy. At least the list of patients and problems seemed pretty straightforward.

Nine o'clock came, and people began to arrive. My first patient of the day was an elderly gentleman whom I had never met before.

"J. Winthrop Seward here," the man introduced himself as we shook hands. "I'm looking for a new doctor. I heard about you from one of my friends and thought I'd come in to see you."

"Glad to meet you," I said.

"I wonder if you'll be able to help me when the others couldn't?"

"I'll try. Tell me about it."

"Well, I've got a few medical problems that don't seem to be improving the way I'd like them to. I've seen several doctors the past couple of years but haven't been happy with any of their treatments. Fact is, I'm suing three of them."

"Oh?" I raised my eyebrows.

"Yes, they just didn't seem to know what they were doing. Now I do smoke and have for many years. I know it's bad for me, and I've tried to quit but haven't been able to do so. It has given me a little emphysema, and I take some medicine for that. But boy, let me tell you, I almost died when I first started having trouble breathing because the doctor screwed up. That was about five years ago. Now I won't tell you his name, but he's a real jerk. He diagnosed my emphysema and gave me a lecture about stopping smoking. He also prescribed some pills. Did I ever have an allergic reaction to them." He shook his head. "I almost stopped breathing! I could have died. He's one of those I'm suing. He should've suspected that I might be allergic to them."

"What was the name of the medicine?"

It turned out to be albuterol, a commonly used drug. I suspected it had been prescribed appropriately and Mr. Seward just happened to react to it.

"I see. You said you have a few medical problems. What are your other ones?"

"Well, I have high blood pressure. And diabetes too. But I can't stand the diet they gave me for that. There's nothing good to eat on it, so I eat what I want. I do take my insulin, though. I also got this darn leg," he pointed at his right one. "Broke it in a car accident three years ago. There were several pieces of bone sticking out. The paramedics had to take me to the emergency room where they got a bone doctor to come in and fix it. He spent four hours working on it in surgery, but it healed slightly crooked." The man pointed at his leg, then added, "So I'm suing him too. He should've made darn sure it was perfectly straight, especially since he took so long in surgery."

I studied the leg. It looked straight to me. I also recalled having seen Mr. Seward walk into the room without a limp.

Feeling my stomach churn at his accusations, I asked politely, "Anything else?"

"No, that's it."

"You mentioned earlier that you're suing three doctors, but you've only told me about two."

"Yes, sir, but I can't talk about the third one now," he confided with an air of importance. "My attorney in that case has advised me not to say anything about it."

New patients sometimes schedule consultations in order to get acquainted and decide if they want me as their doctor. In this case, it was I who had benefited from the meeting. There was no way I was going to be Mr. Seward's physician. For all I knew, I was next on his list of doctors to be sued.

"Mr. Seward, it certainly sounds like you have some complicated problems. Because of that, I'm probably not the best doctor for you. I'm not sure I could do a good enough job. You'd be better off finding another physician who's had more experience with the kind of illnesses you have."

He seemed taken aback by my statement. Getting up, he replied gruffly, "Okay, if that's how you feel." Mr. Seward left in a huff.

The next hour went by uneventfully. I make every effort to see patients on time. Unfortunately, some days there are emergencies, deliveries, injuries, or problems more complex than expected. These throw me off schedule. Today, all the patients seemed straightforward, from a boy whose stitches needed to be removed to a woman who wanted birth control. Then came Eric Noonan, the sixth patient of the day. He had come with his parents from southern Utah to see me on the recommendation of another patient of mine. As soon as I walked into the room, I knew from Eric's appearance that this was going to be one of those patients who throw things off schedule.

Eight years old, Eric was very thin. He was of mixed descent, his mother being Mexican and his father Anglo-American. Straight black hair covered his ears and dangled in bangs over his forehead. His T-shirt displayed a local merchant's logo and hung over faded blue jeans. White socks and worn sneakers completed his attire.

His parents sat quietly, attentive and concerned. Mr. Noonan had tousled, dark brown hair and a weather-beaten, mustached face supported by a squat neck and a short, stocky frame. He wore a red knit shirt, grease-stained overalls, and heavy work boots. Because of his job as a mechanic, his hands were coarse and blackened. Eric's mother was fairly thin and dressed casually in a checkered blouse and jeans. She had a dark, roundish face, large brown eyes, and long, black hair.

"I'm Mr. Noonan and this here is my wife," his father introduced themselves.

"Glad to meet you. What can I do for you?" I asked.

"Well, Eric's been having this problem with his arms and face for many weeks. It started about two months ago, after he had been sick with a sore throat. At that time, we took him to our doctor in Moroni. They got a throat culture and gave him a shot of penicillin. When he didn't get better, we took him back, but the doctor said it was nothing to worry about and didn't give him nothing. Then Eric began to get worse. He kept doing more of those funny movements." He nodded at Eric. "We went back to the doctor again, but he just reassured us and said to wait, that Eric would get better soon. So we took his word for it and waited. But Eric didn't improve.

"Then he started having problems with the other children. They make fun of him because he twitches so much. Now he's doing bad in school too, and he just ain't right. Something's wrong with him."

The reason for their concern was clear. Two or three times a minute, Eric's arms and face writhed, each episode lasting a second or so. The rest of the time he acted normal.

The movements immediately brought to mind chorea, one of the complications of rheumatic fever. Before the days of penicillin, rheumatic fever was a dreaded disease. Thousands of children were affected; some even died. Of the survivors, many developed heart damage, often for the rest of their lives. In fact, rheumatic heart disease sometimes worsens with time. The culprit? A bacteria called *Streptococcus*. How it occurs is interesting:

In the beginning, the bacteria usually attacks the throat, resulting in the common malady strep throat. In response, the body produces antibodies that kill the bacteria. Every so often, however, this response goes awry. In ways that are not well understood, the antibodies sometimes not only kill the strep but attack other parts of the body as well, resulting in the characteristic findings of rheumatic fever: high fever, swollen joints, a heart murmur, a characteristic rash, and chorea. Fortunately, it has become much less common since the advent of antibiotics. By treating strep throat with antibiotics, we can prevent those later complications from occurring. In fact, I had never seen anyone with chorea before. Still, I was pretty sure of my diagnosis. Eric looked exactly as the textbooks describe it.

"Did the throat culture taken at the beginning show strep?" I queried.

Eric's mother nodded as she answered, "Yes."

"Has he had any fever?"

Eric's father now took over. "When he first got sick, he had some really high ones, up to 104 degrees. Lately, they're not as bad, although he still gets an occasional one."

"Now, you said he's had those jerking movements for two months, right?"

"That's right, Doc. It wasn't so bad at first, but just look at him now."

It sounded to me like rheumatic fever. But there were still two more things I needed to know. Watching Eric suffer another contortion, I asked, "Has he had a rash of any kind?"

His father looked off into space for a second as he tried to remember, then replied, "Now that you mention it, Doc, yes, he did. When he first got sick, he had one on his shoulders. It was about . . . oh . . . maybe two weeks after he first seen the doctor. We showed it to him, but he said it was from the strep throat and not to worry about it."

"It was a funny rash," his mother added. "Kinda twisted, almost looked like a snake. And it seemed to come and go. But it only lasted a few days."

"How about any swollen joints?"

Mrs. Noonan looked at Eric, then shook her head no.

Mr. Noonan volunteered more information, "Eric's lost a lot of weight since he's been sick. He just doesn't get hungry anymore. We've tried to get him to eat more but he refuses. My wife even fixes all his favorite foods, but it don't help. And he's always tired too. Every day he comes home from school and goes straight to bed for a long nap. After supper he'll stay up maybe an hour or two, then go to sleep for the night. He just don't seem to have any energy.

"The kids in school have been picking on him because of the jerking. They call him names and push him around. Several times, Eric's come home crying. Lately, he seems to be getting worse, and we're getting real scared of what's happening. So we decided to get a second opinion. We talked to my wife's sister about it, and she told us about you."

It was easy to see why Eric would be derided by his peers. He looked like the picture a cartoonist would draw of a "wimp"—thin frame, pale complexion, and no coordination. His jerking movements and chronic fatigue added fuel to the fire.

I was pretty convinced by now that Eric had rheumatic fever, but before discussing it with his parents, I wanted to examine him. If my diagnosis was correct, we would need to consider doing several tests.

Considering how long he had had the chorea, I anticipated finding more than I did. His throat, of course, had long since recovered from the strep infection. Likewise, his joints were normal, and he had no rash. After two months of rheumatic fever, however, I expected to hear a loud heart murmur but did not. He had only a soft one, no different from that commonly heard in children. The rest of the exam was also unremarkable except for his involuntary jerking—the chorea. It occurred suddenly and caused his arms or face to twitch uncontrollably.

"I'm pretty sure I know what Eric's problem is," I began. "I think he has rheumatic fever."

"That's what we thought too," his mother interjected before I could continue. "But the doctors before told us no."

"Well, the story you've given me plus the chorea—which is what doctors call those jerking movements—strongly suggest that diagnosis. As you may know, rheumatic fever is a complication of strep throat in young children. How serious it is varies from person to person. Some get quite sick, whereas others do fine. The chorea usually improves by itself over time. From what you've told me, though, Eric's still getting worse after two months." They nodded as I continued.

"Rheumatic fever can cause heart damage too. Whether Eric has that is unclear. He definitely has a murmur, but it isn't very loud. Still, the fact that he's always tired and has no appetite makes me concerned his heart has been affected.

"Now, there are two ways we can approach this. One would be to do some tests to see how bad his rheumatic fever is. That would involve three things. First, some blood tests. Second, an echocardiogram. This is a picture of the heart that would give us an idea of how much, if any, damage has occurred. And third, because the chorea's lasted so long, I'd like to have him see a pediatric neurologist. Doing all these would take time and cost money. But we'd have a better idea of the extent of his illness, what to expect in the future, and the best way to treat him.

"The other way is to just treat him for rheumatic fever and see how he responds. This would be much simpler and cheaper. On the other hand, we wouldn't be able to tell you how much his heart has been affected, whether he's likely to have problems in the future, and whether something else is causing the chorea. I'd strongly recommend the first way, but it's up to you. What would you like to do?"

The Noonans had steadily nodded their heads in agreement while I talked. As soon as I stopped, Mr. Noonan said without any hesitation, "I took off several days of work to come up here and get this taken care of. We got insurance, so money isn't a problem. Do whatever you think needs to be done."

"Fine. I'll go ahead then and make the appointments for the other doctor and the echocardiogram while my nurse draws his blood."

Turning to Eric, I explained to him what we were going to do, "Eric, we're going to take some blood from your arm. It'll hurt a little bit, so if you want to cry, that's okay. After we're done, we have a surprise for you."

LeAnne drew his blood and then gave him the certificate for a free ice cream cone that we give every child who undergoes a painful procedure. It is my way of trying to keep a child from associating a visit to the doctor only with pain, but rather with the treat too. Meanwhile, the appointments were scheduled.

"When will all the results be back?" his mother inquired. "We need to decide how long to stay in Salt Lake."

"I should have them in three days. Why don't you come back then and we'll discuss them."

"We'll be here."

"In the meantime," I added, handing them a prescription, "I'd like to start treating Eric. He should take these penicillin pills four times a day. I also want him to take one aspirin with the penicillin. That should help decrease any inflammation of his heart from the rheumatic fever."

After the Noonans left, I wondered what would happen to Eric in the end. Would he suffer complications? I hoped not, for if there was permanent damage, the continued ridicule from his peers might ruin his self-esteem. And Eric seemed like a nice kid.

Driving home later that day, I noticed the mountains were resplendent in the setting sun. This year, the sunsets had been unusually pretty because of the large amount of matter in the air from the volcanic eruption of Mount Saint Helens. I pulled over to the side of the road to absorb the majesty of it all. The cragged tops in the east, covered with snow, were a soft contrast with the darkening sky. Beneath them, the tiny twinkling lights of thousands of homes studded the accumulating dusk. Over to the west, fiery orange clouds floated over the Oquirrh mountains and the Great Salt Lake. The sun, a bold red semicircle, was almost hidden behind those mountains, but not quite. It was still high enough for its rays to turn the water a shimmering, rippling gold.

Over the next twenty minutes, the sky darkened as the sun disappeared. I searched carefully and found Venus on the horizon, setting behind the sun. Overhead, the stars of the Big Dipper began to appear. Following the line formed by the pointer stars, Merak and Dubhe, I found Polaris, the North Star. And there, over to the east, Vega gradually appeared.

Long ago, humans had depended on these stars to navigate, to guide their course on their travels. I wondered about creatures on other worlds—perhaps orbiting those very stars? Did they also view the points of light in their skies with as much wonder as we do? What was their life like? Did they have diseases and doctors too? Perhaps they had become so medically advanced that they had eliminated illness. If so, they probably also knew how to "cure" deafness—or defects of whatever sensory perceptions they used. Even here, we're making a lot of progess in that direction. Researchers are steadily improving the cochlear implant, a mechanical device that transmits sound to the inner ear. I am sure the day will come when complete restoration of hearing will be possible. Then, no one will have to involuntarily face the problems I and other people who are deaf or hard of hearing have had to confront.

Feeling a sense of peace, I took one last glance, pulled back on the road, and headed home in the near darkness.

TWENTY-FOUR

THE THREE DAYS PASSED QUICKLY and the Noonans returned for their follow-up appointment. I had reviewed all the reports and was pleased with the results. Eric did have rheumatic fever, but there was no evidence of significant complications. His heart was only mildly affected; the pictures had shown only one valve involved, and minimally so at that. The cardiologist had examined him too and felt the development of long-term heart disease was unlikely as long as Eric continued on the penicillin and aspirin. Likewise, the pediatric neurologist recommended the same medications. She agreed he had chorea but felt it would disappear with treatment. And the blood tests were normal except for changes consistent with rheumatic fever.

As the Noonans listened attentively, I summarized the findings. "So," I concluded, "Eric should stay on four penicillin pills a day. After a month, we can consider gradually decreasing it to one a day, but he'll be on that dose indefinitely. He should also keep taking the aspirin. I want to stress that this is aspirin, not acetaminophen, like Tylenol tablets. Aspirin reduces the inflammation in his heart and elsewhere from the rheumatic fever; Tylenol doesn't. I wouldn't expect a dramatic improvement in the next few days or even the next two weeks. Eventually, he should get better, but it will take time."

"Do you have any idea how long a time we are looking at before he'll be completely okay?" his father inquired.

"That's hard to say. I hope it will be sooner rather than later, but it may take months. I would like to see Eric again in two weeks, if possible. If not, at least call and let me know how he's doing." They seemed satisfied with this response and returned to southern Utah with a prescription for penicillin.

I really enjoyed the rest of the day. There's nothing like the satisfaction of helping another person feel better.

Two weeks later, Eric's mother called to tell me he had improved. He still had the chorea, but it was less frequent than before. He was also beginning to eat more, gain weight, and be more active. She sounded very happy about his progress. After further discussion, I decided to reduce both pills to twice a day, starting in two weeks. If there were any problems, she was to call immediately.

That evening during supper, I was telling Barbara the happy news about Eric Noonan when the phone rang. It was a message to call Dane Strong. It had been a year since I had hospitalized him for heart failure and pneumonia. Since then, he had remained well. He even came to my office periodically and, unlike before, took his medications.

"Hey, Doc," he bellowed as usual into my amplified phone.

My ears ringing from the loudness of his voice, I turned the volume down slightly, something I almost never did. "Yes?"

"My stomach, it's been hurtin' me something awful bad."

"How long has that been going on?"

"Oh, I reckon 'bout four hours or so."

"I'll meet you at the emergency room in about twenty minutes," I told him. "Go on over there right now."

"Aw, Doc. Can't ya jus' have 'em gimme a penicillin shot? That's all I need. I don't wanna put you to no trouble."

"Mr. Strong, if you're having severe stomach pain for four hours, you need to be seen by a doctor now. I'll meet you there shortly."

"Okay," he agreed reluctantly.

When Mr. Strong arrived at the hospital, he certainly did not look sick. He walked in erect and acted normal. He complained that his stomach hurt "all over" but said it was better than when he had called me earlier. I examined him and noted his abdomen was diffusely tender, but only mildly so. There was nothing to suggest a serious illness. His urine, X ray, and blood count were all normal too. Although he most likely had a virus, I felt a little uneasy. First, he was ninety years old. Older folks often don't have the typical findings of illnesses that younger people do. Second, because he so rarely complained, I worried there might be something more serious than the flu. And third, he had a bad heart. If he did have something serious, he wouldn't tolerate it well. So just in case, I decided it would be safer to put him in the hospital.

"Mr. Strong," I began, "you probably have the flu. If so, there's not much we can do about that. However, I'm not sure about this and am worried something more serious may be going on. Therefore, I'd recommend you stay in the hospital overnight for observation. If you're feeling better in the morning, we'll send you home."

He shook his head vigorously. "I ain't staying here, Doc. No way."

Because of the lack of findings, I couldn't demand he do so. "Then if you insist on going home, you'll need to be rechecked here in four to six hours if you're not better. Of course, if you get worse at any time, don't wait. Come back immediately. Remember, don't see how tough you can be. If the pain is not gone in four hours or if you're worse at any time, come back here, okay?"

"But, Doc, can't ya jus' gimme something for the pain?"

"No, not until I feel more convinced there isn't anything serious going on."

"Not even a penicillin shot?"

"No."

"C'mon, Mabel," he ordered, steadying his wife's arm as they walked out.

I never saw him again.

The following morning, the emergency room called. "Dr. Zazove, we wanted to let you know one of your patients, a Mr. Dane Strong, was just brought here, dead on arrival."

"What?"

"The paramedics were called to his house by his daughter a short while ago."

"What happened?"

"We're not sure. He was dead by the time they got there."

I sat down, stunned, wishing I had been more insistent the night before that he be admitted. He might have agreed to come in. Knowing whether to insist a patient do something or just suggest it can be such a difficult decision sometimes. The only proper thing left to do was to call the family. I couldn't call his wife because she was as deaf as I am, so I called his daughter.

"I just heard what happened to your father, and I'd like to offer my condolences. He was a wonderful man."

"Thank you, I appreciate that."

"Do you know what happened after he left the emergency room last night?"

"Yes," she replied and told me the story. Mr. Strong had gone straight home from the hospital. Over the next few hours, the pain worsened steadily. He had, however, refused to go back to the emergency room or even call anyone, despite his wife's pleas. He told her he wanted to wait and see how he felt in the morning. When dawn came, the pain was excruciating. In fact, he had not slept at all the entire night. By then, he had agreed to call me. Before doing so, though, he went to the bathroom. Since the pain was so intense, he had to crawl to it. When he finally reached the toilet, he pulled himself up, then suddenly fell over dead. We'll never know what killed him, since an autopsy wasn't done. I suspect he had had a blood clot in an artery to his intestine that caused his gut to become infected and eventually burst.

I wished he hadn't been so stoic. Who knows? If he had gone back for the repeat exam when he was getting worse, he might have survived. But then, that wouldn't have been Dane Strong.

TWENTY-FIVE

THE GIRLS, BARBARA, AND I pulled into our driveway, having just finished riding our bikes around the neighborhood. As the children pulled off their safety helmets and ran next door to play with their friends, Barbara went inside to do some work.

It was October, that transitional time between summer and winter. And indeed, the air had been getting cooler the past few days. But it was still warm enough to be outdoors. I slowly walked about the house, inspecting the new trees we had recently put in. By the time I returned to the front again, my daughters were on our lawn, playing a game they had invented with their friends—a sort of reverse tag. Everyone was chasing our dog, Snoopy, who easily managed to avoid being caught. Suddenly, Katie stopped and, pointing above her, shouted.

"Look, Daddy, up there."

I peered up at the cloudless evening sky. Passing over us was a rounded V-formation of birds flying south.

"Those are geese, Katie," I explained. "They're heading south for the winter. When you see them doing that, it means winter isn't very far off."

"But why?"

"Well, winter here is much too cold for them. There's no food, and they'd freeze to death. So they go south where it's warmer and there's plenty to eat. But they'll be back. As soon as spring arrives, you'll see them flying home."

"Oh," she said as her four-year-old sister came over.

"Daddy, I want to tell you a secret," Rebecca said. She cupped her hands and began to whisper in my ear.

I pulled my head away. "Honey, I've told you before, I can't understand you when you whisper in my ear."

"But it's a *secret.*"

"Then whisper in front of me. I'll read your lips."

When Rebecca was young, she loved to tell me secrets. Even though I told her numerous times I couldn't hear her whisper in my ear, she still tried to do so. It is interesting that she did this because she otherwise communicates well with me. There must have been something about whispering in an ear that made the secret more exciting for her.

I sat on the front steps watching my girls play with their friends, feeling a glow inside. Sometimes I am amazed at the depth of my attachment to my children. I'm sure other parents have similar feelings. Explaining this to someone who has never had children would be impossible. It's different from the bond with one's spouse, parents, or siblings. It's not better, worse, or more or less intense than those relationships. Just different.

Over the years, I have delivered about a thousand babies. Although each one was special, seeing my own children born was particularly meaningful to me. I began to reminisce about Katie's birth in the middle of March, a few winters earlier. . . .

The pregnancy had had problems early on. Eleven weeks along, Barbara developed symptoms of gallstones. As a result, she had excruciating pain whenever she ate. Since fat is the cause of this discomfort, she eliminated it from her diet. The pain became less frequent, but she still couldn't eat; her food was so bland it was unpalatable. Then the soreness under her right ribs became persistent. Even after an attack subsided, a dull discomfort remained.

There was only one treatment—surgery. We had hoped to avoid it until after the baby was born. However, if Barbara couldn't eat and had continuous pain, waiting wasn't possible—not with two-thirds of the pregnancy remaining. And our family doctor agreed.

She would be better off having surgery, despite her pregnancy. So thirteen weeks along, her gallbladder was removed.

I had been the typical husband, worried about both Barbara and the baby. I felt helpless too. Being a doctor did not help; even though I knew exactly what was happening, there was nothing I could do. It was not until she recovered from the operation that I was able to relax. Still, although the baby seemed unaffected by the surgery, we both knew one couldn't be sure until it was born.

Things went more smoothly after that. When Barbara reached thirty-weeks gestation, we began Lamaze classes. Along with our classmates, we became more excited about our baby-to-be; only a few weeks remained before we would be a family. It was interesting to hear other couples' perceptions about pregnancy, labor, and delivery, significantly different from our perspective as physicians. After eight weeks of practicing breathing techniques, however, we were eager to tackle the real thing.

We had everything we needed for our first baby. All the furniture, clothes, and other items had either been bought or received as gifts. Even the baby's room had been decorated. Yes, we were ready.

The closer the due date approached, the more impatient we became. We tried everything imaginable to start labor, once even going into the mountains to jog in the snow there. It was all to no avail. Labor wouldn't start.

The evening of her due date, Barbara started having contractions. Excited, we went to bed early to get some rest before they really got strong. We got plenty of sleep too—eight solid hours of it—for the contractions stopped during the night. After the same thing recurred the next few evenings, we began to ignore it. For two weeks, we awoke every morning, hoping that day would be the one, only to find night arriving uneventfully.

Barbara was becoming exhausted. She worked a full schedule right up to her delivery, despite the surgery, the ever-growing baby, and the emotional strain of being overdue. She was remarkable, maintaining her composure in spite of all the demands on her time.

"We're now two weeks overdue," I lamented, exasperated with the waiting. "Do you think we'll ever have this baby?"

"I'm beginning to wonder the same myself," answered Barbara. "Any ideas on how to start labor?"

"No, but I wish I had some."

After supper, the nocturnal contractions began again. As usual, nothing happened, and we later went to sleep.

At midnight I woke up with vomiting and diarrhea. It was so bad the two occurred almost simultaneously, and I had to perform a real juggling act on the toilet. In between attacks, I lay on the bathroom floor, waiting for the next bout. I didn't dare try to return to bed.

Sometime later, I noticed Barbara walking about, pacing the floor. I wasn't sure why she was up but figured she either couldn't sleep or was staying awake in case I needed help. Regardless, I felt too ill to care.

After a while, my sickness ceased. Since I was too fatigued to move, I lay limply on the floor. I must have dozed off because around 5:00 a.m., Barbara awakened me.

"Philip," she said with some urgency as she shook me gently. "Wake up. I have something to tell you."

"What?" I mumbled, probably grumpily, arousing slowly. I wasn't happy about being awakened when I had finally fallen asleep. What could be so important that she had to rouse me in the middle of the night?

"It's finally happening. I'm in labor," she proclaimed. "It started three hours ago, and it's getting steadily stronger."

That statement jolted me out of my stupor like a bolt of lightning. Rearing up, I searched her face and asked, "Are you sure?"

"Yes," she replied, but her grimace from the pain of the next contraction was answer enough. "I knew when it first began at two this morning that it was the real thing."

The impending arrival of our baby energized me as quickly as any miracle cure. Drawing on inner reserves that I would not have thought existed two minutes earlier, I jumped up and started walking with Barbara, coaching her through each contraction. All the practice came in handy now. It made labor more tolerable for her and got me fully involved.

"Okay, now. Take a deep breath and let it out slowly. That's it. Good. Keep it up. Now take another one. Good. Okay, the contraction's over now. Just relax."

I rubbed Barbara's back and abdomen, trying to ease her discomfort as we walked back and forth, breathing through each pain. It was an enlightening experience. It's one thing to know the Lamaze technique and explain it to patients; it's quite another to do it oneself.

Over the next two hours, Barbara's contractions got stronger. At 8:00, she lay down. It had become too uncomfortable for her to walk. Meanwhile I called Steve Adamson, our family physician.

"Steve, this is Philip. Barbara started her labor five hours ago. When do you want us to go to the hospital?"

"How often are her contractions?"

I watched her as another one began. "About every three minutes."

"Have you checked her?"

"No. I'm just the husband in this one. You're the doctor. I'll leave that up to you."

"I'll tell you what," he said. "Since your house is on my way to work, I'll stop by in twenty minutes and check her."

He appeared on our doorstep exactly on time. "Come on in," I said, opening the door and letting him in from the wintry March wind.

"Morning, Barbara," he greeted her. "I hear you're finally in labor."

"Finally," she repeated. "I was beginning to wonder if it would ever start."

"It usually does," he noted matter-of-factly. Another pain began and he laid a hand on her abdomen, assessing the strength of the contraction. When it was over, he continued, "It looks like you're having good ones."

"They sure are," she agreed, panting, as she let out the last of the Lamaze breaths for that contraction.

He checked her cervix; it was dilated three centimeters and completely thinned out.

"You're doing well," he said. "At this rate, I'd go to the hospital around noon unless your bag breaks or you start bleeding. If either of those happen, or if you have any other problems, go there immediately. I'll be in the office if you have any questions."

Noon came. I helped Barbara dress and get into the car, trying frantically to take pictures of the event. At the hospital she was examined and found to be five centimeters dilated. By now, her pain was worse. For those of you who have never been through it, imagine how much it would hurt to flatten your nose to the thickness of a piece of paper and then stretch a nostril open to the size of an orange. That's basically what happens to a woman's cervix during labor.

Barbara continued to make progress throughout the afternoon. By 3:30, her cervix had opened to nine centimeters. Everything looked perfect.

But the smooth sailing didn't last. It took almost three hours, instead of the usual thirty minutes, for the cervix to dilate that last centimeter. Finally it did, and the time had come to push our baby out. With my encouragement, Barbara began to do so with each contraction. This quickly became tiring for both of us, yet we both knew first babies can take up to two hours of breathing and pushing. We had no choice.

Progress was slow. After an hour, Barbara cried, "I can't take it anymore. I want an epidural."

The anesthesiologist tried to place the epidural in Barbara three times but was unsuccessful. Then he attempted a caudal block, a closely related type of anesthesia. That didn't work either. So she was left to rely on the Lamaze breathing. I did all I could to keep her as comfortable as possible, but the emotional letdown must have been tremendous. After a long trial of natural labor, she had finally decided to get an epidural, only to have it unavailable.

I was so involved with Barbara that I didn't pay attention to the things doctors normally watch during labor. Besides, I was the father-to-be, too emotionally involved to be objective. Steve was the doctor—it was his job to worry about the details. We had chosen him knowing he would make all the decisions; we had complete trust in him. I am convinced that a physician who delivers his own wife's baby will have a hard time dealing with any complications that arise. And I better understood the adage about physicians who treat themselves: "Doctors who treat themselves have a fool for a doctor and a patient who's a fool."

After two hours, Barbara began to falter. She was losing her strength. Our baby's head was stuck in the sideways position and wouldn't budge, no matter how hard Barbara pushed. She was going to need some help.

"I'd recommend trying forceps," Steve informed us at this point. "But if the baby won't come out easily, then we'll need to do a cesarean section."

"Whatever you think is best," I answered. Barbara lay on the bed, exhausted, relishing every second of rest between the contractions.

While Steve got ready for the delivery, the anesthesiologist tried one more time to place a caudal block. This one worked. Finally!

It was after 8:30 when everything was ready for the delivery. The forceps were applied, and our baby was delivered without difficulty. Out she came—a beautiful girl. And I saw her let out a lusty cry.

It was amazing. What more can I say? There's nothing like seeing your own child born. Barbara and I both started crying from the excitement and happiness.

I leaned over and looked at the baby closely. Like all expectant fathers, I had worried that there would be something wrong with her. Unconsciously, my medical training took over. I scanned the infant girl totally, from head to foot, searching for abnormalities. She was normal—beautifully normal. Relieved, I watched contentedly while my wife held our daughter.

"Do you know what you went through, Katie?" Barbara crooned at the child she held on her stomach. "You went through a gallbladder operation. Yes, you did."

Katie seemed oblivious to her mother's comments. She was more interested in looking at the wonderful sights she saw for the first time. Periodically she would cry a little but would then stop and open her eyes again. Ten minutes later, I took and bathed her in a lukewarm bath. She seemed to enjoy this, moving her arms and legs in the water. Afterward, I handed her back to Barbara for breast-feeding. Katie took to this readily too.

I knew that having children would change my life drastically, but really had no idea just how much. My whole philosophy of life has changed. Having children has done as much as anything to make me a better person. I'm more self-controlled, more giving, and far more patient. It has also made me a better doctor. I can understand and empathize with parents' concerns much more than before. When a mother or father is exhausted after being up all night, or if a parent comes in because their child won't stop screaming for an hour, I know exactly what they are feeling. I have been there too.

People have often asked me what it is like to be a deaf person raising normally hearing children. I suspect there are not any dramatic differences from any other family. Of course, I have had to make some adjustments. For instance, when my daughters were young, Barbara was sometimes called to the hospital at night. As any father would do, I took total responsibility for my children. However, I had a distinct disadvantage. I could not hear my children crying in their cribs. We solved this dilemma by buying portable intercoms. I would put one extension in each of the girls' rooms and put the third on my bed, next to my ear. With the volume turned all the way up, I could hear if they cried. But I never slept well those nights either. I always dreamed I had knocked the intercom off the bed or that I hadn't heard one of them cry, so I kept waking up to check.

Another way my deafness was a factor with my children was when I decided to buy insurance. When Katie was born, I decided to purchase life and disability policies to provide for her in case something should happen to me. So I called Sam, a longtime family friend and independent insurance agent. He researched the market and recommended two companies, one for disability and the other for life insurance. He filled out the appropriate papers and mailed them in with my checks for the respective premiums enclosed.

My first inkling of a problem came one month later. "Philip," Sam told me, "I've got some bad news for you."

"What?"

"Both companies want to make changes in their policies because of your hearing loss. The disability insurance company wants a rider that excludes them from having to pay for any hearing-related problems, and the life insurance company wants to charge you a higher premium than usual."

"Why? I'm healthy. I don't understand."

The disability company feels that because you have so little hearing, you don't have any cushion. In other words, if you were to lose what little hearing you have, you would be totally deaf and they believe that makes you a higher risk for claiming a disability sometime in the future. The life insurance company said that your hearing loss makes you a higher risk . . ."

"For what?" I interrupted him. "Dying? Sam, my hearing has not changed at all since it was discovered almost thirty years ago. Do they understand that? It's not like it has been getting worse over time. There's absolutely no reason to think it would change. And as a physician, I can tell you unequivocally that my hearing loss is *not* going to kill me.

"Look, Sam, I won't agree to either of those requests. If they won't be reasonable, then I'd like you to find different companies."

"Tell you what. Let me talk to them again and see what I can do. If they won't change, I'll fill out applications for other companies. But I wouldn't be surprised if we found ourselves in the same situation."

A couple of weeks later, he called back. "We're making progress. The life insurance company agreed to charge you the standard rate."

"Good."

"But the disability company still insists on the exclusion clause," he continued. "I have a call in to someone higher up who I know, but I haven't heard from him yet."

"I'm willing to wait but I haven't changed my position. I won't accept an exclusion clause."

"I know. If he won't eliminate the rider, I'll mail you an application to another company I do a lot of business with. Their rates are slightly higher but they're just as solid and well-established a company."

"Sam, do they realize that even were I to lose what little hearing I have, I would probably cope with that much better than most people would if they lost just part of their hearing? I'm used to not hearing things."

"I tried to explain that to them but it didn't work. You see, all insurance companies have written guidelines they pretty much follow all the time. The person I talked to read me their company's guidelines for a person with your degree of hearing loss. It clearly states that the policy must include an exclusion clause releasing them from responsibility for disability claims due to worsening of the hearing loss."

It was almost another month and many discussions later before Sam told me the final decision. "It's all taken care of."

"You mean they dropped their demand for an exclusion?"

"Yes. I finally convinced my friend. You should be receiving the standard policy from them within a few days."

My children consider it normal for me to be the way I am. After all, they have grown up with me this way. They have a good sense of what I do and do not hear. Furthermore, as daughters of a deaf father, they seem to feel a kinship with other deaf persons as well. Still, they periodically ask why I am deaf and why I don't get it fixed.

Occasionally, my deafness has caused difficulties, such as when some of their classmates complain that I don't talk normally. I avoid using my daughters as interpreters in public situations, even when it is difficult for me to communicate. I want to prevent any possibility of the reversal of the parent–child role; childhood is a time that should be as carefree as possible.

My two daughters are an integral part of my life. Being a family doctor, especially one who does obstetrics, takes me away from them more than I . . .

A girl running directly in front of me startled me out of my reverie. It was almost dark. Stretching, I rose from the front steps and started to walk into the house.

"Come on," I yelled to the two girls who were still chasing Snoopy around the yard and laughing. "It's time to go inside and get ready for bed." I shivered a little, for the air was quite cool. Winter was just around the corner.

TWENTY-SIX

I STILL REMEMBER the day she walked in. I was up in the front of the office, talking to another patient when I first saw her. LaNell O'Donaghue was heavyset but short, maybe five feet two inches at the tallest, and looked to be in her mid-thirties. Short-cropped blond hair and a pug nose accentuated her round face, while a protruding abdomen advertised she had been pregnant for some time.

"I'm pregnant," she stated cheerily. "I was referred to you by Lisa Romney who spoke very highly of you. You delivered her last baby. This here is my seventh pregnancy, and I'd like to have you deliver the baby."

"I'll be happy to," I answered, not surprised by the number of children she had. In Utah, families commonly have more than five children, the result of the Mormon emphasis on large families. It was one of the main reasons Barbara and I had originally chosen the residency program at the University of Utah; we knew we would get lots of experience in obstetrics and pediatrics. And whenever we traveled back to the Midwest to visit our families, the relative lack of pregnant women there was starkly apparent.

LeAnne showed Mrs. O'Donaghue to a room, and I joined her shortly thereafter. "How far along are you?"

"I'm not sure," she confessed. "I feel bigger than I remember being with my other pregnancies. Maybe I'm farther along than I thought I was."

"Let's figure that out. When was your last normal period?"

"December 15," she answered. A quick calculation revealed she was due in September, making her five months pregnant at this point.

She certainly looked bigger than that. "Are you sure about that date?" I looked at her lips.

"Positive," she stated. "I looked it up in my journal where I always write it down."

I proceeded to do a complete history and physical, as I do on all new prenatal patients. These histories are essential to detect potential problems that may need treatment. In Mrs. O'Donaghue's case, other than appearing larger than she should, all was normal.

"Were your other babies large?"

"Oh yes. And each one was bigger than the one before. The last three times, the doctor worried about twins, but it never was. I guess I just make big babies." She smiled. "My youngest was really big, eleven-and-a-half pounds. In fact, she was the biggest one in the nursery by far. That's why we named her Victoria." She smiled again as she reflected on that. Then she pointed at her belly. "But I don't think I've ever been quite this big."

"Hmmmm. Sounds like you do have large babies. Still, to be sure there's no other cause for it this time, I'd like to check you for diabetes and get an ultrasound."

"An ultrasound? Oh, for fun," she exclaimed. "I'd like that. I never had one before, but my friends told me all about it. I'll be able to see the baby too, right?"

"That's right, and not only that, you'll probably also see it move and its heart beat. It'll help me too. By measuring the baby's size, we can get a good idea of when your baby is really due. And we'll also be able to check for some of the problems that can make you bigger than you should be."

"Will they tell me if it's a boy or girl?"

"Possibly, if you want to know. At this stage, it depends a lot on which way the baby is facing."

"Oh, I'd rather not know. With six girls at home, my husband would really like at least one boy, but," she shrugged, "there's nothing we can do about it now."

There were several possible causes for her large size, but because all her babies were so big, I suspected she was right—it was a hereditary tendency and the ultrasound would turn out normal. She might have diabetes of pregnancy, but that could be diagnosed only by a blood test. I did not give the impending ultrasound another thought, especially because I had to go home and pack. The next day I was leaving town to attend a conference where Barbara was going to present her research.

The conference itself was a typical medical meeting. Barbara's presentation was at the end of the first day, so we spent the day listening to other speakers. We sat in the front row, where I always sit so that I have a better chance of reading the speaker's lips. Unfortunately, that day almost all the speakers used slides, and whoever controlled the lights turned them completely off, making it impossible to see the lecturer's face. The slides themselves were boring, and I found myself closing my eyes and daydreaming.

Several times I caught myself waking up from a catnap to find the lights on and the speaker answering questions. This situation was no easier for me to understand. I had to follow the direction the speaker looked in when he called on someone, then turn my head and scan the people in that section to see who was talking. By the time I figured out who it was, the questioner was usually finished. Then, I had to quickly turn back to the speaker in order not to miss much of the answer. When someone cracked a joke, I invariably missed it. Sometimes I would smile when I saw everyone else laughing; I did not want to be the only one with a serious face.

Barbara's turn finally arrived. I brought myself to attention. When the lights were turned off for her slides, she asked that they only be dimmed. That way, I could see her lips and easily follow her presentation. It was well-received by the audience, and afterwards, we went out to celebrate.

While we were gone, Mrs. O'Donaghue had her ultrasound. And the results provided us an answer—a surprising one—to Mrs. O'Donaghue's large girth: she was carrying twins. By the time I talked to her, she already knew.

"Well, how do you feel about it?"

"Oh for neat. You know, at first I was shocked. I couldn't believe it. But now that I've thought about it a while, I'm getting excited." She beamed. "I'm looking forward to having two babies. And you should see my husband. He's on cloud nine. Just imagine, Doctor, two babies at one time."

"Mrs. O'Donaghue," I cautioned her, "you'll need to be more careful with this pregnancy than with your others. Twin pregnancies often have more complications, such as diabetes, difficult deliveries, and high blood pressure." I paused, then added, "They're also more likely to deliver prematurely."

"Well, Doctor, is there anything special I need to do?"

"Yes. First of all, we'll see you every two weeks instead of monthly."

"Okay."

"Second, what kind of work do you do?"

"I work in a fabric shop, selling fabric."

"So you're on your feet most of the day?"

"Yes, all the time."

"Then you need to stop work. It's very important that you rest a lot, taking at least one nap daily."

"But I have to work," she protested. "We need the money."

"I'm sorry, but you really need to rest. If you spend all day on your feet, you'll make the complications much more likely to occur. Over the years, doctors have found that women with twins who rest every day seem to do better."

"Well, okay, if I must."

"We will, of course, still watch for the usual problems that can occur with all pregnancies," I continued. "And I'd suggest you schedule an appointment with an obstetrician. That way he'll be familiar with you and can help us with any problems that may develop."

She agreed. "Who should I see?"

I suggested Dr. Parker. She saw him later that week and he consented to follow along with us. This was going to be my first set of twins in private practice. They occur once every eighty or so pregnancies. Although more exciting than normal pregnancies, twin gestations are also often fraught with problems. I was glad Dr. Parker would be backing me up.

But the pressure does not stop after the babies are born. Twins are often small or have other medical problems. Even when normal, they are more demanding than one infant. Everything has to be done twice. The O'Donaghues were going to have their hands full since they already had six other children. Fortunately, their family seemed very supportive. That would go a long way toward helping them cope. And it could have been worse. Mrs. O'Donaghue could have had triplets; the risk of complications with these is even higher than twins. I have seen only two sets of triplets. Those women were truly immense and had been confined to bed in a futile attempt to prevent the complications. Unfortunately, in both cases only one of the babies survived. Thinking about the problems those women faced almost made Mrs. O'Donaghue's situation seem mundane.

Two weeks later, LaNell O'Donaghue returned, much larger than before. "I feel so big, like I'm ready to have a baby now," she complained. "And I get tired so easily. Just walking across the room makes me so exhausted I have to sit down again. It don't seem like my other pregnancies."

Normally, during the second half of pregnancy, a woman's uterus measures one centimeter for each week she is pregnant. Mrs. O'Donaghue had been twenty-eight centimeters at twenty-four weeks. Now she was thirty-one centimeters at twenty-six weeks. She had also gained five pounds rather than the usual one pound per week.

"Are you still excited about having twins?"

"You bet," she replied. "It's going to be real neat."

One month later, I recommended she increase the number of rest periods. It's one of the few treatments doctors have that might reduce the chances of complications. Mrs. O'Donaghue complied faithfully and did well until she developed diabetes of pregnancy. We had been watching for it, however, and were able to control it with a special diet.

"We're so looking forward to having twins," she confided to me at her thirty-two week visit. "We had to get a few extra things, but everything's bought now. We're ready to go." She and her husband were enjoying their notoriety and the attention it generated from family and friends.

"Aren't you worried about the extra workload you'll have with two babies?"

"Oh, for no. I think it'll be fun."

"I'll bet it'll be a real challenge too."

She agreed. "But it'll still be neat. Besides, my oldest daughter is fourteen, and she'll be able to help me."

We had previously reviewed the risks of premature labor. My hope was that she would make it to at least thirty-six weeks, but I knew labor could start any day. And every morning I anticipated that would be the day. Each time someone called the office, I thought it was her. Every night when the phone rang, I was sure it would be labor and delivery. If my beeper went off, I thought, "This is it. She's in labor." Amazingly, none of the calls were about her.

As time passed, Mrs. O'Donaghue became more anxious. Most women measure between thirty-six and forty centimeters at the time of delivery. At thirty-six weeks, she was already forty-eight centimeters. Her abdomen looked like a huge beachball. Just walking from the exam table to the chair, three feet away, made her short of breath. "I can't wait to have these babies," she panted. "I can't do anything. I can't even eat much at one time—there's just no room. A few minutes later, though, I'm hungry again. How much longer do you think it'll be?"

"I don't know. You've already made it farther than many women with twins, and I'm happy about that. The longer you go, the better the chances are for healthy babies and the less likely they'll have the problems many twins have."

Twelve days later, in the afternoon, I got a message on my special beeper while at the grocery store. Beepers had come a long way since I was an intern, and I now had a vibrating beeper. Furthermore, it displays a written message rather than utter a voice one. I pushed the appropriate button and read the words: "Call labor and delivery about your patient LaNell O'Donaghue."

I went to the closest public phone hoping it would be an amplified one, as a few of them are. It wasn't. Deciding to try it anyway, I inserted a coin and called the hospital. The phone rang twice before someone answered it. Or at least I thought someone did. The ringing had stopped, but I could not hear a sound.

"Hello?" I said.

This time I could barely hear a voice. It sounded too faint. There was no way I was going to be able to understand it.

"This is Dr. Zazove. I can barely hear you. Could you speak louder? You called me about Mrs. O'Donaghue?"

I still couldn't hear the reply.

"Look, I'm at the grocery store and can't hear you on this phone. I'll go home and call you back in five minutes," I said before hanging up. Darn! When would they get around to making amplified car phones?

I looked at my cart full of groceries and remembered the line at the checkout counter. I had no time to wait. Mrs. O'Donaghue might be having problems.

Leaving the cart by the phone, I started to run out to my car. Just as I got through the door, I had to swerve abruptly to avoid knocking over an elderly lady who was walking in. I stopped a second to see who it was. Mrs. Conn.

"My goodness, Dr. Zazove, that's no way to go out a door. You could've hurt me if you had run into me. But I am glad to see you. I was just thinking about . . ."

"Mrs. Conn, I'm sorry, but I must leave. I have to go deliver a baby." I turned and ran to my car, not seeing her reply. This was one time I was glad I was deaf, for regardless of what she was saying, I could not hear her and didn't have to answer. And because she knew that, she couldn't be upset with me. I hurried home and, as soon as I arrived, called the hospital on my amplified phone.

"Dr. Zazove? Helen Gallegos. LaNell O'Donaghue arrived here fifteen minutes ago, in labor. She's dilated to four centimeters, is at zero station, and the first baby is headfirst. I'm not sure about the position of the second one, however."

"Do you have them both on the monitor?"

"Yes. Their heartbeats look fine."

"Good. Get an ultrasound of her abdomen so we can see what position the second baby is in," I ordered. "I'll be right over. And please call Dr. Parker and have him come in too."

I arrived at the hospital ten minutes later. Mrs. O'Donaghue was now six centimeters dilated. The first baby was definitely headfirst, but I could not determine the position of the second infant. Both heartbeats were okay, however, just as Helen had said. Then I looked at the ultrasound.

It confirmed that the first fetus was headfirst, but the second fetus wasn't; it was coming down left shoulder first. That position would make for a very difficult, if not impossible, vaginal delivery.

Years ago, Mrs. O'Donaghue would have had her babies at home. Whoever delivered them would not have had ultrasounds or even X rays available, so there would have been no way to determine the position of the second infant. In fact, chances were that no one would have even suspected two babies. In those days, twins were often not discovered until birth. Even today, some come as a surprise.

The second infant would have been a tough delivery too. The doctor would have been forced to put a hand inside the mother's uterus and try to reposition the baby—a risky maneuver. If the baby could not be moved, and sometimes even if it could, it would die or be born severely damaged. Mrs. O'Donaghue herself might not have survived the delivery, and if she did, the high chances of a life-threatening infection from the doctor's manipulations might well have killed her a few days later.

Today we have an alternative—cesarean sections. When these were first done, they too were risky because of poor sterilization and anesthesia, plus a high incidence of complications. Now they are much safer. In situations like Mrs. O'Donaghue's, they are the best way to go.

"I don't expect any problems with the first baby," I told the

O'Donaghues, "but the second one is a different story. It's coming down shoulder first. There just isn't enough room for it to come out that way without risking serious damage to both of you. There'd be a good chance of that baby dying or being brain damaged, and you'd be severely torn up and could die as well. Sometimes, after the first baby delivers, the second one moves into the correct position. If it does, we'll deliver that one naturally too. Otherwise I'd recommend a cesarean section. There are risks with that too—bleeding, infection, and complications from the anesthesia. And, of course, there's still no guarantee the baby will be okay. But these complications are uncommon. I feel they're outweighed by the likely results—namely, a healthy baby and a healthy you."

"Whatever you recommend," the O'Donaghues agreed without hesitation.

"Let's wait and see if Dr. Parker agrees before we make a final decision," I added.

Shortly thereafter, we moved into the delivery room. Normally I do my deliveries on birthing beds in the labor rooms. It's more comfortable for the mother as well as more aesthetic. This time, however, I wanted to be in the delivery room. We might need to do an emergency C-section, and all the equipment we would need was available there.

We barely got Mrs. O'Donaghue on the table when the first baby started coming out. I quickly put on my hearing aid and sterile gloves in time to guide out a six-pound, fifteen-ounce girl. Obviously a healthy baby—and, for a twin, large as well—she immediately let out a robust cry.

"Oh, for cute," Mrs. O'Donaghue cried happily. "A little girl."

"Yes," Mr. O'Donaghue repeated, "a little girl."

While they cuddled their new baby, I checked Mrs. O'Donaghue's cervix again. The second fetus had moved down but had not changed position; it was still shoulder first. Then Dr. Parker arrived. After he reviewed the ultrasound, he agreed a section was indicated.

We performed it without problems. The second girl was also healthy and only slightly smaller than her sister. There was only one placenta and bag of waters, suggesting they were identical twins. The O'Donaghues named them Ann and Alice.

LaNell O'Donaghue recovered quickly from the surgery. During her hospital stay, she was her usual jolly self, ecstatic about the new members of her family. She breast-fed both infants and wasn't bothered by the extra work of twins. Four days later she went home, happy and with a baby in each arm.

The miracle of birth never gets old. It is what makes obstetrics a gratifying part of a family doctor's practice. After all, most of the time things turn out well, and everyone is happy. It's a welcome respite from the illnesses other patients have too. Unfortunately, because of the malpractice crisis, insurance is becoming prohibitively expensive, and many family doctors are giving up this valued part of their practice. If current trends continue, even more family doctors will stop delivering babies. That would be very unfortunate. People will no longer be able to have one doctor care for everyone in the family, from cradle to grave.

The twins, Ann and Alice, are growing up rapidly and are now young girls. Although I still cannot tell them apart, the rest of the family has no difficulty at all. But one question remains—will the O'Donaghues ever have a boy?

TWENTY-SEVEN

THE MORNING WAS a perfect one for skiing. The sun was out, the temperature moderate, and the winter landscape sparkling white. In Utah, there are numerous places to ski—both downhill and cross-country. And this was a particularly good year for skiing because the mountain resorts were loaded with more than a hundred inches of snow.

Barbara, the girls, and I drove up one of the mountain canyons to our favorite spot for cross-country skiing. As Barbara and Katie took off down the trail, I put Rebecca in my backpack carrier, hitched on my skis, and headed off into the pristine wintry wilderness behind them. As an infant, Rebecca loved to ride on my back, watching the sights as we glided over the trail. Sometimes she babbled on and on about various things. She also enjoyed leaning from side to side, trying to throw me off balance.

The trail we took paralleled the course of a meandering stream adorned by icicles of all lengths and shapes. Some hung from limbs of trees, others rose from the banks, and a few were in the creek itself, perched on fallen branches in the water. Together, they looked like the stalactites and stalagmites of caves. Along the trail, branches of pines, spruces, and firs sagged under the weight of the spotless snow. Occasionally, gusts of wind skimmed some off, spraying the cool mist over our faces.

We skied along, the cold stream entertaining us with an ever-changing view, sometimes flowing quietly, other times rushing wildly. Every so often, other skiers would pass us with a friendly greeting, or a dog would romp by, frolicking happily in the powder.

We then came to a steep drop and paused awhile, watching the waterfall cascading over it. Afterwards, we left the cover of the trees. The sun dazzled us with its bright rays reflecting off the snow. We reentered the shade and saw a porcupine perched on the branch of a huge aspen, lazily watching us pass beneath. The four of us stopped here to eat lunch, spending much of the time studying the animal with interest. Three hours later, our trip was over. We felt tired but happy, and at peace with nature.

I really enjoy escaping into the mountains of Utah after a hard week's work. It refreshes my mind and invigorates my spirit—something every doctor, in fact every person, periodically needs. And spending it with my family makes it extra special. I was fortunate to have a wonderful work situation which provided me time off to spend with Barbara and my daughters. Connie, Doug and I all shared a similar philosophy. We try to be home with our families as much as possible, and structured our office hours so that this could happen. We made less money this way, but that was not the most important thing to us.

Besides hiking and skiing in our beloved Wasatch front, my family and I often took short trips around the state. Sometimes, we even traveled to one of the neighboring states. One of the best things about living in Utah is being near the beautiful natural scenery that abounds in the Rocky Mountains. The intermountain West contains all kinds of interesting places to explore, and we enjoyed them all.

Every summer we went to Yellowstone National Park, perhaps the most spectacular place of all. The physicians who worked in Barbara's clinic had obtained a contract to cover the Old Faithful clinic, close to the famous geyser of that name in the middle of the park. Our ten days there were always an exciting time. Six of the ten days, Barbara had to work and I would play Mr. Mom. Still, the girls and I had fun. I especially enjoyed the peace of no distractions from television or telephones, both devices that deaf persons use less frequently than hearing persons. Instead, we went sightseeing all over the park, stopping whenever we felt like it to hike to various geysers, mudpots, or other unusual natural phenomena. The first couple of years, when the children were small, I had to push one or the other in a stroller, sometimes even up steep hills. After a few years however, they were both old enough to walk and we could go further. Although I did not appreciate most of the sounds from the thermal features we saw, the girls did. They often knew we were approaching one because they could hear the noise of boiling water or an erupting geyser. They did not have that much of an advantage over me, however, because all of these places released steam. And with water temperatures in the range of two hundred degrees Fahrenheit, the steam would condense in the air, especially on cooler days. It was easy to spot this above the trees or in the middle of a clearing.

When Barbara was not working, the four of us would leave early in the morning and visit the more distant areas of the park. Yellowstone Park is a huge place, almost as big as the state of Rhode Island. It took hours to reach certain parts of the park. Most years we managed to see a bear; fortunately, every time but one we were in the safety of the car. The exception was in our campground, just before dinner one day. As soon as I saw it, I ushered the kids into our trailer. Not everyone else present was so cautious though. Through the windows we watched two people walk close to the animal slowly, fascinated by it. Fortunately, the bear was not aggressive. It turned and reentered the woods.

Most evenings, we spent with one of the other physicians (and their family if they had one) working in the park. Often, Barbara and that doctor swapped stories about the experiences they had had at the Old Faithful clinic. I always found these interesting, not so much for the stories themselves but for what they revealed about people in general. Many of the tales centered on the denial by many persons of the dangers of various features in the park, despite numerous warning signs along the roads. One tale particularly sticks out in my mind.

"You know how people often try to walk up to bison to try to get close-up pictures of them?" Dr. Wilson was telling us.

Barbara nodded.

"Well, today, some man got this crazy idea of putting his son on top of a bison to take a picture. As he was walking toward his child, he got too close to the bison. The animal became agitated and charged the man. He turned and sprinted back to his car. Fortunately, one of the car windows was open and the man dove through it just in time before the bison ran into the door with his head."

"Was he okay?" I asked.

"Yeah, he just had a few minor cuts. He was so lucky."

"You heard what happened to Mark earlier this summer?" Barbara asked.

Dr. Wilson, who had just arrived the previous evening, shook his head.

"His second day here, two men were hiking near the clinic with their dog. For whatever reason, the dog dove into one of the hot springs." Barbara paused to let the implications of that statement fully sink in.

The physician grimaced in understanding; with average temperatures approaching two hundred degrees Fahrenheit, there was no way the dog would survive his plunge.

"Then the dog's owner dived in after his pet."

"Oh no!"

She nodded, then added, "And his friend waded in up to his waist to pull the other two out."

"You're kidding me."

Barbara slowly shook her head.

"What happened?"

"By the time they reached the clinic, the man who dove in was already swelling up like a balloon from the third-degree burns all over his body. He died before he reached the hospital. The other man at least made it there, although I never heard if he survived."

"I hope I never see something like that."

"Me neither."

It is hard to imagine people who would do such things. But then, the diversity of people who live in the United States is also one of its strong points. The constant influx of new ideas that immigrants bring from their native countries has helped the country be so successful. It must have been hard, however, for many of these people. The lifestyle and language here are vastly different than other places in the world.

Still, as every schoolchild learns, people come to the United States to escape persecution elsewhere and to have the chance to pursue their dreams. My ancestors were a typical example. They had faced similar problems around the turn of the century, problems that led them to emigrate from small towns in Russia to the United States. Being Jewish, they had been the victims of anti-Semitism. They had no opportunity for advancement or even education in Russian schools. Thus, like millions of others during the golden age of U.S. immigration, they came to the promised land. Once here, they could benefit from their individual talents and capabilities. I have spent many fascinating hours listening to stories about their homeland and early twentieth-century America, both different worlds from mine.

My entire family immigrated here during the days of the Russian czars. Those were days of corruption, persecution, lifelong servitude, despair, and poverty. My ancestors had only each other and their Jewish faith to sustain them. Because of outside religious intolerance, they lived with their fellow Jews at one end of town while non-Jews lived at the other end. Their homes were hovels, with whole families in one or two rooms. I remember my maternal grandmother telling me they often brought their animals, including livestock, into the front room of their house for the night, to prevent them from being stolen. Her family of seven slept in the other room.

Her father once was arrested at the whim of a local aristocrat. When her mother heard that the czar happened to be traveling nearby, she went to await his arrival. As he rode by, she flung herself in front of his horse. Fortunately he stopped rather than trample over her, as nobility had been known to do. After hearing her plea for help, the czar ordered my great-grandfather released. Soon after, the family emigrated.

On their arrival here, the name Zazove was conceived. It is a shortened version of a longer Russian name that means "town crier." When my great-grandparents went through the immigration center on Ellis Island, the officer there asked them what their name was. They answered in Russian. Since the officer did not understand this, he wrote down a name that sounded phonetically similar to the first two syllables of the Russian name—Zazove. That has been our family name ever since, and because it was a new name invented upon my ancestors' emigration here, anyone with that name is related to me.

There aren't many of us, but I am proud to be a Zazove. Despite arriving in this country penniless and destitute, my ancestors worked hard and have been extraordinarily successful in diverse fields of work. Some day in the future, I hope my descendants will look back at my life and say the same about me. And I hope they will be able to say, "He helped destroy the stereotype that once prevailed about deaf people. He showed that they can do anything hearing people can, even be a doctor."

TWENTY-EIGHT

It was just before 11:00 a.m. when Carma called. "Dr. Zazove, Patty Anderson is on the line. Do you want to talk to her now, or shall I take a message?"

"I have a minute so I'll take it now."

I picked up the phone. "Mrs. Anderson? How are you today?"

"I'm fine, Dr. Zazove," she answered. "But my grandmother isn't."

"Oh?" I replied, checking to make sure the amplifier was turned on all the way. Mrs. Anderson's voice was somewhat quiet. "What's wrong?"

"She hasn't been doing well for a couple of weeks. She complains of feeling weak and spends all of her time in bed. Lately, she's also had this dry, hacking cough, and sometimes even has trouble breathing. I'm not sure what to do. At first I thought it was just a virus, but Grandma keeps getting worse. Doctor, I'm worried about her. She doesn't even want to eat anymore."

"Would you like me to come over and take a look at her?"

"If you could, I'd really appreciate it. And I know she would too."

"How about today during lunch time, around 12:30?"

"That'll be great."

I finished my schedule of patients for the morning. It was the usual variety of problems. First, a little girl with a urinary tract infection, possibly the result of a bubble bath she had taken, then, a boy who had fallen off his bike and cut his hand. After seeing a prenatal patient and two people with high blood pressure, I was

done. Or so I thought. Just as I started to leave, in walked Wilma Brewer.

I waved "hello" at her. She returned the greeting then pointed at the baby in her arms and made the sign for sick. I turned around and gestured for her to follow me. Once we were alone in a room, I signed, "What's the problem with Lilly?"

"She's been fussy the past two days. She . . ."

The woman used some signs I did not understand.

"Sorry, what's that mean?" I furled my eyebrows as I repeated the signs.

She spelled out the meaning word for word.

"Oh, she's not been eating either?"

Mrs. Brewer nodded.

"Any fever?"

She nodded again.

"How high?"

The young woman shrugged. "We don't have a thermometer."

I recalled the circumstances of Mrs. Brewer's pregancy. Unexpected, it had occurred while she had been living in Nevada. The father of the baby disappeared as soon as he learned about the pregnancy, but Wilma elected to keep the baby. In the seventh month of her pregnancy, she moved back home to live with her parents, both of whom were also deaf. By the time she came to see me, she only had one month left before the baby was due. The delivery, fortunately, had been uneventful and she had bonded well with her daughter.

From the beginning, I had found Mrs. Brewer interesting and intelligent. She had a good relationship with her parents, and they helped her care for her child. Nevertheless, she was also very reserved, and communicated in a dialect of American Sign Language that was hard for me to understand. She volunteered few details about her life and, despite her apparent willingness to do what was best for the baby, she had a habit of not showing up for her appointments.

I studied the seven-month-old infant. Despite a temperature of 103 degrees, she did not look that ill. She was somewhat irritable,

but not unusually so, and my examination failed to reveal a treatable cause for the fever.

"I think Lilly probably has a viral infection that will get better by itself," I signed to her. "However, because I'm not positive of this, I would like to get a blood and urine test to be sure nothing more serious is going on."

She flashed the sign *okay* back at me.

"I'll let you know if the tests show anything we need to worry about. In the meantime, if Lilly gets worse in any way, if she gets a higher fever, more irritable, or lethargic . . ." At this point I paused as I struggled for the correct sign for this word, then elected to fingerspell it out letter by letter. Deciding to elaborate, I said, "that means she's sleepy all the time and you have trouble waking her up." Mrs. Brewer nodded.

"Or if there's anything else that worries you, let me know immediately. Okay?"

"Yes."

"In fact, why don't you call me tomorrow and let me know how she's doing, even if she's better."

"Okay."

As soon as she left, I turned on my beeper, told Carma I would be at the Anderson's, and headed toward the parking lot.

It felt good to be outside. Even the sultry summer air did not bother me. It was a welcome contrast to the air-conditioned office. Besides, I am an outdoors person. There is something about being under a blue sky that makes me feel content. I got into my car and started to drive, all the while thinking about Mrs. Anderson and her grandmother.

Patty Anderson was twenty-eight years old, a petite mother of three children. At first glance, she seemed like everyone else. She had medium length brown hair, an upturned nose, and clear, dark eyes. Although slightly overweight, she was always well groomed. She even looked presentable during labor when I delivered her last child.

But after being around her awhile, one began to notice a certain unique quality. She was interested in people, really interested in

them without being overbearing, and devoted her time to helping others. How she found time to do everything she did was beyond me. She participated in community and church activities in addition to running her own home-based fingernail painting business. But it was her family that she cared for most. Besides being a wife and a mother, she also nursed her ailing grandmother, a full-time job in itself. It was this tireless devotion to everyone and her willingness to help others that most impressed me. And she did it all without a complaint.

Mr. Anderson was a striking physical contrast to his wife. While she was only five feet tall, he was well over six feet. His husky frame featured a small pot belly, blond hair, and a fair complexion. He looked to be of Scandinavian stock, a sharp contrast to his wife's Italian appearance. Yet, as different as they looked, they were similar in temperament. Both were outgoing, friendly, and easy to talk to. I don't think I ever heard a harsh word from either of them.

The Andersons lived three to four miles away, in an isolated group of houses surrounded by farm country. As I drove there, the bright sun warmed the verdant fields of grain and grass. Horses, cows, and sheep grazed contentedly in the pastures. People were out everywhere too: children on bicycles, boys playing baseball, girls riding horses. Every so often, I passed a farmer mowing hay, his dog trotting behind the tractor. People I knew waved as I went by.

I enjoyed this noon drive in the middle of the summer and wished I had more time to drive around. Everything seemed peaceful. Close to a metropolis, yet still rural, the area displayed a rustic charm of its own. I suspected it was probably quite different from Rome, the birthplace of Mrs. Anderson's grandmother, Vera Frendetti.

Vera was actually the family member I had met first. Short like her granddaughter, she looked at least ten years older than her stated seventy-five. Her face was long and wrinkled, and a somewhat aquiline nose sat between dark, sunken eyes. Sparse, unkempt, grayish hair was matted down from lying on her pillow much of the day.

Despite her elderly appearance, Vera Frendetti retained all her mental faculties. A keen observer of people and life, she often entertained me with stories of her younger days, descriptions of places she had been, and tales of situations in which she had found herself. I enjoyed hearing her opinions as well; they were anything but old-fashioned.

She had lived in Las Vegas most of her American life. When her daughter and husband died, she found herself alone, and moved to Plymouth to be with Patty, her sole surviving family. Shortly thereafter, Vera Frendetti came to my office for the first time, complaining of shortness of breath. I had diagnosed heart failure and treated it appropriately. She improved for a while but then developed progressive weakness in her legs. Gradually, she became bedridden.

She also became depressed. At first I did not realize this because she acted so cheerful at times, asking about my children and cracking jokes. But over time her feelings became obvious. She wanted to die, to "get on with it," as she put it. She felt she had lived her life and believed herself to be a burden to her family. Since Patty Anderson was pregnant, all Mrs. Frendetti desired was to stay alive until she could see the baby. After that, she would be content to die.

I turned down the street where they lived and parked in front of their home, a small ranch house in the town of Zion. The neighborhood was new, and the absence of trees made the area seem barren. Mrs. Anderson answered the doorbell promptly.

"Dr. Zazove," she greeted me warmly. "Please come in."

Turning around, she talked as she led me into the house. Fortunately, I was able to see enough of her lips in profile to understand what she was saying. "I really appreciate your coming here to see Grandma. There are so few doctors who make house calls now, I don't know what I'd do otherwise. It's so difficult to get her in and out of a car. As you know, she doesn't move around well, and I have a hard time lifting her—"

"Grrrrr. Grrrrr." Our path was blocked by a snarling English setter, quite unhappy at my presence.

"Cecil, it's just the doctor. You've met him before," Mrs. Anderson reprimanded him gently. "It's okay."

"Grrrrr," he growled a little less loudly, backing up a few steps.

"Cecil doesn't like strangers," she remarked as she tried to calm him down. "But he's a good watchdog." When he continued to snarl, she grabbed his collar and pulled him into the backyard.

"Come this way," she said after returning. She pointed left toward a hallway leading to the bedrooms. "Grandma is in her room, the last one on the right."

Because the blinds were drawn over the windows, it was a little dark. Still, the house was obviously clean.

We walked down the short, carpeted hallway. I always enjoy seeing how my patients live. It gives me a better sense of what their home situation is like. The differences between homes can be marked. This was a well-kept house; everything was neat except for scattered toys left behind by the children. Pictures of the children adorned the off-white walls. There was a definite overall mood of contentment.

Vera Frendetti watched us walk into her room. She looked tiny, lying on one side of a king-size bed. Her room was much plainer than the rest of the house. A bedside commode, banged-up pine dresser, old table with a blue-green lamp, and two pictures on the wall were the only other pieces of furniture in the room. Since she lay either in bed or on a recliner in the family room, Mrs. Frendetti really did not need any other accessories.

"Hi, Doctor," she said very quietly with her distinctive accent. But I had no trouble understanding her as long as I could see her lips.

I returned her greeting, squeezing her left hand lightly between both of mine. "How are you?"

"Not too hot," she used one of her favorite expressions.

"Why not?"

"I've been coughing and I just don't feel good. Besides, what use is it my being here, Doctor. I can't move my right hand much." She continued talking, but I didn't catch what she said because I could no longer read her lips. The woman had turned her head to look at her arm.

"Mrs. Frendetti," I interrupted, moving around the bed to see her lips again. "I'm sorry. I didn't hear what you said."

"Look at it," she repeated as she held up her arm. "I can't even eat with it anymore. And oh boy, does it hurt. I do the exercises the therapist showed me, but they just make it worse. The pain pills don't help much either."

"Is it any different from before?"

"About the same," she admitted. "But tell me, Doctor, what's the use of my being alive and having to put up with this? All I do is lie in this bed." Her eyes, however, belied her statements. They still showed a twinkle of life in them.

It was easy to understand why Mrs. Frendetti was depressed. Despite everything we did, she continued a downhill course. One thing after another seemed to befall her. First, high blood pressure and heart failure. Then, weakness of her legs and, to a lesser extent, her arms. Next, a continuous tremor. And on top of all this, she was taking medication upon medication.

I suspected she had Parkinson's disease but was uncertain. Because her symptoms were not typical, I wanted to get an opinion from a neurologist before we tried medication for that. However, she firmly refused to see one.

Her prolonged inability to get out of bed had caused other problems too. One year earlier, she developed blood clots in her lungs. At that time, I had been sure she was going to die. But Mrs. Frendetti survived, demonstrating remarkable resilience for a woman her age.

She had also been hospitalized recently for heart problems that required a pacemaker. There was no denying it. She was getting worse, slowly but steadily.

"Are you still going to physical therapy?" I asked while examining her.

"No, I stopped three weeks ago. It's too tiring. By the time I get there, I can barely make it back home, let alone do the therapy. Doctor, I have pain in my leg. The same place as before. It hurts all the time."

"Right here?" I asked, touching her left ankle.

"Yes." She flinched. "It just won't let up."

"Can you touch my fingers with your left foot?" I asked, holding them about five inches above her foot.

"Not at all," she replied. Sure enough, there was no perceptible movement of her leg.

"How about the right foot?"

"I can't, Doctor," she repeated as, for maybe a second, her right foot lifted an inch or two above the bed.

"Let me see your arms." I lifted her right one. The hand was bent forward stiffly about ninety degrees at the wrist in what is called a flexion contracture. In this position it was useless. This problem was the result of still another misfortune. When someone pulled on her arm too hard, she had developed bleeding into her armpit because of blood thinners she was taking. This in turn damaged the nerves going to that arm. Despite surgery, the wrist never regained useful function.

"Try to squeeze my finger," I encouraged, putting one into her left palm. "Let's see if you can do it."

She barely grasped my finger. "I can't do it any better, Doctor. My hands shake too much. I can't even hold a spoon now."

I acknowledged her statement with a nod, then said, "You said earlier you've been coughing."

"Yes. And I can't sleep well either. The cough keeps me up. Do you think maybe I've got pneumonia, Doctor?"

"Possibly. Any fever?"

"No," interjected Mrs. Anderson, who had been listening closely.

"Here, let me listen to your heart and lungs."

With our help, Mrs. Frendetti slouched forward in bed, and I quickly listened to her chest. It was unchanged from before. We then laid her back down on the crisp, white sheets. Her legs were slightly swollen, especially the left one, and covered with varicose veins.

"What medications is she taking now?"

Mrs. Anderson pulled out the blue, spiral-bound notebook in which she carefully kept a daily record of her grandmother's health. In the back was a list of the medications. She was taking many more than I wanted her to, and I constantly tried to decrease the number. Yet, each time we stopped one, she worsened and had to resume the drug.

Throughout all these ordeals, Patty Anderson continued to attend to her grandmother. The endless hours of nursing care must have been taxing. Even at night there was no respite; she had to help Mrs. Frendetti go to the bathroom. Near the end of her fourth pregnancy, Mrs. Anderson also raised three children, maintained the house, and pursued her own interests. Still, I never heard her complain.

"Mrs. Frendetti, I think you probably have a viral bronchitis, not pneumonia. Unfortunately, not much can be done for it," I explained. "However, because of your lung disease, I think it's worth trying some antibiotics just in case a pneumonia is developing."

"Anything that'll help, I'll take," she consented.

"I still believe physical therapy is your best hope for feeling better," I continued. "You need to try it again and work on regaining your strength and mobility. People who stay in bed all the time get weak from the inactivity. Eventually, they become unable to do even the simplest of daily tasks."

"But I'm too tired to go there."

"Well, as I see it, you have two choices: either remain as you are and slowly get weaker, or try the physical therapy and see if it helps."

"But what about my tremor? I can't hold on to anything."

"We've talked about that before. I don't know anything else to do for it. I still recommend you see a neurologist."

"No, no, no. I don't want to see anyone else. Once Patty's baby comes, I just want to die and get this over with. What's the use, Doctor? There's nothing for me in life anymore. I just want to see her new baby and then go on."

I am sure I would feel the same way if I were immobilized like Mrs. Frendetti. After a lifetime of independence, being bedridden and helpless would devastate me.

"Did you hear what the doctor said, Grandma?" asked Mrs. Anderson. "I agree with him. I think you should go to therapy. I'll be glad to take you."

"That's too much work for you."

"Grandma, I've told you many times that it's no problem. I'd be glad to take you. What have you got to lose? If it works, you'll feel better and be able to do more. If it doesn't, you're no worse off than you are now."

"Oh, I don't know," said Mrs. Frendetti, feeling both hopeless and helpless. Antidepressants had done little for her depression, yet she had also refused counseling.

"Well, I'm not sure there's anything else I can do for you at this point," I told her. "It's up to you. Here's the prescription for the antibiotic. If you change your mind, just let me know and I'll arrange for physical therapy. I really do think it'll help."

"All right," she finally conceded after a pause. "I'll try it, but I don't know if I'll be able to do it. And if I'm going there, I might as well see the other doctor too."

"Great!" her granddaughter exclaimed joyfully as she grasped the elderly lady's hand. "It really helped before, and I bet it'll help again."

"One more thing," I said. "I need to draw some blood to check how the blood thinners are working. And as long as I'm getting that, I'll check a blood count too."

As she held out her left arm dutifully, a warm glow came into her eyes. "How are your little girls?" she asked.

"Wonderful," I told her.

"How old are they now?"

"Five and three."

"They grow older fast. Before you know it, they'll have children of their own," she assured me. "Do you have a picture of them?"

I showed her one from my wallet.

"They're precious," she crooned as she looked at the photograph. "Take good care of them."

"Thank you. I will," I said while leaving her room. "And I'll talk to you soon."

TWENTY-NINE

PATTY ANDERSON STOPPED ME before I left the house. "I've done everything I can think of, but nothing seems to help Grandma's depression," she confided in me. "She's so unhappy."

"I know, and I don't know what else to do at this point. She won't take antidepressants, and she refuses counseling. The fact that she lies in bed all day, doing nothing, makes it even worse. If we could only figure out how to get her interested in a hobby or something, she might feel better."

"I've tried, Doctor, believe me, I've tried. She just won't consider doing anything. She's not interested in crafts, reading, or even TV. Before, she'd at least watch that."

"Well, at least she'll go to physical therapy now. Maybe she'll even do the exercises at home. Either way, she'll be getting out of the house. That kind of stimulation has to be good for her, and hopefully it'll help pick up her spirits."

"I sure hope so."

"It must be hard for you," I said. "I'm impressed at how much time you selflessly devote to your grandma. And not only that, you still manage to have a normal family life too."

"Yes, it's hard, but I don't mind it. Grandma doesn't have anyone else to care for her. And I don't want her to go to a nursing home, especially after what happened before. She really hated it there. Remember how she was even more depressed than she is now?"

"Yes, I do," I murmured, recalling how sad Mrs. Frendetti had become during her short stay there. Physically, she had actually improved with the twice-daily therapy treatments she received, but mentally she had deteriorated. So her granddaughter had brought her back home. She had become a little more cheerful, but she had also stopped the exercises, and her physical condition degenerated again, reaching the point where it was now.

"But it seems as if you devote all your free time to your grandma. Don't you feel the need for some time for yourself?"

"I get some," she assured me. "My husband is very understanding and helpful. He often tends to Grandma so I can get away. And for two hours everyday we have a home nurse care for her. Grandma has a trust fund that covers the cost of that."

"What about your kids? How do you think this has affected them?"

"They love Grandma. She really dotes on them too. In fact, they're about all that's keeping her going. Anyway," she added, "I'll take her to the other doctor as soon as I can. Maybe he'll be able to help with her weakness. You know, if we could just get her strong enough to move around, I think she wouldn't feel so helpless."

"I agree."

"Well, thanks for coming."

"It was my pleasure," I replied. "If she gets worse or develops a fever, let me know immediately. Otherwise, why don't you call me in a couple of days and let me know how she's doing."

"I will."

I glanced at my watch. I had seven minutes before my first afternoon patient was scheduled—enough time to get to my office but not enough for lunch. Oh well, it wouldn't be the first time I missed a meal.

I arrived at the office just in time to learn that the emergency room had called. Mr. Gatto was there, quite sick. His daughter had brought him in, complaining he was depressed again. Since I had been at the Andersons' when he had taken a sudden turn for the worse, his daughter had taken him to the hospital. I went over to see him immediately.

Meanwhile, the emergency room doctor examined him. One look

at Mr. Gatto, and she knew it was more than depression. Her evaluation confirmed this—it revealed pneumonia. The physician tried to convince Judy Harding that her father was suffering from pneumonia and cancer rather than depression, but was unable to do so.

As soon as I saw Mr. Gatto, I agreed with the other physician. He might be depressed too, but that was not Mr. Gatto's main problem. He was dying. Compared with his wretched state the last time I saw him, he looked even worse. It was as if he had aged twenty years instead of five months.

"Mr. Gatto," I addressed him. There was no answer.

"Mr. Gatto?" I repeated louder.

Still no response.

"Papa's getting really depressed," his daughter spoke up. "And I don't blame him. The antidepressant pills aren't working. They just make him sleepy."

I looked at the concerned woman, then walked around the bed to her. "How are you doing?" I asked. "It must be hard for you watching him get worse."

She paused, then nodded. A tear began to roll down her cheek.

I handed her a tissue from the box next to the bed. "I know it's hard. Have you talked about it with anyone?"

"My husband. He's been real supportive."

"Good. That helps."

Another pause, then she nodded her head at her father. "What do you think's going on with him?"

"Did he have that operation to remove his testicles?"

"Yes, right after we last saw you. He felt better for about three months, but lately he's gotten bad again."

My examination confirmed the other doctor's findings, and I told Mrs. Harding so.

She looked at me a second, then blurted out, "Do you think if I had brought him to you sooner, they could have cured the cancer? I thought about doing so when he first told me about his dripping, but decided to wait instead and see if his problem would go away by itself. I feel so guilty now."

"Mrs. Harding, it's not your fault. I think the cancer had spread long before your dad came out here. Even if you had brought him the very day he arrived, it wouldn't have made a difference. There's absolutely nothing else you could have done. In fact, I'm impressed how well you've cared for him. He's been very lucky to have you."

"Thanks," she replied softly. "I feel better knowing that."

I admitted Rico Gatto to the hospital for the pneumonia. He was totally listless and did not have long to live. I treated the pneumonia with antibiotics but, in accordance with his previously expressed wishes, did not give him drugs to fight the cancer.

Fifty minutes later, I finally got back to the office. I smiled at people I knew while walking through the packed reception area. I felt a little sheepish, obviously late when they were on time for their appointments. Hoping futilely they would realize that I had been working the whole "lunch" hour, I walked into the first exam room. Mrs. Martinez was there with her oldest daughter, a seven-year-old. She looked at her watch when the door opened.

"Good afternoon, Mrs. Martinez. I'm sorry I'm late, but I had to make a house call to see a very sick woman. Thanks for waiting. What can I do for you two today?"

Her glare softened by my apologetic explanation, she began. "Megan has a runny nose. She's had it since she woke up this morning."

A runny nose for one day, I thought. How trivial compared with Mrs. Frendetti and Mr. Gatto, who were slowly dying. Runny noses are usually caused by either allergies or viruses. The former are treated with antihistamines, while the latter just need to run their courses. And this woman was upset with me for being a few minutes late because I was trying to help people who are deathly ill? Calming down, I concentrated on the problem at hand. Mrs. Martinez was very concerned about her daughter's nose, and she had every right to be. It was as important to her as Mrs. Frendetti's or Mr. Gatto's illnesses were to them and their families.

I asked the necessary questions and did the appropriate examination. It appeared Maria Martinez had a viral illness. I discussed this with her mother and, because Maria also had a sore throat, obtained a throat culture. I promised to call them back the next day with the results. The Martinezes left, seeming satisfied. I finished the day without further incident, feeling more relaxed as time wore on.

The following morning, Mrs. Frendetti saw the neurologist. Afterwards, he called me to explain that he agreed she had atypical Parkinson's disease and recommended trying some medication. I did not have long to ponder this because LeAnne handed me the lab tests on Lilly Brewer. The urine culture was normal but the blood test showed a high white count, suggesting a possible bacterial infection that needed treatment with antibiotics. I called Mrs. Brewer on the TTY only to learn that the line had been disconnected. Worrying about the baby, I decided to go to their apartment and check on her.

I looked up the address on a map. It was near the office—five minutes by car at most. As soon as I had a break in my schedule, I hopped in my car and drove straight there. It was a small duplex, on a circular cul-de-sac lined with other low-income duplexes. The street appeared deserted, perhaps the result of the hot temperatures outside. I found the address and parked alongside the curb in front of the building. The shutters were drawn, and no one seemed to be home.

I did not ring the doorbell at first, thinking no one would hear it, then realized they might have it hooked up to some type of signaling device as many deaf people do. So I pushed the button and through the front window saw a bright light flicker on and off inside the home. A minute later, the door opened to reveal Mrs. Brewer holding Lilly. When she saw who I was, she smiled and beckoned me inside.

The house was scantily furnished, and the structure itself poorly maintained. The ceiling sagged a little in the center, and in the far corner I saw a large water spot where the roof had leaked. The walls were in need of a fresh coat of paint, and one of the windowpanes was cracked. The furniture was not in any better condition: the living room contained an old sofa with a hole in one cushion, two worn chairs, and a badly scratched end table with a lamp on it.

"How is Lilly doing?" I signed.

"Much better. She slept good last night and the fever is gone now."

I did not understand half of the words but managed to get the gist of her statement. After verifying my understanding with her I added, "How about her appetite?"

"She's eating better today."

I examined the infant again. She did indeed look better. I felt comfortable the baby would do fine and no treatment was necessary. After all, doctors do not treat laboratory tests; they treat patients. And white blood counts often rise with viral infections, especially in infants.

After explaining this to Mrs. Brewer, I added, "Do you have a new phone number?"

She shook her head.

"I tried calling you on the TTY but your line was disconnected."

"We did not have the money to pay the phone bill," she explained.

I nodded. "Well, it looks like Lilly will do fine," I concluded. "If you have any questions or there are any other problems, let me know."

Two days later, Patty Anderson went into labor. The labor went fine, and I delivered the Andersons' third boy. Mrs. Anderson decided to stay in the hospital for two days, a wise choice, I thought. She needed a well-earned respite from the pressures at home. But lo and behold, that night the emergency room physician called me about Mrs. Frendetti. She had been brought in because of a seizure she had had thirty minutes earlier. I went to see her. Although I could find no reason for the seizure, I decided to admit her because of her precarious health. It was possible the new Parkinson's medication had caused the seizure. So I had Mr. Gatto, Mrs. Frendetti, and Mrs. Frendetti's granddaughter in the hospital at the same time.

Mr. Gatto did poorly. He would not eat, despite his daughter's strong encouragement, and was totally listless. The pneumonia did respond to treatment, though, and he left the hospital alive but apathetic, emaciated, and pale. I never saw him again.

Mrs. Frendetti did better. She had no more seizures and was her usual witty self. What struck me most, however, was how Patty Anderson became fully involved. Even in the hospital with a new baby, she found time for her grandmother. And she did so cheerfully. Two days later, when Mrs. Frendetti went home, Patty Anderson went with her. So she never did get the rest she deserved.

Shortly after the birth of their son, Mr. Anderson lost his job. He accepted another position in Arizona, and the family moved, taking Vera Frendetti with them. I have not seen them since. I often wonder whether Mrs. Frendetti is still alive, and if so, whether she is any better. Or perhaps she finally got her wish.

THIRTY

"BRAD IS VERY SHY," explained his mother. "It takes a while before he'll talk to people he doesn't know."

"Hi, Brad," I smiled at the youngster curled up in his mother's arms as he sized me up shyly out of the corner of his eye. "How old are you?"

There was no answer. When he saw me watching him, he looked away and stared at the floor.

"It's okay to talk to the doctor, Brad," encouraged his mother. "Tell him how old you are." He still wouldn't speak.

Brad was a short, skinny five-year-old. Light brown hair in a mop style cut hung halfway over his ears. His upper two front teeth were quite prominent, jutting out at an angle from the others. Whenever he smiled, which was rare, he looked like Bucky Beaver. He also had big hazel eyes that kept darting over to glance at me. Setting off these features was his fair skin, generously covered with freckles and slightly reddened, as if he had just come in from being outside the whole day. All in all, he looked like a typical American farm boy. Well, almost. What set him apart was the melancholy look his face conveyed, as if he had been badly hurt.

I opened the door to the cabinet where I keep toys for children. "Look, Brad," I pointed at them. "You can play with these if you want."

Suddenly, as if a warning had flashed through his mind, he backed up, cuddled resignedly in his mother's lap, and gazed at the toys.

"It's okay to play with them if you want." His mother caressed his hair gently. With this encouragement, he stood up again and walked gingerly over to the cabinet, ready to scurry back to her if need be.

As he started to play, I turned to his mother and asked, "What can I do for him?"

"We're here because Brad's had a sore throat for two days," she answered. "He was also complaining earlier this morning that his right ear hurt."

"Has he had any fever?"

"For sure."

"How high was it?"

"I don't have a thermometer," she apologized. "He's felt warm, though."

I am amazed at how many families don't have thermometers. Considering how inexpensive they are, I wish people would think ahead and buy one. It would make it easier to tell if a patient really had a fever and, if so, how high it was.

"Does he get this kind of problem often?"

"I don't know," she answered. "To tell you the truth, we just got Brad and his sister a week ago from the Department of Family Services. They was being abused by their real parents, so the state took them away and gave them to us."

"How do they seem to be doing in their new home?" I wondered out loud.

"So far, okay. And you know, I've seen a difference in him already. When we first got him, he was very withdrawn and wouldn't say anything. His sister was better; she talked to us a bit. Now Brad's starting to be more open too. He still has some problems, but he seems to be improving. We're very optimistic we can help him."

"How are your own children reacting to them?"

"Well, at first it was hard," she admitted, "but things seem better now. They're getting used to it."

Looking over my shoulder, I saw Brad playing with a truck. He seemed less tense and was wrapped up in his game. Turning back to his foster mother, I asked a few more questions about Brad's symptoms. "Has he had a runny nose, diarrhea, or vomiting?"

"No."

"Anyone else at home been sick?"

"Yes, his sister. She had the same thing a few days ago, but she's better now."

Although now more relaxed after playing with the toys, Brad still had a reserved manner about him. Unlike most kids his age, who go through all the toys quickly and often run around the examining room with them, he sat in front of the cabinet and played quietly with one or two at a time. I wondered how deep his emotional scars were from being abused. I recalled the times as a youngster when I had been ridiculed because of my speech and how it had hurt. It must have been much worse for him. Would he ever regain the boisterousness and confidence of most children? Perhaps a little magic would help. I occasionally use sleight-of-hand tricks to capture the attention of younger kids. And they are not the only ones who enjoy it—their parents do too.

"Come on up here on the table, Brad." I pointed to one side of it. "Let's see if we can find out why you're not feeling well."

He gave his foster mother a brief, frightened glance, then got up slowly and walked over to the exam table. He climbed up on it and sat there passively, shoulders hunched over, as if he were waiting to be hit or punished. I asked his foster mother to stand next to him so he would feel more secure.

"Brad, will you look in my ears first and tell me if they're okay?" I put the otoscope in my left one and let him look inside. Then we did the same with the other side. "Do they look okay?" I asked, making a worried expression with my face.

He nodded as he mumbled, "Yes."

"Whew! I'm glad to hear that. Now let's look at your ears. Am I going to find anything in there?"

"No," he replied with a little smile.

"Okay." I looked in. "You're right. Nothing in this ear. Let's look in the other one. Nothing there, either."

He looked at me with large soulful eyes. The sadness that poured out of them was immense. Again, I wondered about his past. Whatever had happened must have been awful.

I examined his neck, noting the swollen glands on both sides of his jaw. Then, skipping the throat deliberately for the moment, I asked, "Would you like to listen to your heart?"

He nodded joyously. I put the earplugs in his ears and the stethoscope on his chest. A big grin lit up his face as he listened.

"Does it sound all right?" I asked after a few seconds.

He nodded again as he listened intently to his heartbeat.

"Okay, now it's my turn." Brad was becoming more comfortable and was able to meet my gaze without difficulty. His heart and lungs sounded fine. "Hmmmm. What next. Oh yes, your tummy. Let's have you lie down."

For a second, his apprehensive self returned, and he froze, looking at his foster mother with fear.

"It's okay," she reassured him quietly. "The doctor just needs to check your stomach. It won't hurt."

He lay down hesitantly. Smiling at him while checking his abdomen, I asked, "What did you eat for lunch today?"

"Hot dogs and potato chips."

"You did!" I exclaimed. "That sure sounds tasty. And what did you drink?"

"Milk."

"Well, let's see if I can find them in your tummy. No, they're not here," I said. Brad, enjoying the game we were playing, began to giggle. "No, not here either. Ahhhh! Here they are. I feel them right here!" I pointed to the area under his belly button. Brad laughed. His foster mother did too.

"Okay, Brad. So what do you think is the problem?"

He looked at me sheepishly and shrugged his shoulders. "I don't know," he said. "All I know is that my throat hurts."

"Oh my," I held my head in my hands, as if in dismay. "I forgot to check your throat, didn't I? Do you mind if I take a look?"

He shook his head. By now Brad was at ease and even somewhat animated, although still not talkative.

I got up and grabbed hold of a light. "Okay, let's look at it."

He opened his mouth immediately and said, "Ahhhhhhhh." I barely had enough time to glance inside before he closed it. I let out a gasp and shook my head with disbelief. "So that's why. No wonder you have a sore throat. I'm surprised you haven't had more problems with it than you have. How long has that been in your throat?"

Brad looked at me, befuddled by my statements. He shrugged his shoulders, too confused to respond verbally.

"Here, open your mouth and let me look again,"

This time he did so more cautiously. I looked in and again shook my head. "Amazing. And you say you didn't put it there yourself?"

"I didn't put anything in there," Brad insisted.

Both of them looked at me as if I had suddenly gone crazy. Finally his foster mother asked, "What do you mean, Dr. Zazove? Is there something in his throat?"

I nodded. "There sure is. Here, let me see if I can get it out so you can see it."

I faced Brad. "I'll be reaching in with my fingers to remove it. It's very important that you don't bite my hand as I take it out."

At the thought of that, Brad started to giggle again.

"Okay, Brad. Are you ready?"

"Yes," he answered, then sat as still as he could with his mouth open.

"Here we go."

Using the light in my left hand and peering intently into his mouth, I started to reach in with my right one. Then I jerked it out and asked, "You're sure you're not going to bite me?"

Laughing, he promised, "I won't."

"Okay, I believe you. Then let's get it out." My fingers reached in again. After a few seconds of moving them around, I declared with excitement, "I got it!" and slowly pulled out a magic red sponge ball. With a satisfied expression, I showed it to them.

Brad sat with his jaw open and his eyes wide with disbelief. He, of course, had never even seen the ball before, let alone known where it came from.

After a few seconds of silence, his foster mother burst out laughing. I'm not sure which amused her more—the expression on Brad's face or the surprise of the magic itself.

"I didn't put that in my mouth," Brad finally insisted. "I didn't."

Holding the ball out for Brad to see, I said, "Well, however it got there, it's a real ball. Here, feel it and see for yourself." He took the ball and, after squeezing it, looked at his foster mother. "I don't know how it happened. I don't remember putting it there."

"Does your throat feel better now?" I asked him.

He nodded.

"Good. It should continue to improve over the next few days."

When his foster mother finally stopped laughing, I explained to her that Brad probably had a viral infection. There wasn't a treatment for it; it would just have to run its course. However, since there was a small chance it was strep throat, and because at Brad's age that could potentially evolve into rheumatic fever, I recommended we do a throat culture. She agreed. Brad, meanwhile, was so engrossed in the ball that he didn't hear my explanation.

After the culture was done, Brad and his foster mother left the room to go home. Brad still had an astonished look on his face and walked out reverently. Even so, he was more talkative than when he first came to the office. He showed the receptionist and nurse the ball. "Look what the doctor found in my throat. No wonder it hurt. I feel so much better now."

Right before he left the office, I told him it was just a magic trick. "Since it's my magic ball, may I keep it, Brad? It will help me remember you."

Smiling, he handed it over with awe.

That evening, before going home, I stopped at the store to pick up some groceries. As I walked by the snack bar, I saw Mrs. Conn sitting at a table with another woman, talking as they smoked cigarettes and drank coffee. I tried to sneak by without being seen, but Mrs. Conn spotted me.

"Dr. Zazove," she called, waving at me.

"Oh, Mrs. Conn. Nice to see you tonight." I smiled at her before turning down an aisle in the opposite direction. Thirty seconds later, while I was reaching for a jar of peanut butter, I felt a tap on my shoulder. I turned to see Mrs. Conn standing next to me.

"I called you back there, Doctor, but you didn't hear me. I'd like to introduce you to my friend. Come with me and meet her."

As we walked back down the aisle, Mrs. Conn spoke. "I've been telling her all about you, Doctor, and what a good doctor you are. There aren't many doctors around who understand us old people, you know." She winked at me before continuing. "We have a lot of concerns younger people don't. And Gertrude needs someone who can help her. You see. . . . Oh, Gertrude," she called as we approached the snack bar, "this is Dr. Zazove, the young doctor I've been telling you about. Doctor, this is Gertrude Spinnaker."

"How do you do, Mrs. Spinnaker."

Before she could answer, Mrs. Conn interrupted. "I was telling the doctor about you, Gertrude. You see, Doctor, she's been having some heart problems. You know, it skips a few beats here and there. And she's worried about it. I don't blame her. I would be too. At least it hasn't been giving her any pain. Now, she does have a doctor who's been treating her for her heart, but his office is way on the other side of town, up in the Heights. That's such a long way to drive, especially in the winter. Don't you think so?"

Without waiting for my answer, she continued. "I've told her what good care you take of me. And you're so much closer. You know how we old folks don't like to drive far, especially in winter. Oh yes, she's also having some female problems that have been hurting her. She'll need some pain pills for that. Gertrude, while the doctor is here, why don't you tell him about the bleeding you've been having," she crowed in the midst of all the people in the snack bar. "Don't forget to tell him how it soaked through your clothes. And also, as long as he's here . . ."

About five minutes later, I was finally able to excuse myself and get the groceries. I used the checkout counter on the other side of the store to avoid having to walk past Mrs. Conn again.

Over the next few months, I saw Brad several times. From all indications, he appeared to be flourishing in his new home. During the office visits, he acted more and more relaxed because of the rapport

I had established with him. In fact, he was downright boisterous at times. Each time, he asked to see the ball and would examine it carefully, wondering out loud how it had gotten into his throat and hoping I would find more. I did look several times but never found one again.

A few months later, his foster mother came to the office to see me about a medical problem of her own. After we were done, I asked about Brad.

"He's not with us anymore."

I was stunned, as much as Brad had been with the sponge ball. "What happened?"

"Well, it became too much of a problem with our real children," she explained. "Brad had such a history of neglect that he demanded constant attention for himself. It was like he was trying to make up for lost time. He got into a lot of fights too. After a while, it seemed like there was constantly one problem after another. It was really a hard decision because we were getting attached to him and his sister. Finally, however, my husband and I decided that our own children were more important. There just didn't seem to be an end to the continual commotion. So we sent Brad and his sister back."

THIRTY-ONE

I AM PERIODICALLY ASKED to speak at gatherings about what it is like to be a person with a profound hearing loss. Once, I was part of an assembly to an elementary school trying to explain what it's like to be deaf in a hearing world. The meeting had been organized by a special group of children whose classroom was based at the school. Most of them were totally deaf; the few who weren't were almost so.

These children performed several short silent skits illustrating some of the problems faced by people who are deaf. One in particular especially appealed to me. It was about a deaf child in a classroom, busy reading in the front row. The bell rang, and everyone else left. The child, who could not hear the bell, continued reading a while before she looked up and found herself alone. She checked her watch, shrugged her shoulders, and left.

Although my hearing loss is not total, the children's portrayals were familiar. Not hearing bells is a typical example of the barriers faced by people who are deaf. The only time I ever hear a bell is when a loud one rings right next to my ear. Still, people who are deaf have to deal with bells all the time, for they play a large role in our society. It's not until one stops and thinks a minute that this becomes apparent; school bells, doorbells, telephone bells, church bells, all kinds of bells are essential to our life. So, like other people who are deaf and hard of hearing, I have had to compensate in various ways. For instance, my telephone has the previously described special low-frequency buzzers. And for the doorbell, I have my trusty dogs. They never fail to let me know when someone's there.

Numerous other types of assistive devices are available. A popularly used one is flashing lights. These can be connected to almost anything electrical. Thus, they can be used to alert a person with a profound hearing loss that the doorbell, telephone, fire alarm, or even alarm clock has gone off. Hearing people are often surprised to learn that flashing lights are as effective in waking up deaf people as audible buzzers are for hearing people.

Even when I do hear sounds I often don't understand them. TV is a good case in point. I rarely know what the conversation is about, no matter what type of show is on. Only when the camera is focused on the speaker's face, such as during the news, do I have a chance of understanding what someone is saying. Fortunately, many programs, including some of the better ones, are now closed-captioned. With this technology, the words that are being said by the actor or newscaster appear, one sentence at a time, on the bottom of the screen. With my closed-captioned decoder, I am able to get as much out of these shows as people who hear.

Sometimes, closed-captions are helpful even for hearing people. A perfect example was when "Shogun" was shown as a TV miniseries. On that show there were many Japanese phrases, some of which were hard for non-Japanese speakers to understand. On our TV, however, these phrases were printed as part of the dialogue, enabling both Barbara and myself to easily understand them. When Barbara watched one of the episodes at a friend's house one evening (I was on call), she and her friend had a hard time understanding the Japanese words. That was the first time she realized how much the captions helped. More and more video rentals are now also closed-captioned, allowing me to enjoy movies as well.

Seeing movies in the theater has traditionally been a problem for me. Except for subtitled films, I have missed almost all the conversation and have not enjoyed them very much over the years. The recent passage of the Americans with Disabilities Act (ADA), however, will change things. The law requires that cinemas make assistive listening devices available for people who need them. Several types of closed-circuit amplification systems can be used by persons with hearing losses to enhance their perception of sound in the theater. One way is to wear headphones connected to a transmitter that interacts with a central device broadcasting the words. A volume control allows the intensity of the sound to be adjusted to the person's needs. Recently, I tried this and, although I still missed the vast majority of the conversation, I understood more than I otherwise would have.

The ADA will benefit people with a hearing loss in other ways, too. For example, hotels and motels will now make available amplified phones and closed-captioned televisions. It will also ensure the viability of telephone relay systems. These enable conversations to occur between a hearing person who does not have a TTY and another person who can only use a TTY. Either party calls an 800-number. Then a trained operator with a TTY acts as an intermediary between the two parties. She reads the TTY message from the deaf person word for word out loud to the hearing person, and likewise transmits via the TTY to the deaf person every word the hearing person said.

Radio is a different story. Voices on it are usually just a jumble of noises to me. There is one exception, however. When the news is on, especially if a man is speaking and the volume is loud enough, I can sometimes understand some of what is being said. Otherwise, the radio is useful only for listening to the rhythm of music. I can appreciate this pretty well, although I rarely hear individual notes and I never understand the lyrics.

Records, tapes, and CD players present the same problems as the radio. Nevertheless, I enjoy music. I recognize some tunes and even play the piano. What's more, for the low-pitched notes within my hearing range, I happen to have perfect pitch. Still, it's harder for me to play the piano than other people because I don't hear many of the notes and often cannot tell when I play a wrong one. But I don't think I have found it more frustrating than other people. As with everyone, the pieces usually sound pretty good with a little practice. Higher-pitched instruments such as the piccolo, however, are beyond the range of my hearing. In fact, someone playing such an instrument seems very strange. I see the person moving his or her fingers and blowing into the mouthpiece, yet it seems to me that nothing else is happening.

I feel fortunate to have the little hearing I do. This has allowed me to appreciate some of the hearing world. But in other ways, it's made life more difficult. Because I am part of mainstream America, people often expect me to understand more than I do, especially in group conversations. And when I don't—and I often don't—they occasionally get upset. Numerous experts and people who work with deaf and hard of hearing individuals have stated that being hard of hearing is in many ways more difficult than being totally deaf. For the most part, people who are totally deaf use only sign and become part of the Deaf community. People who are hard of hearing, however, are caught in between. They are not really part of the Deaf community (especially if they don't sign), yet they often have problems integrating with the hearing world. It is a Catch-22. Despite this, however, I feel like I have succeeded in being part of the American mainstream.

THIRTY-TWO

"MAY I HELP YOU?" Carma asked as the patient approached the counter.

"Well, yes," the woman murmured as she glanced around the office. "My name is Wendy Downing. I have an appointment tomorrow with Dr. Zazove, but am thinking of not keeping it. I mean, I just don't know if he'll understand my situation."

"What's the problem?"

"Well, it's kind of complicated, and I just don't know what to do." She shook her head and inspected her shoes nervously. Looking back up, she suddenly asked, "Is Dr. Zazove open-minded?"

"I'm not quite sure what you mean," Carma replied. "Is there something in particular you'd like to know?"

Ms. Downing fidgeted in front of the counter, trying to decide whether to pursue the matter. Fortunately, no one else was around. Finally, she spoke quietly. "Well, I feel like I can talk to you, but I want you to keep this confidential."

"Absolutely. I won't tell a soul."

"Well, ummm. . . . Okay, ummm. . . . Well . . . I'm pregnant."

"Congratulations, Ms. Downing."

"Well, but you don't understand. I'm . . . well . . . okay, I'm gay," she blurted, watching closely for Carma's reaction.

"That's okay," was the immediate response. "The doctors in this office do their best for everybody. They don't let things like that affect how they care for people. I guarantee you that won't be a problem."

"Oh, good," sighed Wendy Downing. "I feel so much better

about seeing him. I'll be here tomorrow then." She started to walk out, then stopped and turned around. "Well, but are you really sure he won't mind taking care of me and my pregnancy?"

"I'm positive. He'd be honored to do so."

"Well, would you kind of warn him about this so he knows and I won't have to tell him? That way, if he doesn't want to see me, just call and let me know."

"I'll be glad to," Carma agreed.

"That sounded interesting. What was that all about?" asked Mrs. Conn, who had walked in the office at the end of the conversation.

"Mrs. Conn, how nice to see you." Looking at the schedule, Carma continued, "You don't have an appointment today. Is there some way we can help you?"

"Yes. I need to have the doctor refill my prescription. Now, I know he's a very busy man, so you can tell him that he doesn't have to take any time to see me. Just have him write out a prescription for meprobamate. Here, let me spell that out for you, m-e-p-r-o-b-a-m-a-t-e. Did you get that?" When Carma nodded, she added, "Are you sure? I'll be glad to spell it out again if you want me to."

"I have it, Mrs. Conn."

"Good. Now you see, I only need a few pills. Fifteen should be more than enough. And tell the doctor if he wants to, he doesn't even have to write it out. He can just call it in to Valley Pharmacy. That way they'll have it ready for me when I get there."

The elderly lady then snuggled up to the counter, leaned over, and whispered, "You can trust me. I won't tell anyone. What was that lady talking to you about?"

"I'm sorry, Mrs. Conn. That's confidential. Now if you'll just have a seat and wait a minute or two, I'll see what Dr. Zazove says about the prescription you want."

And that's how I found out about Wendy Downing. Her partner, whom I had seen a few months earlier for a cough, had referred her to me. I was curious to meet her because of the unusual circumstances. The dynamics of it might be interesting. However, if I had known then just how interesting, I would not have been so eager.

Wendy Downing came on time for her appointment. She was in her late twenties, of medium height but slightly heavy, with dark features suggesting an eastern Mediterranean ancestry. There was a quiet demeanor about her, which seemed to be complemented by her tasteful clothes and short hair. At first she seemed embarrassed and avoided eye contact. Gradually, as we talked, she relaxed and spoke more freely. Soon she began to look at me.

"Is this your first baby?" I inquired.

"Oh, no," she shook her head emphatically. "My third."

"Did you have any problems with the others?"

"No, everything went fine. I had both my boys naturally."

"Were all three pregnancies by the same father?"

"Well, no," she answered. "My husband died two years ago from leukemia when he was only twenty-eight. My two boys are his, but this one is by a different man."

"Are you married to the father of this baby?"

She let out a short gasp, seemingly startled by my question, then gazed at me with wide-open eyes. Snapping out of it, she stuttered, "Well, no. I'm living with another one of your patients, Lorna Blank." As she plunged into the details, her speech became more fluid. "You see, after my husband died, I began to realize I was attracted to women. At first I was very upset with myself, thinking there was something wrong with me. But as time passed, I came to grips with the fact that I really am gay. I don't see anything wrong with that. I loved my husband and all that, but he couldn't satisfy me like a woman can. Soon I met Lorna, and we fell in love. She moved in with me about a year ago, and we've been together ever since."

"I see," I acknowledged her confidence quietly. "So the two of you will raise the baby?"

"Well, yes, we wanted to raise a girl. Because we only have my two boys, we needed another child. Since Lorna's never been pregnant and I have, we decided it would be easier if I were the one to have the baby."

"I understand all that, Ms. Downing, but you must know there's at least a fifty-fifty chance you'll have a boy. In fact, statistics show that more boys are born than girls."

"Well, we've arranged things to make sure it'll be a girl. We consulted the horoscope and found out that the first week of March was the best time for me to get pregnant in order to have a girl. We also wanted the baby to look and be as much like Lorna as possible. Since her brother is the spitting image of her, we decided to have him get me pregnant. So the first weekend in March, I flew to California where he lives, and spent the weekend with him."

"Sounds like he knew about your plans."

"Well, yes, he did. At first he was quite cooperative too. But by the time I left, there was a problem. He was falling in love with me and wanted to continue seeing me. Well, he's a nice guy and all that, but I don't want to spend the rest of my life with him. I'm happy with Lorna. Besides, she made me promise before I went that I wouldn't enjoy sex with him.

"Then he threatened to tell their parents that Lorna is gay if I got pregnant. So we haven't told him yet, even though we've known for two weeks."

I was surprised by the complexity of the story but, at the same time, found myself intrigued. No wonder she had had that conversation with Carma. I obtained the rest of the pertinent history for her pregnancy. There were no further surprises.

While I examined her, I asked, "How do your parents feel about your pregnancy, or do they know about it yet?"

"Well, they don't, and it's going to be a real problem when they find out. I don't know what I'll do about that. You see, they just found out I'm gay three months ago. They're very upset about that and are furious I'm living with Lorna. In fact, my dad's threatened to separate us. Unfortunately, he might be capable of doing that."

"Really?" I said, stopping my exam. "Why do you think so?"

"Now this is a secret," she stated. "Promise you won't tell anyone?"

"I promise."

"I've never known for sure, but I've always thought he was involved in some sort of underworld activity. Seeing how upset he is about my being gay, I'm afraid what he'd do if he found out I got pregnant by Lorna's brother. That might be too much for him, so we aren't going to tell him how I got pregnant."

I was no longer intrigued. Instead, second thoughts about caring for Ms. Downing began to rise. I had visions of being embroiled in a violent family dispute merely because I happened to be the doctor delivering the baby. I didn't want people threatening me or my family, or even trying to coerce me to kill Wendy's baby.

"What are you going to do?"

She shook her head ruefully. "Well, I don't know yet. At least for now we're not going to tell him I'm pregnant."

I changed the subject as I examined her abdomen. "What about your other children, your boys? Do you think there'll be any problem with them growing up in a family with two women as parents?"

"Well, I don't think so. Lorna really cares for them too. We're going to raise them as normal boys."

I finished my evaluation with a pelvic exam. It confirmed she was about eight weeks pregnant, consistent with the fact that her last period was two months earlier.

We discussed prenatal care, good nutrition, avoiding alcohol and smoking, and other factors that may affect pregnancy. Because of her family's objections, Ms. Downing might well need more moral support than most prenatal patients. I asked her to follow up in one month but to feel free to call me anytime if any problems arose.

The faint smell of cows scented the brisk breeze. The cool evening air felt good on my sweating skin as I jogged with my neighbor in the open country. Above us a hawk was floating lazily in the sky, around us were farm animals, and wherever there was water, we also saw migrating ducks.

The road made a sharp turn right, toward the Wasatch front. We crossed a stream and noticed that the spring runoff from the melting mountain snows had caused the water level to rise. Just north of the bridge the stream passed over a short drop-off. Although not a true waterfall, it was enough of a plunge to generate a low-pitched roar as water cascaded over. I turned my gaze eastward to the mountains. The haze shrouding their bases gave them an eerie appearance. The peaks were still white, but the snow line had begun to recede.

The sights, smells, and even occasional sounds were helping crystallize my thoughts. Often, while running, I'm able to sort through difficult subjects and make decisions I have agonized over for days. Today was no exception. My mind had been dwelling on Wendy Downing. I had been debating whether to continue being her doctor. If there was a risk of violence being involved, I did not want to. At this point, however, I really had no idea how realistic my fears might be. She had even stated that she herself was not sure about her father. In a way it was a fascinating situation. What would happen, and how would she deal with it?

In the past, I have occasionally had to terminate care with patients, but never for this type of reason. Usually, the need to do so had been much clearer. The first person I ever released from my practice had been stealing our office supplies, including calculators and other small machines. Another patient had been continually verbally abusive to my employees. But Ms. Downing's situation was different, one I had never even dreamed of facing. I pondered the circumstances a while before finally opting to wait a little longer before making a final decision. By then, I hoped, the answer would be more obvious. If at any time, however, I became more uncomfortable, I would ask her to find another doctor.

I felt a tap on my shoulder and looked at my friend Peter. He gestured behind us at a car coming down the road. We stepped off the pavement until the car passed. Usually I do not hear cars until they are next to me, so if I am running alone on a street, I have to keep checking behind me. That's one advantage to jogging with friends. On the other hand, however, I have to try to watch the road ahead and someone's lips at the same time. It's a miracle I have never hurt myself doing this.

I turned my attention to the hill ahead of us. We were near the end of our run, and this was the last hill left. Suddenly we ran into the pungent smell from a skunk. Whew! It tainted the air most of the way up the slope. I felt sorry for the poor animal that received the brunt of the skunk's wrath and was glad it had not been me.

One month later, Wendy Downing showed up for her scheduled prenatal visit. "How's everything going?" I greeted her as I walked into the room.

"Well, I feel fine."

"Let's see." I looked at her chart. "You've gained two pounds, your blood pressure is fine, and your urine's okay. Good." I then examined her abdomen. "I can't feel your uterus yet, but you look like you're starting to get bigger."

"Well, yes." She frowned slightly. "I am. I'm beginning to feel fat. My pants are getting tight. I'm about ready to start using my maternity clothes."

"Let's see if we can hear the baby's heartbeat today."

Despite listening with the microphone for five minutes, I couldn't. "We can't hear it yet, but you're only twelve weeks pregnant now. We often don't hear the baby until it's fourteen weeks old. So why don't you come back then; we should be able to hear it at that time. Otherwise, everything seems fine. Any questions?"

When she didn't have any, I asked one of my own, "Have you told your parents yet?"

"No. I haven't even talked to them since I was last here. They're so mad about Lorna they're ignoring me. And I'm afraid to call them myself."

"What about Lorna's brother? Have you heard from him?"

"Oh, he calls once in a while, but we haven't told him either."

"I'm sure they'll all find out eventually."

"Well, I know, but I'm still too scared to tell them now."

"That's up to you. If there aren't any questions, then I'll see you in a couple of weeks."

Two weeks later, when she returned, she voiced some concerns.

"You know, Doctor, I feel funny. I just don't feel as pregnant as I did before. Actually, I feel weird."

"What do you mean by that?"

"Well, my breasts aren't tender like they were before. Also, I don't have to go to the bathroom all the time anymore. Before, I couldn't pass one without having to stop and use it. Now I only go a few times a day. And I used to always be hungry, although I couldn't eat much at one time. Now I rarely get hungry at all."

I examined her and still could not feel the uterus in the abdomen. This was disturbing. By now it should have been partway to her navel. I then listened for the baby's heartbeat—it was still not audible. Something was wrong.

I did a pelvic exam to determine how big her uterus really was. Perhaps it was tilted backward and had not grown up into the abdomen yet. But that was not the answer. The uterus was small, much more so than it should have been. That meant one of two things: either Wendy Downing was due later than we thought or her baby had died. Because of the change in her symptoms, I suspected the latter.

We discussed my findings, and I recommended an ultrasound. Ms. Downing readily agreed. It was done later that day and confirmed my fears—the baby was dead. Furthermore, its remains were still in the uterus.

I met Ms. Downing at the hospital to discuss the results. I began with the facts, watching her reactions closely. "The ultrasound shows that the baby has died. It appears this happened recently because your uterus is now ten-weeks size instead of the fourteen weeks it should be."

"Well, I was afraid of that," she stated almost matter-of-factly. Strangely enough, she didn't seem very upset. I would have expected more grief, considering the extensive arrangements she had undertaken to get pregnant.

"It's very common for miscarriages to occur in the first three months of pregnancy," I continued. "In fact, some reports suggest one of four pregnancies ends in a miscarriage. When studies are done on these fetuses, most are found to be abnormal, so it's felt that somehow the body knows the baby is not normal and aborts it. In other words, it's nature's way of minimizing abnormal births.

"It's nothing you did wrong. Nothing you ate or didn't do that you should have. It's just one of those things that happen. After we finish taking care of this, there's no reason you can't get pregnant again if you wish to."

She said something, but I couldn't read her lips because she had moved into the glare from the window. I moved too, to where the light no longer blinded me, and asked her to repeat herself.

"Well, I already told Lorna that if I didn't get pregnant when I went to California, I wouldn't try again. I'm too old for this stuff and don't want to go through it again. Besides, this takes all the pressure off with my family. And I won't have to worry about Lorna's brother either. I was really starting to worry about what I had gotten myself into."

Me too, I thought to myself, also relieved as far as her father was concerned.

"That's up to you. But first we need to decide what to do about the dead baby inside you, which is called a 'missed abortion'. Usually, the tissue is gradually absorbed until it's all gone. Sometimes, however, life-threatening complications occur. Because of this possibility, some doctors do an operation called a D and C. But since that has its own risks, such as putting a hole through the uterus, other doctors don't like to operate. As you can see, there's a difference of opinion on how best to treat this."

After pausing to let her absorb all this information, I added, "I tend to favor the approach where we follow you closely and not do any surgery. However, I'd like to discuss it with my partners first to see how they feel."

"Well, okay, but please don't tell them how I got pregnant and all that. I don't know if they'd understand."

"Don't worry. That part is strictly confidential."

Relieved, she sighed long and low. "You know, I'm sure glad I'm done having babies. I'll never go through this again."

I reviewed the situation with both Connie and Doug. They agreed with my approach. I then told Ms. Downing about our consensus.

"Great. I'm happy you want to do it that way," she said. "I really don't want an operation unless I absolutely need it."

The thermometer read ninety-eight degrees. Although still officially spring, it felt like a typical Utah summer day. Only the lack of humidity made the heat bearable. Thankful for the air-conditioning that kept my office cool, I walked into one of the exam rooms to see my next patient, and was surprised to see the Reed family sitting there. Mr. and Mrs. Reed looked the same as before. Eric was perched on the edge of the exam table, also as before. What a change there was in him, however! He had gained weight and grown taller. Even his complexion appeared healthier. He no longer looked feeble but appeared like a normal boy now. But the most dramatic change of all was that he was in complete control of himself. His chorea was gone.

"We thought we'd come up here for a checkup," his dad said. "We were so happy with the care you gave Eric before that we wanted you to see how well he's doing and make sure he's okay."

"I'm glad you did. I had often wondered what happened to him," I paused as I looked him over. "You know, I can't believe how much better you look, Eric. One would never know now how sick you were a year ago. You look like a totally different boy."

"Isn't it something," his mom commented.

"He plays with the other kids now," his father exulted. "They don't make fun of him no more. He eats like a horse and is full of energy."

"Wonderful!" I replied. "Is he still taking the penicillin?"

"Yes, one every day."

Eric's exam was completely normal. Not even a heart murmur remained of his previous illness.

"It seems like he's totally recovered from the rheumatic fever," I informed them.

"We thought so too," his mother concurred.

"However, since he'll always be at risk for having another infection of his heart valves, I'd recommend he keep taking the penicillin. He needs to increase the dose to four times a day if he gets a sore throat, if he has an operation or dental work, or if he has any injuries that break the skin. That should reduce the chances of any further heart problems from occurring."

"That's what we thought too," his mother repeated, satisfied with everything.

The following week, Wendy Downing came in to be rechecked. Not only had her uterus gotten smaller, but her symptoms of pregnancy had also disappeared. She felt good. And two weeks later, her uterus was back to its normal size. At no time were there any complications.

"I don't think you'll need to come back again for this unless you have further problems," I told her. "It looks like everything has returned to normal."

"Great," she laughed, carefree and with more zest than I had ever seen her show before. "I'm glad it's all over. You know, I'm not sure I really wanted to go through with it anyway. Now I don't have to worry about it anymore. And the best thing of all," she added, "is that I don't have to worry about birth control either!"

True to her word, she never got pregnant again. Not only that, she and Lorna separated within one year. I guess it really was for the best that she never had the baby. Was it possible that the stars did play a role after all?

I have since seen Wendy Downing and her boys for various commonplace problems. But she has never mentioned her pregnancy again.

THIRTY-THREE

"THERE ARE TWO THINGS I like about being a small-town family doctor," Dr. Oldenburg explained to me. "First, you get to know your patients quite well. After all, they're your neighbors, and in my town, everyone knows each other. It's much more fun dealing with friends too. There's nothing like delivering babies, watching them grow up, and then delivering their babies.

"Second, the variety is wonderful. I never know what's going to walk in the door next. Just when I think I've seen it all, something new comes along. Of course, being the only doctor in the county, I have to take care of everything that comes in. But that sure makes it more interesting too."

"Don't you get scared sometimes?" I wondered. "For instance, what do you do when you face an emergency for which you haven't had the training or your hospital doesn't have the equipment?"

"I just do the best I can. What else can I do? It would be nice to have other specialists nearby to help out, but I don't. I've come to realize, though, that if I use common sense along with the extensive training we've all had, I can handle most things. At least I can stabilize someone until he can be transferred." He leaned back and continued, "I remember once I had a patient who ruptured her spleen in a car wreck. In that case, there wasn't enough time to send her to a surgeon. By the time we made the arrangements and flew her there, she would've died. So I discussed the situation on the phone with the surgeon, then took the patient to the operating room and removed the spleen, following his instructions and with a surgery book in front of me. She did fine."

"I would've been petrified."

"I was too. But I had no choice. By remaining calm and thinking the situation through, I can usually come to a satisfactory conclusion. Sure, I've made my share of mistakes, but we all do. I'm human and can only do my best."

We were at a picnic sponsored by the University of Utah family practice department. Dr. Oldenburg and I had sat next to each other at one of the tables and were talking about our lives as doctors. Gradually, our conversation had focused on life as a family doctor in an isolated town.

"I once had a doctor from Texas spend six months with me to see what life as a small-town doctor was like. At that time, I was writing a book and needed some free time, so I turned my entire practice over to him except for every other weekend, when I covered him so he could get some time off. I told him not to call me for anything unless he absolutely couldn't handle it. That way he could get a feel for what it's really like.

"One morning I was home writing when I got a frantic call from the hospital. He wanted me there immediately. So I put down my pen and drove over. I found him with a woman who had just delivered a baby. And there was her uterus hanging out, turned completely inside out."

"A uterine prolapse!" I exclaimed. "I've never seen one."

"Neither had I. But there we were. She was bleeding heavily, and something had to be done."

"What did you do?" I asked.

"Well, I looked at her and thought about it. I figured the most sensible way would be to push it back in the way it came out. So we tried that and it worked. She did fine too."

I pondered this story. "You know, even though my practice isn't as isolated as yours, I've had my share of interesting experiences, too."

"If you're in family practice, you're bound to have them," Dr. Oldenburg stated. "I've done it for thirty-four years and have never regretted my choice."

Later that day, I told Barbara some of Dr. Oldenburg's stories.

We both admire people with the fortitude to practice in remote areas. We too handle most problems by ourselves, but feel safer having other specialist backup nearby.

Being a board-certified family physician does not imply one is capable of treating all medical problems. By no means. It does imply, however, that the doctor is familiar with all fields of medicine and can handle at least ninety percent of problems he or she sees. Even in cases where a patient is referred, family doctors know how to initiate the correct treatment until the other specialist can be seen. Family physicians also have extensive training in managing stress-related illnesses like depression, headaches, and stomachaches. Since these are among the most common problems seen by all doctors, we are specially qualified to handle them.

The day after the picnic, the office was busier than usual. It was one of our "emergency room" days, when it seems like every patient is an injured one. One after another, they came in, suffering from lacerations, bruises, and broken bones. We were running constantly, taking X rays, sewing cuts, and putting on casts. A concurrent flu-like epidemic was also going on, and we saw several people with this illness. Finally, only one patient remained—a new one. I glanced at my watch. It was just before eight. Despite having been so busy, we had managed to stay on schedule.

Picking up the chart, I noted the patient's name—Steven Buttrick. LeAnne's note read: complains of dizziness, fever, sweats, and muscle aches.

"Another case of the flu," I thought and walked into the room.

"Mr. Buttrick, I'm Dr. Zazove. I don't think we've met before, but I do believe I know your wife and daughter."

"Yes, you do. In fact, it was my wife who sent me here because she thought this has been going on too long. She wanted me to get it taken care of."

"Tell me about it." I sat on my stool to listen.

"Two weeks ago I went on a business trip to California. I felt just fine when I got to my hotel. It was late, so I went right to sleep. The next morning I was shaving, getting ready for my meeting, when all of a sudden I felt really dizzy and started sweating. Before

I knew what happened, I passed out. Or at least I think I did—I found myself on the floor. I must've hit the table behind me because I got this bump on the back of my head." He pointed at it, then resumed his story.

"I went to the emergency room, where they checked me out and told me I was okay, not to worry about it. And the next day I did feel better. Two days later it hit me again, exactly the same way. So I came straight back home. Since I've been back, the darn thing keeps recurring every couple of days. I get a severe headache, can't stop shaking with fever, and ache all over. It gets so bad I'm totally wiped out and can't do anything while it lasts. I just lay in bed until it passes."

"Are the fevers high?"

"They sure are, Doc. The last time, my wife checked it with a thermometer. She said it was 103."

"How long do they last?"

"Oh, about four to six hours. The day after I feel okay. But then it happens again the next day. Now I'm starting to feel tired all the time, even when I don't have the fevers. I don't seem to completely recover before it hits me again. My wife's worried I have Rocky Mountain spotted fever."

"That's possible, Mr. Buttrick, but if you had that, you'd be a lot sicker by now, if not dead." This was starting to sound quite interesting. It sure did not sound like the flu I had been seeing all day. The spiking fevers made me think of malaria but, despite being the most common infectious disease in the world, malaria is unusual in the United States.

I wondered where he could have acquired it. "Have you done any traveling outside the country the past few months?"

"No."

"Have you been bitten by any insects, such as mosquitoes or ticks?"

"Now that you mention it, yes. I went camping three or four weeks ago in Moab, near Arches National Park. While there, I found a tick on me. It wasn't like the usual ticks I've seen before. This one was quite soft; you could squeeze it easily. I felt another one crawl up my leg but couldn't find it. I was bitten by a few mosquitoes too, but no more than usual."

It was getting more interesting all the time. "Did you do any hunting or skin any animals, like rabbits?"

Suddenly, as fast as Mr. Buttrick could answer no, he began to sweat profusely. I've never seen anyone sweat so quickly. Within minutes, rivers were running down his cheeks, dripping off his chin, drenching his clothes, and falling on the floor. He looked as if someone had just poured a bucket of water over him. "I'm getting another one of those attacks," he volunteered weakly as he lay down. "I feel dizzy and nauseated."

I stood by his side, watching him as I checked his blood pressure. It was normal. Then he began to have teeth-chattering shakes, called rigors by doctors. It had all happened so fast. He had gone from looking merely a little tired to being pale, sweaty, and extremely sick. I touched his skin. It felt warm and wet, as if he had just gotten out of a hot tub. Just as I was deciding to transfer him to the hospital, the rigors stopped. He began to look better too, so I quickly finished my history. The only other clue it provided was that he'd lost seven pounds since his illness had begun.

"How are you feeling now?"

He nodded slightly. "The dizziness isn't as bad as it was a minute ago."

Grunting, with a lot of effort, he raised himself to a partially sitting position, wavering slightly for a few seconds. Supporting himself on his elbows, he noted, "The attacks come and go for about four to six hours. Then I'm better for a day or so before they come back again. And each time, they seem to get worse."

I examined him, then checked his urine and the red blood count. All were normal. Just as I finished, the dizziness recurred, and he lay back on the table. Soon sweat began to pour out again.

I rechecked his temperature: 103.6. With the cyclical fever every thirty-six to forty-eight hours, I suspected malaria even more, although I had no idea how he would have gotten it. Malaria is transmitted by a mosquito that is not indigenous to Utah or California.

Still, it seemed like a real possibility. And we needed to check him for all the possibilities. He had been sick long enough.

Wheeling my stool to the exam table, I sat down again and began to discuss my assessment of his illness. "Mr. Buttrick, I'm not exactly sure what your problem is, but I'm very concerned. You're a sick man, and you seem to be getting sicker. Something is causing the fevers, sweating, weakness, and weight loss, and we need to find out what it is. Now, that'll require doing several tests. It may cost more to do them all at once, but in the long run I feel you'd be better off because the sooner we find the cause, the sooner we can start treating you."

I paused a moment, watching the pale, thin man lying quietly in his soaked clothes, probably feeling desperate in his weakened condition. "Now we have another decision to make. Because you've been slowly getting worse, I think you'd do best in the hospital. However, if you want to go home and your family can help you, I'm willing to try it that way. It's up to you."

"If at all possible, I'd like to go home," he declared without any hesitation. "I don't like hospitals and don't want to go there unless I absolutely have to. My wife can help me in any way necessary."

"Fine. Then we'll try it that way. But if you get worse, we'll have no choice but to put you in. Even if it's two in the morning, if you're worse, call me. Okay?"

He agreed.

"Good. Let's start by running some blood tests. Depending on how they turn out, we'll decide what our next step will be. In the meantime, we should touch base tomorrow to see how you're doing."

"Whatever it takes to get to the bottom of this," he agreed as he rolled onto his left side and got up slowly.

After LeAnne got the specimens, Mr. Buttrick stood up to leave, then sat down again. "Hey, Doc, aren't you gonna give me something for this?"

"I'd love to, but I don't know what to give you until we find out what the cause is. Most of the test results should be back tomorrow, and I'm hoping they'll give us an idea of what's going on. I'll call you as soon as we have them. Remember, though, if you get worse before then, call me immediately.

"Okay, Doc. And thanks," he said as he stood up, wobbly. After pausing to get his balance, he walked slowly out the room. His wife came up to him immediately, grabbed his arm, and helped him out to their car.

"Whew," I thought as I walked back to my desk. "This is going to be a tough one to figure out." I wondered if he did indeed have malaria. If so, from where? The mosquitoes that bit him while camping? I doubted it. Perhaps a tick-borne disease? Humans get other illnesses from them besides Lyme disease.

It was now 9:00 p.m. Going into my private office, I sat down and looked at the pile of twenty charts that awaited completion. I also had ten phone messages to return. There was no way I would get home tonight in time to see my daughters before they went to sleep.

Later that evening, before bed, I discussed Mr. Buttrick's illness with Barbara. "What do you think he has?" I asked her.

She thought about it a few seconds and then said, "I'm not positive, but I wonder about malaria. Yet I can't figure out where he would have gotten it."

"I agree. Still, I ordered thick- and thin-smear blood tests to look for that. I'm really anxious to get the results."

"The word isn't pronounced like it's spelled—it's pronounced a-n-g-s-h-u-s," Barbara told me. She spelled out the word phonetically so I understood how it was spoken.

"Anxious," I repeated, correctly this time as her nod indicated.

Because I can't hear many sounds, I often pronounce words the way they're spelled. Given the fact that English is not a phonetic language, this leads to mispronunciation of certain words. That's why I was in high school before I discovered that the *ch* in Chicago is pronounced like *sh*. Likewise, it's only when someone has corrected me that I've learned the *c* in scene is silent, the *ch* in chef is pronounced like *sh*, and the second syllable of debris sounds like *bree*.

"Do you think you should have hospitalized him? He sounds really sick."

"He didn't want to go unless it was absolutely necessary. I felt he was reliable and it was reasonable to try it on an outpatient basis." As I spoke, I had second thoughts about that decision. What if he developed problems and didn't know to seek medical attention until too late? Often many variables must be considered when deciding whether to hospitalize someone. From the patient's viewpoint, the financial and emotional costs of hospitalization both play large roles in the decision. As a doctor, I'm caught in the middle. I may recommend that people be admitted, but they may refuse. So I do my best to treat them at home. That can be difficult, though, because people often do not realize how sick they are. Some don't even comply with their treatment and get worse. Perhaps I should have been more assertive with Mr. Buttrick in recommending hospitalization. I began to worry.

Since I had the following day off, I called Connie and told her about Mr. Buttrick to familiarize her with the situation. Still feeling uneasy, I went to bed.

The next day around 10:30 in the morning, Rebecca and I had just returned from taking Katie to kindergarten. We were getting ready to play when the phone rang.

"Hello?"

"Hi, Philip. It's Connie."

"Yes?"

"I just got a call from one of the infectious disease doctors in Salt Lake. Apparently, the pathologist looked at the thick- and thin-smear slides on Mr. Buttrick and called me to look at them, too. They have a diagnosis. What do you think it is?"

"Malaria," I guessed confidently.

"No."

"No? Then what is it?"

"Borrelia."

"Borrelia?" I exclaimed, puzzled. I searched my memory, vaguely remembering hearing the name once in medical school. It was an extremely rare disease, so unusual that no lectures had ever been given on it. "I've never known anyone who had that!"

"Neither have they. That's why they were so excited about it. They saw the *Borrelia* organisms on the slides."

I quickly looked it up. Although related to syphilis, the borrelia bacterium causes a disease that is completely different. Usually transmitted by tick bites, it can cause periodic fevers, just like malaria. Fortunately, it is easily cured by antibiotics.

"Have you called Mr. Buttrick yet?" I asked.

"No, but I will right now. Both the infectious disease doctor and the textbook recommend tetracycline for ten days, so I think I'll go ahead and give him that."

"Fine. I'll call him tomorrow and see how he's doing."

Putting the phone down, I recalled Dr. Oldenburg's statement: One never knows "what's going to walk in the door next." He was right. Here was a case that even the infectious disease specialist had never seen.

The next morning, all the doctors I saw had already heard about it. In fact, the case was so unusual that the pathologist planned to present it at a conference he was to attend later in the year. Apparently, no one else had ever seen a patient with borrelia either.

I called Mr. Buttrick as soon as I arrived at the office. The phone rang three times before his wife answered.

"Mrs. Buttrick? This is Dr. Zazove. I'm calling to find out how your husband is doing."

"Oh, yes. He's sleeping right now. Do you want me to wake him?"

"No, don't do that. Just tell me how he's been feeling."

"Better. Since he started taking the pills, he hasn't had any more fever. But he isn't due for the next round of it until later today, so we'll see how well they're working then. I sure hope they help, though, because he's been really sick."

"It might take a few days before the fevers disappear completely," I warned her. "I'd suggest he continue taking the antibiotics even if he has another episode today. And I'd like to see him in the office on Monday."

"You bet."

Three days later, he came back to the office, looking much improved. No longer pale, he appeared more robust and in good spirits.

"Mr. Buttrick," I greeted him. "You look better."

"I am," he responded happily. "I haven't had a fever since I started the antibiotics."

"Are you still tired?"

"Yes, a little. But I can feel myself improving every day."

"Good. You had the infection for a long time, and it took a lot out of you. I wouldn't be surprised if it takes a while before you're completely normal again."

"That's okay. As long as I continue improving, I'll be happy."

I examined him. As before, there were no abnormal findings. The difference was that he now looked healthy.

"Doc, do you think I'll be over this in two more weeks?"

"I hope so. But even if you aren't, you should be most of the way there."

"Good, because bow-hunting season starts then. I'm going to go elk hunting."

"You are? Boy, you must really be feeling better if you're already planning on that. Where are you going to go?"

"Back to Moab," he answered. "I go there every year. It's the best place in the state for elk."

"Aren't you afraid to go back after getting the borrelia there?"

"No. I lived there for seven years before moving here and never got borrelia before. It was just a fluke thing. I'll be careful not to let any ticks bite me this time."

"Well, it's up to you. Whatever you do, though, be sure to take all the tetracycline pills. And I'd suggest you use an insect repellent this time too. That should help keep the ticks away. If you have any problems, just let me know."

"Okay, Doc," he smiled. He got up without difficulty and walked steadily out of the office.

Mr. Buttrick hasn't had any problems since. And every fall, he still goes elk hunting in Moab.

THIRTY-FOUR

I PUT THE REMAINING ITEMS on my desk in the box, closed the lid, and taped it shut. Then I stood up and paused to look around the room. I saw the walnut-colored desk and recalled the excitement I had felt eight years earlier when I first bought it along with the swivel chair behind it. The chair showed its age now, what with frayed edges and all, but the desk still looked almost new. I sighed and sat down in the familiar chair one last time. My gaze swept over the now-barren walls, which had once been covered with diplomas, pictures my daughters had drawn, and a wall hanging my mother-in-law had made. I leaned back slowly, relishing the warm memories of the place that flooded my mind, and found myself reviewing the events that led to this fateful day in August.

After Doug joined us, the practice had continued to grow, at a pace well beyond my wildest dreams. A wonderful associate, both professionally and personally, Doug quickly acquired a loyal following and within a year was as busy as Connie and I. At that point, the three us decided to recruit a fourth physician and once again expand the office. We were confident we could still maintain the intimacy our patients had come to expect from us, despite our increasing size.

We used the same recruiting approach that had been so successful with Doug, and were again fortunate to have several people to choose among. After interviewing the various applicants, we narrowed the choices to two. We could not, however, decide between these people and finally elected to hire them both—the man to start in three months and the woman in nine.

This time, the amount of construction required would be far more extensive than anything we had done before. We had to completely renovate the front office and reception room, as well as move my private office. At the same time, however, this gave us the chance to incorporate improvements we had been planning for several years, changes that would benefit our patients as well as us. Fortunately, the contractor was easy to work with. So despite the major alterations in the office, the workmen structured their jobs around our schedule and we again managed to see patients the entire time renovations were being done.

I leaned back in my chair a little further and stretched. As I did, I saw a spider in the corner of the ceiling, spinning its web. I watched it work for a few minutes. Certainly different from its life, my life was more varied, stimulating, and secure. For that matter, however, my life was different from that of many humans too, all because of my hearing loss.

What would life be like as a normally hearing person? In some ways, a lot different, I suspect. Perhaps someday, if the technology is perfected during my lifetime, I will consider having a cochlear implant. If I did I would then hear many sounds I miss now, and would no longer be dependent on the special equipment that is currently essential to me. It would also be nice not to have to ask people to repeat themselves so often. And people who didn't know me wouldn't stare at me because of my "accent." Movies and television shows would probably be more interesting too, even considering today's closed captions.

On the other hand, if I had never been deaf, I would be a different person. Having a hearing loss has helped make me who I am. All the experiences I have had because of my deafness have played a vital role in shaping my attitudes and beliefs. And, of course, it has affected the lives of everyone who has lived and worked with me. I like to think they have developed more tolerance and compassion for people with handicaps.

I wondered what direction my life would have taken if I had had normal hearing. Would I have become a doctor? And if so, a family doctor? Even if I had, would I be as interested in getting to know my patients? That's what I enjoy more than anything else about my practice. Medicine itself is intriguing, but it is the people themselves who make being a doctor especially attractive. I get to know many of my patients: who their family members are, what they do for a living, what's going on in their lives, who is having a baby. And when I can help them feel better, I like it even more. Perhaps I was destined to be a deaf family doctor. Besides, I am happy with the way my life turned out. Or at least I had been until recently.

In contrast to the success of my practice, things were not going so well for Barbara. She had originally chosen an academic career because of her strong interest in research as well as in caring for patients. So after completing a two-year faculty training fellowship, she joined the family practice department of the University of Utah. Before she could establish a research program, however, she was appointed residency director, a time-consuming position responsible for supervising all the housestaff. The hours required by this, in additional to those spent seeing patients, left little time for anything else. Eighteen months earlier she had voluntarily resigned this position to allow herself to concentrate more on research. After all, one of the purposes of a university is to advance the frontiers of knowledge.

In the interim, the department had chosen a new chairperson. The new person, unlike the previous one, was not very supportive of clinical research. In fact, she wanted the faculty to spend more time seeing patients instead. Even when Barbara learned she would probably be awarded a substantial and prestigious grant from the National Institutes of Health, the situation did not change.

So despite her thriving practice, Barbara was unhappy. She began to study the want ads and expressed a strong desire to look at other university positions. At first, I was not interested. As time passed, however, her job situation deteriorated further. So I agreed to consider moving, and we came up with two conditions the new place would have to meet. First, it would have to be supportive of her research, and second, there had to be a good practice opportunity for me within reasonable driving distance of the university.

Barbara contacted the top family practice departments in the country. Many responded, and she interviewed at several of them. None of the locations, however, met one, let alone both, of these criteria. Then she received a call from the Midwest.

The University of Michigan, one of the top research institutions in the world, had just hired a new chairperson for the family practice department with the explicit charge of making that department a nationally recognized center for research in the specialty. Because he had been a faculty member at the University of Utah while we were residents, he already knew of us and invited Barbara for an interview. She went in December 1988, and came home very impressed. A second visit was arranged for two months later. This time I was to go too, to investigate practice opportunities available in the Ann Arbor area. When it became apparent that there were very few possibilities, I also arranged an interview for a faculty appointment in the family practice department.

The two private practice opportunities I investigated were disappointing. They were not places I could feel good about practicing in: one focused on how much money they could make and the other was very poorly run (it has since disbanded). The academic interviews went better, but I was really not interested in that either. The inhibitory effect of the university bureaucracy compared to my practice was readily apparent, and the clinic itself seemed depressing compared to my office back home. Barbara, on the other hand, was ecstatic about Michigan. Unlike Utah, both the department and school were quite supportive of research. Still, only one of our two conditions was met, and we would have eliminated Michigan from our list if it had not been for one thing: Barbara learned she would receive the National Institutes of Health grant. A five-year award, it would have required Barbara to remain in one place the entire time the study was being conducted. She wanted to conduct the study in a supportive environment, one with long-term potential. She had to move.

We debated the issue for several weeks. I had no desire to leave a dynamic practice to become a medical school faculty member; the other options in Ann Arbor were not even plausible. In addition, I knew I would find it hard to be told what to do after years of being actively involved in the decision making. My vote was clear—stay in Utah. Barbara felt just as strongly that we should move. She was excited about the possibilities in Michigan and looked forward to working in a place where people felt appreciated. Depending on who was more enthused about his or her position, our joint decision swayed back and forth.

We had promised Michigan that we would make our decision by April 1. As the time approached, our final decision slowly became clear. We really had no choice. We had to move, for Barbara's sake. No other academic possibilities existed in Utah. Besides, as Barbara pointed out, despite the apparent bleakness of the job situation for me in Michigan, things might be better than they appeared. And other possibilities might arise over time. Still, we waited until the last day to accept Michigan's offer.

It was with a heavy heart that I told my four colleagues as well as our employees that I would be leaving in six months. My associates were not totally surprised; I had warned them of the possibility earlier. My employees, on the other hand, had had no forewarning. Although they understood my reasons, they were nevertheless upset.

Time flew more quickly than it had for years, as it often does when one does not want it to. Two months before leaving, I sent a letter to all my patients informing them of my move, explaining why, and pointing out that the office and my partners would still remain. As my last day approached, patients began to say good-bye. Some came in, others called. Some wrote notes, while others brought gifts. I found myself spending more time than usual with each person, enjoying every precious minute with people I had come to know.

I sighed and stood up from the chair. Thirty minutes earlier I had seen my last patient in Utah. It was time to leave.

I walked slowly around the office one last time, hesitant to depart. I tarried in each room, savoring the memories bursting from each one, lingering in the building much longer than I had planned. Finally, I finished and walked into the front where my staff and associates were waiting for me. After saying good-bye and shedding a few tears, I walked out the door, an empty feeling growing in my stomach. A piece of me had stayed behind. I would no longer be seeing my patients and associates, people I knew so well, people I considered my friends. And I knew I would never hear from most of them again.

I tried hard to suppress the tears as I reached my car and turned to look back at my office. More memories of my eight years there flashed through my mind: the difficulties getting money and building the office, the first year when people didn't yet know we were there and I had so few patients, the addition of the various partners over the years, the numerous families I had gotten to know—it all came back in a rush that almost overwhelmed me.

I managed to escape back to the present and took a deep breath. I scanned the view around me, cherishing the sight of the mountains I had grown to love. Even though it was late August and it had been a hotter-than-usual summer, several peaks on the Wasatch front still had white tops. As I looked, I recalled when I first got into medical school and my professors had entreated me not to choose family practice because I would later regret my choice. The thought brought a transient smile to my face. How wrong they had been. It was the best choice I could have made.

The thought of leaving came back and caused a few more tears to roll down my cheek. I turned around and glanced at the office one last time. Then I got into my car and drove off. Suddenly I could not hold it back any longer. The magnitude of my loss was overwhelming. I pulled over to the side of the road and cried.

EPILOGUE

It has now been more than three years since we moved to Ann Arbor, and I am finally beginning to adjust to the fact that I am a Michigander. Although quite different from Utah, there are many nice things about this state. It is truly a water wonderland, not only because it abuts four Great Lakes but also because of the thousands of lakes within its borders. This is quite a change from the desert climate of the Wasatch front. The northern part of Michigan—in particular the Upper Peninsula—has a lot of spectacular scenery, although of a different sort than Utah's mountains and red-rock country. And because it rains a lot here, it has been nice not to have to water the lawn and garden several times a week.

Katie and Rebecca adjusted to the move much faster than I anticipated. They are are fully integrated in their respective classes, have many friends and are University of Michigan Wolverine fans. Utah is just a distant memory for both of them; they almost never mention it anymore. It is interesting to note, however, that both copied their father's childhood experience with the bus after the first day at their new schools. Both girls failed to get off their respective buses at the right place. Fortunately, I was watching for them and chased after them until they did get off.

Barbara is content and happy with the move too. The job turned out to be everything she had hoped for, and more. Her research is thriving, she is gaining a national reputation, and she recently received tenure.

I am still employed as a faculty member in the family practice department of the University of Michigan Medical School. In addition to caring for patients half-time, my duties include research, teaching, and various administrative duties.

People here are nice and I have met many members of the Deaf community, as well as educators and interpreters who work with them. This has probably been the most enjoyable aspect of my work here. The university bureaucracy is as pervasive as I feared, and practicing medicine under it is often a frustrating experience. What's more, I've come to realize that the quality of care in that little town in Utah is as good as it is in this medical mecca.

I have not forgotten that town and the wonderful people who live there. Nor has time diminished my recollection of the practice I started, and it never will. I still remember in vivid detail everything about that office. The smell as one walks in the front door, the contents of each room, the cluttered lab in the center, and the unique idiosyncracies of each person in that dynamic, dedicated group of individuals who worked there are indelibly imprinted in my brain.

Sometimes, when I am particularly nostalgic, I close my eyes and imagine I am there once again. If I do this long enough, it feels like I have actually returned home after a long absence. I see myself pausing in the parking lot outside my office, taking in the magnificent view of the Wasatch front against the typical Utah royal blue sky. Then I enter through the doors and walk through the reception room to my private office, to check my desk for messages. Before long, I see LeAnne in the doorway signaling that a patient is in a room, using one of the signs that only she and I know. I get up from my desk, walk to the examination room and open the door. And then, before the door closes and cuts off the view, I see my hands sign, "Mrs. Smith! How nice . . ."